Understand Crypto Before You Invest

Understand Crypto Before You Invest

A Simple, Safe, and Smart Introduction for Curious Non-Techies

Ethan Rowe

Mindful Pages

Published in 2025

ISBN: 9789371776608 (PB)
ISBN: 9789371775533 (eBook)

Published by

Mindful Pages
Imprint of Alpha Editions LLC
312 W. 2nd St #1834
Casper, WY 82601, USA

This book was developed using advanced writing tools to support the drafting and ideation process. All content has been thoughtfully curated, refined, and reviewed to ensure quality and relevance.

Content

Introduction
Why Crypto Feels So Complicated—And Why It Doesn't Have to Be

Most people encounter cryptocurrency much like a foreign tongue dropped into conversation—there is activity, excitement, gains and losses, yet the logic remains obscure. Coins and tokens, miners and validators, blockchains and smart contracts crowd the landscape. Prices swing wildly, often without warning. For many, crypto seems like a high-stakes game designed for insiders, a digital gold rush conducted in a dialect they never learned.

This sense of exclusion is hardly accidental. Cryptocurrency arrived amid fanfare and confusion, draped in arcane terminology and championed by communities that prided themselves on opacity. Touted as revolutionary, it was too often explained with the density of a doctoral thesis. The paradox: a technology promising inclusion, sovereignty, and structural change became one of the most misunderstood arenas of modern finance.

Yet the truth is simple: cryptocurrency is not inherently beyond comprehension. You do not need a computer science degree, an economics background, or a taste for day trading. What is required is a framework—an organised way of thinking that cuts through hype, jargon, and peer pressure. That is precisely what this book provides: a clear, cautious, and considered introduction for intelligent readers ready to think critically.

At its core, crypto is about trust, not mere money. Human exchange has always relied on shared belief. Gold, shells, paper notes, or digital entries—money has always been an agreement, a story we tell about value and exchange. What evolves is not the necessity of trust, but its structure. Cryptocurrency challenges the traditional model by removing the middlemen—banks, governments, corporations—replacing them with distributed trust enforced by transparent rules and cryptographic verification.

This shift—substituting institutional trust with algorithmic consensus—is both captivating and disruptive. It reimagines the dynamics of power, money, and coordination in a digital era. The implications are tangible: remittances across borders, digital art markets, online communities, even individual wealth protection. One need not be a crypto evangelist to recognise the significance.

The problem is often how crypto is presented. Resources either promise get-rich-quick schemes or offer impenetrable technical manuals for insiders. This book avoids both extremes. It neither seeks to convert nor demands blind faith. Its aim is understanding—clear, deliberate, and on your own terms.

We start by stepping back: what is crypto truly about? Beyond volatility and headlines lies a trust revolution, a shift in how societies coordinate, assign value, and govern themselves. We trace its historical roots—from gold and central banks to Bitcoin's emergence post-2008—moments that intertwine economics with culture, authority, and risk perception.

Next, we demystify the building blocks. What is a blockchain? What do "proof-of-stake" and "private keys" really mean? Here, we favour accessible analogies—Google Docs, public noticeboards, safe deposit boxes—turning abstract concepts into tangible understanding. Precision is maintained, but presented in human terms.

We then examine motives: why do people participate? Pursuits range from financial independence to fairness and innovation. Alongside opportunity lie volatility, misinformation, and fraud. This is where behavioural insight complements technical literacy: often the greatest hazards are cognitive blind spots, not the market itself.

Security demands attention. Wallets, exchanges, and custody are explored in depth. Platform failures, the mantra "not your keys, not your coins," and storage strategies are dissected, giving practical clarity for safe engagement.

Understanding crypto also requires cultural literacy. Memes, jargon, and insider codes shape perception, erect barriers, and sometimes obscure risk. Interpreting them provides a clearer lens on authenticity versus theatre.

Chapter 6 addresses scams: pump-and-dumps, fake coins, and toxic communities. Awareness and sceptical curiosity allow readers to protect themselves without succumbing to paranoia. Knowledge here is preventative, not fear-driven.

Investment strategy is treated thoughtfully. No hot tips or predictions are offered. Instead, the framework emphasises alignment with goals, risk comprehension, and long-term perspective. Timing, diversification, and decision-making are explored in a landscape often dominated by impulse.

Stablecoins receive scrutiny. Some function well, others are fragile. Guidance is provided to distinguish utility from hazard, clarifying when such assets can be useful or risky.

NFTs and tokenisation are examined critically. Beyond digital art, they illuminate ownership in a dematerialised economy and demonstrate practical applications of blockchain technology.

Legal context is addressed, surveying taxes, privacy, and compliance. While regulations lag innovation, individuals can adopt clear practices today to remain safe and lawful.

Looking ahead, the book explores emergent technologies: Ethereum, decentralised finance, and new digital infrastructures reshaping finance, governance, and the internet itself. Some promises may materialise; others may falter—but understanding the trajectory is vital.

Finally, readers are invited to define their own engagement. You need not be a trader, developer, or evangelist. Guidance is offered to establish a personal rulebook, maintain informed awareness, and navigate without overwhelm. The goal is independent thinking, wise action, and grounded participation.

Cryptocurrency embodies both opportunity and uncertainty. Its potential is real; its hype is equally present. This book offers clarity without blind optimism or undue scepticism. You are not late, nor underqualified. You are exactly where you should be: questioning, observing, and entering a conversation still unfolding.

Welcome. Let us begin.

Chapter 1
What Is Crypto Really About?

The story of money is one of constant evolution. For millennia, humans have reshaped how value is represented—barter gave way to coins, coins to paper, paper to digital balances. Each step reflected the forms of trust underpinning society. Yet, over the last fifteen years, a profound shift has occurred: a form of money has emerged not from governments, banks, or corporations, but from open-source code distributed across countless machines. This is not simply a new payment mechanism; it is a reimagining of trust itself.

To understand cryptocurrency, one must begin with trust, the invisible scaffolding of every economic system. Its presence is assumed until it falters. When you deposit funds in a bank or tap a card for coffee, you trust a cascade of institutions to operate competently, honestly, and reliably. History, of course, reminds us that such trust can fail. Cryptocurrency asks a provocative question: what if trust could be embedded in the system itself, enforced not by reputation or authority, but by transparent, verifiable mathematics? In other words, crypto does not merely digitise money—it decentralises trust.

For many, this notion feels radical—or even utopian. The term "cryptocurrency" conjures images of start-ups, hype-laden social media, and sensational headlines. Jargon abounds, speculation runs rampant, and the serious innovation risks being lost beneath the noise. Yet beneath it all lies a historically significant development: a technological and social experiment in how humans can coordinate value without relying on central authorities. Even if you never invest, understanding crypto engages you with one of the most consequential questions of our time: how should trust be constructed in a digital world where traditional institutions are faltering?

This chapter strips away the misconceptions to reveal crypto's deeper dimensions: philosophical, historical, and social. We begin with what might be called the Trust Revolution. Cryptocurrency is not merely an app or asset class; it is a model that enables strangers to reach consensus without personal acquaintance or hierarchical oversight. Blockchain technology facilitates this, allowing verification and accountability to exist in code, not charisma. It challenges the centuries-old assumption that only governments or corporations can arbitrate financial truth.

The distinction is subtle yet profound. Traditional institutions rely on delegated trust: you trust a bank because it is regulated, a currency because the state guarantees it, an auditor because of professional accreditation. In contrast, crypto distributes trust. Participants verify the rules, every transaction is publicly recorded, and the ledger enforces protocol regardless of identity. Imperfections remain, certainly, but the departure from centralised trust is unprecedented.

Critics often point to crypto culture as exclusive, insular, or dominated by a narrow demographic—the so-called "tech bros." And at times, that is true: the rhetoric can be self-referential, performative, and occasionally alienating. Yet culture does not define the technology. Beneath the memes and market frenzy lies a toolset with transformative potential—especially for those questioning the distribution of power in finance, or seeking systems that are transparent, accountable, and accessible.

Consider the millions excluded from formal financial systems across Africa, Southeast Asia, or Latin America. Their exclusion is rarely due to irresponsibility; it is structural. Cryptocurrency enables secure storage and transfer of value with just a mobile device—agency previously denied. Similarly, creators can reclaim ownership of digital works via decentralised platforms, circumventing exploitative intermediaries. Citizens in countries facing inflation can preserve savings where traditional currencies fail. These examples illustrate that crypto, at its best, is about empowerment and inclusion.

To appreciate why crypto emerged, we must examine money's evolution. Historically, money has always embodied belief. Ancient Mesopotamian clay tablets tracked debts long before coins existed; medieval tally sticks performed similar functions. Gold's value stemmed not from its material but from collective trust. Paper currencies emerged first backed by gold, then by state decree, each step provoking anxiety and requiring new trust mechanisms. Cryptocurrency continues this lineage, questioning whether code, rather than coercion or charisma, can guarantee value.

Bitcoin, launched in 2009 by the enigmatic Satoshi Nakamoto, exemplifies this shift. Born in the aftermath of the 2008 financial crisis, it responded to eroding trust in banks and bailouts of "too big to fail" institutions. Embedded in Bitcoin's genesis block was a message: "The Times 03/Jan/2009 Chancellor on brink of second bailout for banks." More than a timestamp, it was a provocation: a digital currency designed to operate under rules enforced by code, not decree.

Since then, the ecosystem has exploded. Thousands of coins and tokens exist, ranging from innovations addressing Bitcoin's limitations to opportunistic cash grabs. The landscape is chaotic, often contradictory, and still developing. Yet the consistent thread is a reimagining of collaboration, transaction, and governance in a decentralised world.

This chapter unpacks the foundations of that shift. It examines how the trust revolution reshapes finance and broader questions of power and coordination. It debunks the myth that crypto is only for insiders, revealing why it deserves attention from anyone interested in how technology is redefining public life. Tracing the arc from gold to code, and examining Bitcoin's origin not as folklore but as a lens, we explore the motivations, promises, and limits of this experiment.

By the end, you will not merely understand a technology—you will grasp why it matters. To understand crypto is to confront deeper questions: how trust is built, broken, and rebuilt in a digital age increasingly defined by decentralisation and innovation.

The Trust Revolution

For most of human history, trust has been the central operating system of economic life—so fundamental that it rarely needed naming. People trusted kings to mint coins of reliable weight. They trusted banks to hold their deposits and honour withdrawals. They trusted courts to enforce contracts. The infrastructure of commerce, trade, and finance has always run on this invisible fuel. But trust, while essential, is not fixed. It shifts with culture, crisis, and technological change. Today, we are witnessing one of the most significant shifts in the architecture of trust in modern memory—one that challenges centuries of institutional dominance and proposes an alternative embedded not in reputation, regulation, or authority, but in code.

Cryptocurrency is often misunderstood as simply another financial product—an exotic form of digital money, speculative in nature, and mostly relevant to those with a tolerance for risk or a fondness for technology. But this interpretation misses the deeper story. The true significance of cryptocurrency lies not in its price volatility or its potential for returns, but in its radical proposal: that it is possible to coordinate human activity, transfer value, and reach consensus without relying on centralised institutions. *It is, at heart, a trust system without trust brokers.*

To appreciate the magnitude of this shift, consider the traditional scaffolding of financial trust. When two parties engage in economic exchange—say, transferring money across borders, securing a loan, or purchasing an asset—they are not merely transacting with each other. They are transacting through layers of intermediaries: banks, payment processors, notaries, regulators, clearing houses, and often multiple layers of bureaucracy. Each intermediary exists to verify, record, enforce, or secure the transaction. Their role is to reduce the risk that one party will default, deceive, or disappear. The price of that risk reduction is friction: delays, fees, barriers to access, and vulnerability to mismanagement or corruption.

This model has served its purpose—many of the institutions we rely on were created to solve very real problems of fraud, coordination, and trust at scale. But it also embeds structural inequalities. Millions of people remain unbanked not because they lack the will to participate in the economy, but because they fail to meet arbitrary thresholds of credibility defined by gatekeepers. Small businesses are denied loans due to lack of formal credit histories. Cross-border workers pay exorbitant fees just to send money home. Ordinary citizens watch as inflation, poor governance, or institutional failure erodes the value of their savings—often with no meaningful recourse.

Cryptocurrency enters this landscape with a different proposition. Rather than placing trust in fallible intermediaries, it offers a system in which the rules are transparent, the ledger is public, and enforcement is automatic. The core innovation here is the *blockchain*—a decentralised database maintained by a distributed network of participants, each of whom validates and records transactions according to agreed-upon protocols. No single entity controls the ledger. No central party can rewrite history. This architecture dramatically reduces the need to trust individual actors because trust is embedded in the system's structure.

To illustrate how radical this is, imagine a public noticeboard in a town square where every transaction, contract, or financial agreement is posted in real time, visible to all, tamper-proof, and automatically enforced by community consensus. Now imagine that this town square exists across thousands of interconnected computers around the world, immune to censorship, government seizure, or corporate manipulation. That is, in essence, what blockchain-based systems attempt to create. They decentralise not only data, but authority.

This model reframes a foundational question of economic life: *Who gets to say what happened?* In traditional systems, the answer is: those in power—banks, courts, regulators. In decentralised systems, the answer becomes: anyone who plays by the rules and participates in the protocol. *It is a shift from trusted third parties to trustless coordination.*

Of course, the term "trustless" is misleading. These systems do not eliminate trust; they reallocate it. You still have to trust that the code is well-written, that the majority of participants act honestly, and that incentives are aligned to prevent manipulation. But the trust required is different in nature—it is structural, not personal; procedural, not relational. This difference matters because it allows for new kinds of collaboration between strangers, across borders, without a shared language or central authority.

Critics rightly point out that this model is far from perfect. Technical complexity, governance disputes, and the risk of malicious actors remain real challenges. The early history of crypto is littered with failed experiments, collapsed exchanges, and speculative manias. But to dismiss the entire field on these grounds is to miss the broader context. All trust systems evolve through trial and error. Modern banking was once a chaotic patchwork of private currencies and unregulated institutions. Stock markets, now pillars of the global economy, began as speculative dens rife with manipulation. Progress in trust architecture is rarely linear, and never clean.

What makes this moment different is the *programmability* of trust. For the first time, we can encode rules of economic coordination directly into digital systems—rules that are executed automatically, without the need for discretion or enforcement by central authorities. Smart contracts, for instance, allow agreements to self-execute when predefined conditions are met. These contracts can facilitate everything from decentralised lending platforms to supply chain traceability to artist royalties paid instantly upon resale. What once required multiple intermediaries and legal enforcement can now be governed by code.

The implications extend far beyond finance. Consider identity. In many countries, the lack of formal identification bars individuals from accessing essential services. Decentralised identity systems, built on blockchain, could allow people to prove who they are without relying on a central registry. In global philanthropy, funds can be distributed with greater transparency and accountability using blockchain-based tracking. In governance, decentralised autonomous organisations (DAOs) offer new models of collective decision-making, where votes are recorded immutably and rules are enforced by protocol rather than by fiat.

These developments raise profound questions. *Can we trust systems we do not fully understand? Who is accountable when the code fails? What does justice look like in a trustless world?* Such questions are not distractions—they are essential to any serious engagement with the field. The trust revolution does not eliminate the need for ethics, design thinking, or legal oversight. It simply shifts the terrain on which those conversations must occur.

It also reshapes the geography of power. In a world where code mediates trust, those who write the code—and those who control its deployment—become crucial actors. This raises concerns about hidden centralisation within supposedly decentralised systems. If a small group of developers can push through a software update, or if a few mining pools control the majority of a network's computing power, the promise of decentralisation becomes fragile. Transparency, auditability, and community governance become not just technical issues, but civic imperatives.

Despite these tensions, what distinguishes the crypto trust model is its *openness*. Anyone can inspect the code. Anyone can run a node, validate transactions, or propose changes. Participation is permissionless. This openness has enabled rapid experimentation, but it has also made the space vulnerable to opportunism and misinformation. As such, the burden shifts to users—not to trust blindly, but to *verify intelligently*. In this context, literacy becomes a form of self-defence. Understanding how trust is structured—who controls the keys, what the code enforces, how decisions are made—is essential for meaningful participation.

Perhaps the most radical aspect of this trust revolution is not technological, but cultural. It challenges a centuries-old habit of deference to authority. It says: *Don't trust institutions just because they have always been there. Don't assume that centralisation is the only path to order. Don't accept opacity when transparency is possible.* That ethos, when stripped of ideological extremism, carries the seeds of something genuinely transformative.

But revolutions in trust are slow, uneven, and often misunderstood in their early stages. The printing press decentralised knowledge but took decades to reshape power. The Internet decentralised communication but has only recently begun to challenge media monopolies. Crypto is still young. Its infrastructure is evolving. Its norms are immature. But the questions it raises—and the alternatives it offers—deserve serious, sustained attention.

Because at its heart, cryptocurrency is not a bet on the next big thing. It is a wager on a different way of organising human systems—one where transparency replaces opacity, where open participation replaces institutional gatekeeping, and where trust is not granted, but built into the structure. For anyone who has ever looked at a collapsing institution, a frozen account, or an unjust decision and thought, *There must be a better way*, the trust revolution offers a new terrain of possibility.

That possibility is neither guaranteed nor complete. But it is real. And it is unfolding.

Why It's Not Just for "Tech Bros"

The caricature of cryptocurrency as the playground of arrogant technologists and speculative young men in hoodies is not entirely unfounded—but it is incomplete, misleading, and increasingly obsolete. To reduce crypto to a subculture of "tech bros" is to mistake the most visible participants for the purpose of the system itself. It's a distortion that obscures what's really at stake: the redesign of some of society's most fundamental systems of power, ownership, and coordination. What's unfolding is not merely a technological curiosity or a financial sideshow; it is a global debate about who gets to control the tools of economic participation, and on what terms.

Technology, finance, and culture are converging in ways that demand broader civic literacy, not narrower tribalism. Cryptocurrency, decentralised finance, digital identity, and tokenised assets are not just engineering feats. They are political acts—encoded proposals about how society could function differently. And the ability to understand, critique, or engage with them must not be outsourced to a small elite with technical or financial privilege. *Crypto is not just for people who can write code or trade tokens—it's for anyone who wants to understand how power is shifting in the digital age.*

When Bitcoin was introduced in 2009, it was not pitched as a speculative investment. It was a rebuke to the existing financial system. Satoshi Nakamoto's white paper proposed a system that would operate independently of trusted third parties—banks, governments, clearinghouses—by replacing them with open-source code and cryptographic proof. The first block in the Bitcoin blockchain even included a pointed message referencing the UK Chancellor's second bank bailout: a signal that the system was a response to institutional failure, not just a novelty.

Over time, however, public perception of crypto has drifted. As media coverage became saturated with tales of early adopters becoming overnight millionaires—or losing everything—interest in the philosophical foundations gave way to interest in price charts. This shift allowed crypto culture to be defined largely by its loudest participants: high-risk traders, meme coin promoters, and maximalist evangelists. It fostered an environment that often felt unwelcoming to newcomers, especially those outside the tech or finance sectors. Technical language became gatekeeping. Jargon signalled insider status. Communities grew insular, at times hostile to dissent or scepticism.

But beneath the noise, a broader and more inclusive set of use cases was emerging—use cases that had little to do with speculation and everything to do with access. Consider the role of crypto in economies with high inflation and unstable governance. In Argentina, for example, citizens have long used the dollar as a shadow currency to preserve the value of their savings, often via informal or black-market channels. With increasing restrictions on currency exchange, many turned to stablecoins—cryptocurrencies pegged to the US dollar—as a more accessible and secure alternative. This wasn't about betting on Bitcoin's price. It was about surviving an economic system that offered few reliable options.

Similarly, in Nigeria, where the naira has depreciated rapidly and capital controls restrict foreign exchange, crypto adoption has surged among young professionals and entrepreneurs. Platforms like Paxful and Binance P2P facilitate peer-to-peer trading, allowing users to transact outside of traditional banking rails. In these contexts, crypto functions less as a speculative asset and more as an informal financial infrastructure—one that is increasingly critical to economic agency.

Beyond the global south, marginalised communities in developed nations have also begun to explore crypto not out of ideology, but out of necessity. In the United States, Black and Latino investors are statistically more likely to own cryptocurrency than white investors, according to surveys by Pew and NORC at the University of Chicago. This may seem surprising, but it reflects a deeper mistrust in traditional financial institutions—a mistrust born from experience. From discriminatory lending practices to systemic underinvestment in minority communities, the legacy financial system has often failed to deliver fairness or opportunity. Crypto, for all its flaws, offers an open door: permissionless access, borderless networks, and programmable alternatives to legacy systems.

That doesn't mean the door is easy to walk through. The usability gap remains steep. Wallets are confusing. Key management is intimidating. Scams are rampant. Regulatory ambiguity deters innovation in some jurisdictions and leaves consumers exposed in others. These are real problems—but they are also symptoms of immaturity, not inevitability. And they are being addressed not just by developers, but by educators, designers, policy thinkers, and community builders who recognise that *technology alone does not drive change—accessibility does.*

This is why the idea that crypto is only for the technically inclined is not just incorrect—it's dangerous. It perpetuates a cycle where only a narrow slice of society shapes the systems that will govern everyone else. That same fallacy once surrounded the early Internet. In the 1990s, understanding the web required a working knowledge of IP addresses, FTP protocols, and HTML. Today, children intuitively interact with platforms layered on top of those same technologies—platforms designed with usability and mass adoption in mind. Crypto is undergoing a similar shift. The design of the next generation of crypto tools will determine who benefits from them, who is excluded, and how power is distributed.

Indeed, the question of inclusion goes beyond race, gender, or geography. It extends to philosophical orientation. One need not be a libertarian, a capitalist, or a digital utopian to care about decentralised systems. Feminist scholars, for example, have explored how decentralised finance (DeFi) could reimagine economic participation without the biases embedded in traditional underwriting models. Environmentalists are asking how blockchain can incentivise regenerative practices through tokenised impact.

Urban planners are examining how DAOs might enable participatory governance in community projects. These are not fringe speculations—they are early signs that crypto, as a set of tools, is being tested in many directions by many different kinds of thinkers.

Still, critical engagement is essential. Not every project is meaningful. Many are derivative, predatory, or opportunistic. But this, too, is a reason why broader participation matters. If only technologists and investors shape the space, then the incentives will reflect their priorities. The more diverse the perspectives in crypto, the more robust its ethical, cultural, and social frameworks can become. *Crypto needs critics who understand it, not just cheerleaders who profit from it.*

To frame the field as irrelevant unless one plans to invest is to misunderstand its relevance. Most people don't plan to "invest" in the Internet, electricity, or language—yet each of these infrastructures shapes their lives daily. Similarly, crypto's impact is not limited to wealth creation. It is also about how communities coordinate, how value is created and exchanged, and how rules are enforced without centralised authority. These questions matter whether or not one ever owns a coin.

That said, opting out of ownership is not the same as opting out of consequence. As governments explore central bank digital currencies (CBDCs), as corporations deploy private blockchains, and as data sovereignty becomes more contentious, the public will increasingly confront decisions about which models of trust, control, and participation are acceptable. If the only people informed enough to shape those decisions are early adopters, the rest of society will be subject to systems they did not help design and cannot meaningfully challenge.

This is not an argument for crypto evangelism. It is an argument for crypto literacy—as a civic skill, not a financial strategy. It means knowing how to interpret technical claims, spot misaligned incentives, and ask the right questions: Who controls the code? What happens in failure scenarios? Who profits from adoption? What assumptions are baked into the protocol? These are not questions for specialists; they are questions for anyone who believes that systems should be accountable to those they affect.

There is no doubt that the field is still noisy, volatile, and uneven. But dismissing crypto on the basis of its loudest advocates is as short-sighted as dismissing the Internet because of early chat rooms. The signal is there, beneath the surface. It is in the open-source developers building tools for financial autonomy. It is in the artists reclaiming value from extractive platforms. It is in the refugees using crypto to escape surveillance or hyperinflation. It is in the thinkers wrestling with the governance of code and the ethics of decentralisation.

To see crypto clearly is to move beyond caricature. It is to recognise that beneath the speculation lies a legitimate debate about the future of money, governance, and technological agency. And that debate is far too important to leave to the self-appointed insiders. Crypto is not just for "tech bros." It's for anyone who believes that the design of our systems matters—and that we all have a stake in the rules that shape our shared digital future.

From Gold to Code: A Quick Money Timeline

Money has always been a story we agree to believe. Whether pressed into the form of a coin, printed on paper, or rendered as digits on a screen, its power has never resided in its material substance alone, but in the collective trust we place in it. To understand cryptocurrency as more than a passing trend—or a purely technical artefact—it must be seen within the broader lineage of money itself. Because money, historically, has not evolved in a vacuum. It has mirrored the structures of belief, authority, and coordination that define human civilisation at each stage of its development. When we trace its arc from gold to code, what emerges is not a straight line of technical progress, but a series of adaptive responses to the question: *How can we reliably assign and transfer value across time, distance, and trust gaps?*

Long before coins or banknotes, early economies operated on systems of credit and obligation rather than direct exchange. In

Mesopotamia, some 5,000 years ago, clay tablets recorded debts and payments in units of grain or silver, administered through temple or palace bureaucracies. These were not free-market interactions, but centrally mediated relationships that relied on administrative trust. The objects used were not "money" in the modern sense but instruments of accounting. What mattered was not the token, but the record—and the legitimacy of the institution keeping it.

The invention of coinage in Lydia around the 7th century BCE introduced a subtle but powerful shift. By minting metal discs with standardised weights and sovereign symbols, states could issue portable, divisible, and durable tokens of value. Crucially, these coins were stamped with the mark of political authority—a signal that they were not only physically valuable, but institutionally sanctioned. Gold and silver held intrinsic worth, but what transformed them into currency was the guarantee of the state. Coinage enabled economies to scale by reducing the friction of barter, and by embedding trust in metallurgy and monarchy rather than personal relationships.

As empires rose and fell, so too did the systems that supported their currencies. In mediaeval Europe, a shortage of precious metals led to the widespread use of tally sticks—carved wooden rods split into matching halves, each side bearing a record of debt. One half remained with the creditor, the other with the debtor. Though rudimentary, this system functioned for centuries as a decentralised yet trusted form of exchange. Here again, the material was secondary. What mattered was that the system was legible, durable, and hard to forge—a recurring theme in the evolution of money.

The advent of paper money, first in Tang dynasty China and later in Europe, was a turning point not because it introduced new materials, but because it required a deeper layer of trust. Paper notes had no intrinsic value. They were promissory claims on something else—usually precious metals held in reserve. Their credibility depended entirely on the belief that they could be redeemed. When central banks eventually decoupled currency from gold—a process that culminated globally in the 20th century—they were not abandoning the idea of backing, but replacing it with a different kind: sovereign credibility. The value of fiat money became tethered not to metal, but to the perceived stability of the institutions issuing it.

This shift made money more flexible, but also more political. Governments could now expand or contract the money supply in response to economic conditions, finance wars, or stimulate growth. Monetary policy became a tool of macroeconomic management—but it also introduced new forms of opacity and risk. Inflation, devaluation, and debt monetisation became tools that could be used judiciously or irresponsibly. The average citizen, once able to judge the worth of a coin by its metal content, now had to rely on a complex chain of abstract guarantees: central banks, interest rates, inflation targets, and fiscal policy. Money became more efficient, but also more fragile—especially in contexts where institutions lacked legitimacy.

The rise of digital banking in the late 20th century marked another transformation. Money became almost entirely dematerialised. Balances existed as database entries, accessible through cards, apps, or electronic transfers. Trust now resided in software, encryption, and the institutional infrastructure of centralised ledgers. These systems brought speed and convenience, but at the cost of increasing centralisation. A handful of entities—commercial banks, payment processors, and national regulators—now controlled the flow of money for billions. For the most part, users had no visibility into how the system worked. They simply trusted that it would.

But that trust has not been evenly distributed. In regions plagued by inflation, capital controls, or banking exclusion, the limits of the system have long been visible. Even in advanced economies, financial crises have repeatedly demonstrated how centralised systems can fail—or be gamed—at immense cost. The 2008 global financial crisis was, at its core, a crisis of trust: trust in banks, in ratings agencies, in regulators, and in the assumption that financial innovation was synonymous with financial safety. When Lehman Brothers collapsed, and central banks stepped in to bail out "too big to fail" institutions, the public was reminded that the existing system could absorb massive losses and still function—so long as the right people were making the calls.

It was in this context that Bitcoin appeared—not as a technical novelty, but as a direct critique. Its white paper, published under the pseudonym Satoshi Nakamoto, proposed a form of digital cash that would require no trust in intermediaries. Instead of relying on central authorities to verify transactions, it would use cryptographic proof and distributed consensus. Instead of being issued by decree, it would be created through transparent rules encoded in software. The aim was not just to create a new currency, but to demonstrate that monetary systems could be decentralised, auditable, and resistant to manipulation.

Bitcoin's value, like all money, depends on belief. But the nature of that belief is different. It is not faith in a government's fiscal discipline or a bank's solvency, but belief in the integrity of a protocol. Bitcoin users trust that the system will function as specified: that blocks will be mined roughly every ten minutes, that the supply will cap at 21 million, and that no one can unilaterally change the rules without majority consent. In a sense, this is a return to the tangible logic of earlier forms of money. Just as the weight of a gold coin once guaranteed its worth, the mathematical constraints of the Bitcoin protocol serve as a visible anchor for trust.

Of course, Bitcoin is only the first chapter in the story of digital-native money. Since its inception, thousands of cryptocurrencies have emerged—some building on its principles, others deviating entirely. Some seek to offer privacy, others programmability, others speed. Ethereum introduced the concept of smart contracts, enabling money to become *conditional* and *autonomous*—a fundamental departure from the passivity of fiat. Stablecoins attempt to blend crypto's programmability with the price stability of traditional currencies. Central bank digital currencies (CBDCs), now being explored in over 100 countries, represent an institutional response: an attempt to harness the benefits of digital money without ceding control to decentralised systems.

This proliferation can be overwhelming. But what unites these innovations is not their form, but their underlying inquiry: *What should money be in a networked, programmable world?* That question is no longer academic. As transactions migrate to digital spaces, as monetary policy confronts new tools and pressures, and as individuals seek alternatives to systems they perceive as exclusionary or unstable, the debate over money's future is no longer confined to banks or policy circles. It is playing out in open-source code, in digital wallets, and in the courts of public opinion.

Money has never been static. Each stage in its evolution—from clay tablets to blockchain—has responded to the needs and constraints of its time. What makes the current moment distinctive is not just the speed of change, but the degree of decentralised participation. Today, a teenager with an Internet connection can issue a token, build a financial protocol, or join a decentralised autonomous organisation. The barriers to entry are technical, not institutional. The rules are enforced by code, not by decree.

This is not to say the system is mature. Far from it. Volatility, fragmentation, and exploitation remain serious concerns. But the very existence of a parallel financial infrastructure—operating without centralised control, across borders, in real time—is historically unprecedented. And it is the logical outgrowth of a long tradition: the belief that money can—and must—adapt to the contours of human trust.

From gold to code, the story of money is a story of belief systems made tangible. The form changes, the instruments evolve, but the underlying question remains the same: *What do we trust, and why?* Cryptocurrency does not answer that question definitively. But it reopens it—forcefully, controversially, and at scale. For anyone seeking to understand where the world is heading, that makes it too important to ignore.

The Bitcoin Origin Story

On 3 January 2009, a quiet but irreversible event occurred. A small piece of code was executed by a pseudonymous figure known only as Satoshi Nakamoto, creating the first block of a digital ledger now recognised as the Bitcoin blockchain. Embedded within the metadata of this genesis block was a plain sentence lifted from the front page of *The Times* newspaper: *"Chancellor on brink of second bailout for banks."* It was more than a timestamp. It was a declaration of intent—a subtle, almost poetic indictment of the financial system's fragility and a gesture toward an alternative future.

To understand Bitcoin, one must start not with technology but with context. The year 2008 marked one of the most severe systemic failures in modern financial history. The global economy teetered on the edge of collapse as banks fell under the weight of opaque derivatives, excessive leverage, and regulatory blindness. In the United States, Lehman Brothers—an institution with over 150 years of history—filed for bankruptcy in September. What followed was a cascade of collapses, bailouts, emergency lending programmes, and a pervasive loss of public trust. Credit froze. Stock markets plummeted. Central banks scrambled. And for millions of ordinary people, savings evaporated, jobs were lost, and homes were foreclosed.

While governments and financial institutions were preoccupied with preventing total collapse, the legitimacy of the system itself was unravelling. The crisis exposed what had become a brittle architecture of confidence: institutions that were "too big to fail" proved also to be too complex to manage and too interconnected to regulate effectively. Those responsible for the meltdown, whether through negligence or complicity, faced few consequences. Meanwhile, the costs were socialised. In the years that followed, austerity measures, rising inequality, and institutional cynicism deepened the sense that the system served the powerful at the expense of the public.

It is within this atmosphere of disillusionment that Bitcoin quietly emerged—not as a fully-formed financial product, but as an idea encoded in software. The Bitcoin white paper, released in October 2008, proposed a "peer-to-peer electronic cash system" that would allow two parties to transact directly without the need for a trusted third party. On the surface, it was a technical specification. But at its core, it was a philosophical provocation. Bitcoin was not only a digital currency; it was a thought experiment in institutional bypassing.

Its architecture was deliberately hostile to centralised control. There was no central bank to adjust the supply, no corporate board to steer policy, no nation-state to underwrite value. Instead, scarcity was enforced by code: a maximum supply of 21 million coins, released at a diminishing rate, with new units issued as rewards to those who helped secure the network through a process called mining. Transactions were validated by a distributed network of nodes rather than a central clearinghouse. Every action was recorded on a public ledger—transparent, immutable, and synchronised across thousands of machines.

The motivation behind this design becomes clearer when contrasted with the mechanics of the system it sought to replace. In traditional finance, trust is institutional: you rely on the integrity of a bank, the credibility of a regulator, or the legal enforceability of contracts. Bitcoin inverted this. It placed trust not in people or organisations but in protocol—a predefined set of rules that anyone could inspect and no single actor could arbitrarily alter. In essence, *it turned trust from a social promise into a cryptographic guarantee.*

Satoshi Nakamoto's identity remains unknown. Despite countless theories, investigations, and self-proclaimed inventors, the creator of Bitcoin has never been conclusively identified. Some believe it was a single individual; others suspect a group. Satoshi corresponded publicly with early developers and contributors, but by 2011, they had vanished from the project entirely. This anonymity has only heightened the symbolic power of Bitcoin: a system launched without a central figure, a founder's fortune untouched, and no one to prosecute, lobby, or co-opt. In contrast to the founder-centric narratives of Silicon Valley, Bitcoin's origin is almost mythological—an artefact left behind like digital scripture.

But mythology alone does not sustain value. What gave Bitcoin traction in its early years was a small but determined group of technologists, cryptographers, and ideological misfits who saw in it a real-world application of earlier efforts to build sovereign digital money. These efforts date back to the cypherpunk movement of the 1990s—a community of privacy advocates, mathematicians, and digital libertarians who believed that strong cryptography could serve as a tool for individual empowerment in the face of growing surveillance and centralised control. Many cypherpunks had experimented with digital cash before—projects like DigiCash, Hashcash, and b-money—but all had either failed to gain adoption or relied too heavily on central authorities. Bitcoin succeeded not because it was the first attempt, but because it solved key problems others had not: the double-spending problem, the coordination of consensus without trust, and the embedding of incentive structures to maintain security at scale.

Still, for the first few years, Bitcoin was mostly a curiosity. Early adopters were drawn by ideology, curiosity, or technical challenge—not profit. Coins were mined on laptops, transactions took place in niche forums, and prices hovered around pennies. But this changed gradually as more people recognised that Bitcoin was not just an academic exercise but a working system—a network that continued to function, resist attack, and grow in value without a central operator.

The moment Bitcoin first truly entered the public consciousness came not from a breakthrough, but a pizza. In May 2010, a Florida programmer named Laszlo Hanyecz paid 10,000 BTC for two Papa John's pizzas—now worth hundreds of millions in hindsight. While often retold for its absurdity, this event marked a milestone: a theoretical currency had become a medium of exchange. Later, exchanges like Mt. Gox allowed users to trade Bitcoin for fiat currencies, and by 2013, Bitcoin was being discussed in mainstream financial press—not just as a novelty, but as an emerging asset class.

But with visibility came volatility. The same attributes that made Bitcoin immune to censorship also made it attractive to criminals. The Silk Road, an online black market, used Bitcoin as its primary payment method until it was shut down by the FBI in 2013. Regulatory scrutiny intensified. Questions emerged about whether Bitcoin was a currency, a commodity, or something else entirely. Governments were unsure how to classify or tax it. Banks were reluctant to touch it. And still, the network grew.

Each time Bitcoin was declared dead—after a major hack, a price crash, or a regulatory crackdown—it re-emerged with more resilience. Part of this durability lies in its decentralised structure. But it also lies in the fact that Bitcoin, despite its clunky interface and slow throughput, solves a specific problem that has not gone away: the fragility of institutional trust. In countries with capital controls, inflation, or banking crises, Bitcoin is not theoretical—it is practical. In authoritarian regimes where financial activity is monitored or restricted, the ability to store and transmit value outside the state's purview is not just a convenience; it is protection.

Bitcoin's critics rightly point out its limitations. It is slow by design, processing only a handful of transactions per second. Its mining process consumes enormous energy, raising environmental concerns. Its price is highly volatile, making it unsuitable for everyday payments. It has spawned a cottage industry of speculation, scams, and ideological extremism. But these issues, while significant, do not erase its core achievement: Bitcoin demonstrated that a decentralised, trustless system of digital value could not only exist, but persist.

It also forced a conversation that traditional finance could no longer ignore. Central banks began researching digital currencies. Governments debated regulation, taxation, and enforcement. Developers launched second-generation platforms like Ethereum, expanding on Bitcoin's principles to support programmable contracts and decentralised applications. The wider crypto ecosystem now includes everything from lending platforms to governance tokens, from NFTs to decentralised autonomous organisations. But it all began with one simple but radical proposition: *that money could be disintermediated.*

The birth of Bitcoin was not a product launch. It was a political act, disguised as code. It offered no grand promises, no marketing campaign, no founder roadshows. Just a white paper, a message in a block, and a system that has continued to operate—without downtime, CEO, or central server—for over a decade. Whether one views Bitcoin as an asset, a tool, or a symbol, it remains an artefact of a historical moment: the moment when the question of who controls money was asked not by petition, but by protocol.

And once asked, it could not be unasked.

Chapter 2
The Building Blocks of Crypto

Ask most people to describe cryptocurrency, and Bitcoin inevitably comes up. Ask them how it works, however, and the conversation often fizzles. Public awareness has grown, yet the mechanics remain opaque to anyone not immersed in software engineering or financial jargon. Intelligence isn't the barrier here—framing is. Much of the confusion stems from how crypto has been taught and marketed, often assuming the learner is either an aspiring developer or a day trader. This chapter takes a different approach: it begins with the assumption that you are capable of understanding crypto, provided the explanation respects your time and intellect.

Cryptocurrency is built on principles that are, in essence, familiar. What often gets lost is the bridge connecting abstract technical concepts to intuitive, real-world ideas. Words like blockchains, tokens, proof-of-stake, and private keys can seem exotic, but they solve very human problems: recording agreements, proving ownership, preventing fraud, and coordinating strangers around shared rules. These issues are hardly new—they have existed since the earliest markets. Crypto's innovation lies not in inventing problems, but in offering new solutions to long-standing ones.

Central to this system is the blockchain. Often described as a "distributed ledger," this term captures the technical truth but misses the deeper significance. Imagine a Google Doc shared across thousands of participants, where every change is recorded, verified, and visible to all. Now imagine that this document cannot be altered retrospectively, and each entry links cryptographically to the one before it. That is a blockchain: a continuously updated record of transactions with no single controller but universal transparency. Its significance lies not in the data itself, but in the trust architecture it establishes. Blockchains replace institutional trust with procedural certainty, ensuring no transaction can be falsified or hidden—a crucial innovation in a world where centralised databases are vulnerable to manipulation or attack.

On this foundation operate the assets, agreements, and interactions that comprise the crypto economy. Coins are the native currencies of their blockchains—Bitcoin on Bitcoin, Ether on Ethereum. They function not only as digital units of value, but also as instruments of coordination: incentivising behaviour, securing networks, and enabling transactions. Tokens, by contrast, are layered atop existing blockchains. They can represent anything: dollars (via stablecoins), equity in a decentralised application, or voting rights within a governance system. The distinction is subtle but critical: coins underpin the infrastructure, tokens leverage it. Protocols—often encoded as smart contracts—define how these assets behave. If blockchains are the roads, tokens are the vehicles, and protocols are the traffic laws. Grasping these layers is essential to navigate crypto without being misled by hype or mislabelling.

Security, however, is not just abstract—it lives in the interface between users and assets: wallets and private keys. Private keys are strings of characters akin to a master password, proving ownership of crypto assets. Lose it, and access is gone; share it, and anyone can seize your holdings. There is no "forgot password" option. Wallets store and manage these keys: hot wallets remain online and convenient but vulnerable, cold wallets offline and secure but less accessible. The choice of wallet is as much philosophical as it is technical: how much control are you willing to assume, and what are you prepared to entrust elsewhere?

Custody is the fulcrum of crypto literacy. In traditional finance, institutions hold your money; in crypto, you can be your own bank. That empowerment carries responsibility. Exchanges can fail, devices can malfunction, keys can be lost. Awareness of these risks is essential. Understanding self-sovereignty versus delegated security is not optional—it distinguishes informed participation from reckless speculation.

This chapter equips you with the conceptual toolkit to navigate crypto confidently. Not through rote memorisation of acronyms, but by grasping the logic underpinning each element. Blockchains record truth without arbiters. Coins and tokens coordinate value and governance. Consensus mechanisms maintain integrity without trust. Private keys define ownership without intermediaries.

Individually, each component is powerful; together, they form a programmable, permissionless economic system that is still very much under construction.

Crypto is often portrayed as a destination requiring mastery or investment. In reality, it is a set of building blocks. Understanding them requires curiosity and clarity, not adoption or allegiance. You do not need to become a developer to comprehend the architecture. Without that understanding, decisions—whether to engage, abstain, or critique—will be shaped by assumption rather than insight.

In the chapters ahead, each component will be unpacked not as technical jargon, but as a puzzle worth solving—because it underpins a system quietly rewriting rules most people do not yet realise are negotiable. Crypto's complexity is not impenetrable; it is legible to those who ask the right questions. And crucially, those questions are not only technical—they are human: who decides? Who benefits? Who is accountable? The answers start here.

What the Heck Is a Blockchain?

The most transformative technologies often hide behind language that makes them sound more complicated than they are. "Blockchain" is a prime example. The word itself is awkward and opaque—conjuring images of machinery or cryptic code rather than something practical or relevant. But at its core, a blockchain is simply a way of recording information so that no one person or institution can change it after the fact, and everyone can see exactly what has happened. It is a public memory that cannot be quietly rewritten. Once you understand that, you're already closer than most to grasping why this technology matters.

Imagine for a moment a public noticeboard in the centre of a town. Anyone can pin a note to it—say, a record of a sale, a contract, or a declaration—and everyone else in the town can read what was posted, when it was posted, and who posted it. Once pinned, the note is permanently visible and cannot be removed without leaving an obvious trace. Now imagine that this board exists not in one place, but is mirrored across thousands of other town squares around the world. Every time someone adds a new note to any board, all the others automatically update to match, and everyone in every town can see the exact same, verified version. That is, in essence, how a blockchain works. It is a *distributed ledger*—a shared digital record-keeping system that updates simultaneously across a network of participants and is practically impossible to tamper with after entries are made.

This sounds simple, and conceptually, it is. But the implications are anything but trivial. Historically, keeping trustworthy records has always required trust in a central authority—a bank to record balances, a government to record land titles, a notary to witness contracts. These intermediaries are necessary because people don't inherently trust one another, particularly when money, ownership, or identity is involved. Blockchain technology proposes a different route: don't trust a person or institution; trust a system that doesn't allow anyone to cheat. Rather than relying on a gatekeeper to validate or store information, you allow anyone to participate, while the system itself ensures the integrity of the records through mathematical rules and distributed consensus.

Each record on a blockchain is stored in a "block," which contains a bundle of data—typically a list of transactions—and a unique code called a cryptographic hash. This hash is a fingerprint of the block's contents. Any small change to the data completely alters the hash, making tampering obvious. Each block also contains the hash of the previous block, linking them together in chronological order—hence, a chain of blocks. This design is what makes blockchains *immutable*: once information is added, it's locked into the structure of the chain, and rewriting it would require altering every subsequent block across every copy of the ledger, simultaneously—a task that becomes exponentially more difficult as the chain grows and as more participants join the network.

This structure solves two enduring problems in digital record-keeping: *data integrity* and *distributed consensus*. The Internet made it easy to copy, edit, and transmit data. What it lacked was a native mechanism for guaranteeing that a digital record was accurate, final, and agreed upon by all parties without relying on a central server or authority. Blockchain fills that gap. It provides an infrastructure where everyone can see the same version of events and know that those events haven't been retroactively changed. This doesn't mean blockchains are magical or perfect—only that they offer a novel set of trade-offs: transparency over opacity, decentralisation over control, and verifiability over trust.

Different blockchains can serve different purposes. Bitcoin, the original blockchain network, was designed as a ledger for financial transactions—a way to track who owns what without a central bank. Ethereum, a later development, expanded this concept by allowing users not just to transfer tokens, but to run code on the blockchain in the form of "smart contracts." These are self-executing agreements with the logic of the contract written directly into code. Imagine an escrow agreement that releases payment only when certain conditions are met, and enforces those conditions automatically without needing a lawyer or an institution to mediate. That is what smart contracts enable.

There are now blockchains designed for supply chain traceability, digital identity verification, intellectual property management, and even voting. What unites them is their reliance on a shared, tamper-resistant record that everyone can audit but no one can singlehandedly control. This is what makes blockchain a general-purpose technology—*not because it solves every problem*, but because it reconfigures how we think about record-keeping and authority in a networked world.

That said, the question of who gets to write to the blockchain—and how—is not a trivial one. For a blockchain to work, there must be a reliable method for determining which new blocks are valid and who gets to add them. This is where consensus mechanisms come into play, which we'll examine in detail later. For now, it's enough to understand that consensus is how a decentralised group agrees on what happened without trusting each other. That consensus is then encoded into the blockchain itself, so that the system's memory reflects only agreed-upon events.

To bring this into a more familiar context, consider Google Docs. When multiple people collaborate on the same document, each participant sees updates in real time, and the history of changes is tracked automatically. You don't need to trust that your colleague typed what they claimed—they did it right in front of you, and the document itself records the revision. Blockchain works on a similar principle, but without Google as the host. The document is not stored on a company's server; it's distributed across many nodes, all of which verify and store identical copies. Instead of trusting Google to enforce permissions and retain history, the rules of participation and record-keeping are embedded in the blockchain's protocol and enforced collectively.

The implications of this go well beyond cryptocurrency. In a world where data breaches are common, where central databases can be hacked or corrupted, and where institutional trust is weakening, blockchain offers a fundamentally different model for maintaining integrity. But it also raises new challenges. Blockchains are transparent by design, which can be a benefit or a liability depending on the use case. Public blockchains expose all transactions to scrutiny—great for auditing, problematic for privacy. The technology is also slower and more resource-intensive than traditional databases. You don't use a blockchain because it's fast or efficient. You use it because you don't want to rely on any single actor to tell the truth.

This shift—from trust in people and institutions to trust in protocols—is what makes blockchain significant, and also controversial. It challenges deeply entrenched roles: banks, registrars, custodians, and central authorities of all kinds. It also demands a different kind of literacy. You don't need to write code to understand the social implications of this technology, but you do need to grasp what it changes: who verifies the facts, who owns the data, and who controls access to participation.

At its best, blockchain is a democratising force—not because it guarantees equity, but because it reduces the barriers to building, verifying, and transacting in open systems. At its worst, it can become another buzzword for speculative projects or poorly thought-through applications. The distinction lies not in the technology itself, but in how it is applied and who gets to shape its rules.

Understanding what a blockchain is, then, is not just a matter of technical fluency—it's a form of conceptual readiness. It allows you to assess claims, spot exaggerations, and evaluate whether a blockchain is actually necessary in a given context, or simply being used for marketing gloss. The core idea is not mystical. It's a public ledger secured by code and shared across many participants. The promise is not that it will solve everything, but that it allows us to build systems where records cannot be quietly altered and truth cannot be monopolised.

In that sense, blockchain is not a product you buy or a service you subscribe to. It's a foundation—a new way of structuring shared digital reality, one entry at a time. And understanding that foundation is the first step toward navigating a world where decentralised systems are no longer hypothetical, but increasingly real.

Tokens, Coins, and Protocols

The moment someone begins exploring cryptocurrency, they're likely to encounter an apparently simple question that quickly proves frustrating: what's the difference between a coin and a token? And what exactly is a protocol? The confusion here is understandable. Crypto terminology has evolved faster than consensus about its usage. Terms are often deployed loosely, inconsistently, and without explanation—sometimes even by people building the systems in question. But these distinctions are not trivial. They reflect fundamentally different architectures, incentives, and use cases. Without clarity on these concepts, it becomes difficult to evaluate what a crypto asset actually *does*, how it works, or whether its underlying system is credible.

Start with coins. In the crypto context, a *coin* is typically the native digital asset of a blockchain protocol. Think of Bitcoin (BTC) for the Bitcoin network, or Ether (ETH) for Ethereum. These assets are integral to the functioning of their respective chains: they're used to pay transaction fees, reward participants who maintain the network, and in many cases, to signal governance preferences. Coins are not created or issued arbitrarily—they are produced according to the specific rules of the protocol they inhabit. Bitcoin, for example, has a maximum supply of 21 million coins, released through a mining process governed by proof-of-work. Ethereum has no hard cap, but issues Ether as part of its proof-of-stake consensus system, with recent changes introducing mechanisms to burn or reduce the supply over time. In both cases, the coin is inseparable from the network—it *is* the network's lifeblood.

Tokens, by contrast, are created *on top of* existing blockchains. They do not require their own network infrastructure. Instead, they leverage the computational and security guarantees of a base layer, such as Ethereum or Solana, to operate. This distinction is analogous to building an app on an operating system. Tokens are governed by smart contracts—pieces of code that define how the token behaves, how it can be transferred, and what rules govern its issuance or destruction. There are standards that help ensure compatibility—for example, the ERC-20 standard for fungible tokens or ERC-721 for non-fungible tokens (NFTs) on Ethereum. But fundamentally, tokens are modular instruments. They can represent currencies, shares, governance rights, access passes, loyalty points, and more. Their versatility is part of what has made platforms like Ethereum so vibrant, but also what makes due diligence so important. Two tokens can be functionally identical in code, yet radically different in credibility.

The rise of tokens created a new class of assets that blurred the boundary between money, equity, and utility. Some are pegged to fiat currencies—so-called stablecoins, such as USDC or USDT—which aim to offer the price stability of dollars with the flexibility of crypto. Others are governance tokens, granting holders a vote in the future of a protocol, such as UNI for Uniswap or MKR for MakerDAO. Still others are more speculative, created for decentralised applications with niche purposes, or launched as part of a funding mechanism through initial coin offerings (ICOs). While tokens can often be traded like coins, their underlying logic—what they represent, how they are issued, and what rights they confer—is dramatically more varied. *Not all tokens are currencies, and not all should be treated as investments.*

This brings us to the concept of protocols. A *protocol* in the crypto world is a set of rules, often encoded as smart contracts, that define how a system operates. It's the software layer that governs behaviour—not just of machines, but of people interacting through digital infrastructure. Bitcoin is a protocol. So is Ethereum. But so too are the rules that govern decentralised exchanges like Uniswap, lending platforms like Aave, or stablecoin systems like Maker. These protocols can be open-source, modular, and composable—meaning that they can interact with one another, build on each other, or be forked into new versions. Understanding the design of a protocol is crucial to assessing a crypto asset's legitimacy and durability. Is it decentralised or reliant on a central admin key? Are its rules transparent and upgradeable through consensus? Are incentives aligned to encourage responsible use and disincentivise abuse?

The distinction between coins, tokens, and protocols isn't academic—it's structural. It affects how systems behave under stress, how governance decisions are made, and how users interact with the ecosystem. Consider the collapse of TerraUSD (UST), a so-called algorithmic stablecoin that promised dollar parity without being backed by actual dollar reserves. UST was a *token* governed by a protocol that attempted to stabilise its price through an interplay with another token, LUNA. When confidence in the mechanism faltered, the entire system unwound rapidly, wiping out billions of dollars in value. This wasn't a failure of crypto broadly—it was a failure of protocol design, compounded by user misunderstanding of how the system actually worked. Many participants assumed that "stablecoin" implied dollar safety, when in fact, UST was an experimental mechanism with no fiat backing and a reflexive feedback loop that amplified volatility.

Contrast that with USDC, a stablecoin issued by Circle and backed 1:1 by reserves held in regulated financial institutions. USDC is also a *token*, but its stability is maintained not by algorithmic arbitrage, but by the promise—and auditability—of fiat backing. It's not trustless, but it is transparent. This example illustrates why surface labels aren't sufficient. You must understand *how* a token is stabilised, *what* a protocol guarantees, and *where* the pressure points are.

Similarly, governance tokens often sound empowering—giving users a voice in protocol development. But the mechanics vary widely. In some cases, a small group of insiders holds the majority of tokens, rendering "decentralised governance" little more than a marketing term. In others, voting participation is low, decisions are opaque, or technical barriers limit meaningful engagement. This isn't to say governance tokens are worthless—only that they are not equivalent to democratic control unless backed by meaningful participation and transparency.

Ethereum provides a useful case study in how all three elements—coin, token, and protocol—interact. Ether (ETH) is the coin. It pays for transaction fees and secures the network through staking. Tokens—ranging from stablecoins to governance rights—are built on top of Ethereum using smart contract standards. And the Ethereum protocol itself is a continuously evolving set of rules, upgraded through a decentralised process involving developers, validators, and community stakeholders. This layered structure is what enables Ethereum to function not just as a currency, but as a *platform*—a base layer for an entire ecosystem of financial and social experiments.

Bitcoin, in contrast, is intentionally minimal. It has no native token system or smart contract language. Its focus is singular: to be a decentralised, censorship-resistant store of value and medium of exchange. Its protocol is more conservative, its development process more cautious, and its monetary policy fixed. This design ethos reflects different priorities—security, simplicity, and predictability over flexibility. Neither approach is universally superior. Each reflects a set of trade-offs that matter depending on your goals: whether you want to build, store, transact, govern, or speculate.

Altcoins—a broad term for any coin that isn't Bitcoin—occupy a wide spectrum of seriousness and credibility. Some, like Litecoin or Monero, offer tweaks to Bitcoin's design—faster block times, enhanced privacy. Others, like Solana or Avalanche, aim to compete with Ethereum as smart contract platforms, optimising for speed or scalability. Still others are barely disguised cash grabs, created to capitalise on hype without offering technical or economic substance. Understanding which is which requires more than tracking price charts. It requires evaluating the protocol's architecture, its incentive design, its security model, and its community governance.

For thoughtful participants—whether they are users, regulators, builders, or critics—these distinctions matter. A coin is not just a digital asset; it reflects the economic engine of a blockchain. A token is not just a tradeable unit; it can represent anything from collateral to membership to creative rights. A protocol is not just code; it is a constitution—defining who can do what, under which conditions, and with what consequences.

This conceptual clarity allows for sharper questions. If a project claims to be decentralised, where is power actually concentrated? If a token claims to be stable, what backs it—and what happens when trust breaks down? If a coin claims to be scarce, who enforces that scarcity? If a protocol promises fairness, who designed the rules—and who can change them?

Crypto is full of marketing noise, often masking fragile assumptions with impressive language. But the underlying architecture is not unknowable. It is inspectable, debuggable, and increasingly standardised. The challenge is not inaccessibility—it is translation. Once you grasp the difference between a coin, a token, and a protocol, you are no longer in the dark. You have a map. You can ask the right questions, reject the wrong premises, and begin to engage not as a passive observer but as an informed participant. And in crypto, that distinction is not semantic. It is everything.

Mining, Staking, and Consensus

The single most important feature of a decentralised network is that it must function without relying on any one person to tell the truth. This isn't a philosophical stance—it's a practical necessity. If there's no central authority keeping the ledger, how do you prevent fraud? How do you ensure that people aren't spending the same coin twice, or creating money from nothing? These questions are at the heart of what makes cryptocurrency function. And the answer, broadly speaking, is *consensus*. But not consensus in the conventional, boardroom sense. In the world of blockchain, consensus refers to the method by which distributed participants agree on a single, accurate version of history—*without knowing or trusting each other*. It's a remarkable coordination problem, solved with mathematics, incentives, and carefully engineered constraints. To understand how this works, and why it matters, you need to understand two dominant models: proof-of-work and proof-of-stake.

Let's start with proof-of-work, the consensus mechanism behind Bitcoin and several other first-generation blockchains. Conceptually, it's easy to grasp if you reframe it as a race to solve a cryptographic puzzle. Imagine a giant lottery that resets every ten minutes. Participants—known as miners—compete to find a solution to a complex mathematical problem. The problem is hard to solve but easy to verify, much like a Sudoku puzzle: checking the answer is quick, but arriving at it takes time and effort. Once a miner finds the solution, they broadcast it to the network. If valid, they are given permission to add a new block of transactions to the blockchain and receive a reward, paid in newly minted coins and transaction fees.

The brilliance of this system lies in its simplicity. To attack the network or rewrite history, you would need to control a majority of the total computational power—an immense and costly undertaking. It's not impossible in theory, but in practice it becomes prohibitively expensive. This is why Bitcoin has remained secure for over a decade. The cost of dishonesty is high, and the reward for playing by the rules is steady. *Proof-of-work transforms electricity into security*—a mechanism that makes cheating more expensive than cooperation.

However, this security comes at a cost. Proof-of-work is energy-intensive by design. Its effectiveness hinges on making it expensive to participate dishonestly. This has sparked legitimate concerns about sustainability, especially as the network scales. Critics point to the carbon footprint of Bitcoin mining, especially when powered by coal or other non-renewable energy sources. Supporters counter that a growing proportion of mining now uses renewable energy, and argue that the energy use is justified by the robustness and independence of the system. Either way, it is clear that *proof-of-work prioritises security and neutrality over efficiency*—a trade-off that not all blockchain networks are willing to make.

Enter proof-of-stake, a newer consensus mechanism that aims to secure networks without the need for massive computational effort. Ethereum, the second-largest blockchain, transitioned to this model in 2022 in an upgrade known as "the Merge." The core idea is elegant: instead of expending electricity to win the right to validate blocks, participants lock up—or *stake*—a portion of their cryptocurrency as a form of collateral. Validators are then chosen to create new blocks based on the amount of stake they have and, in some models, how long they've been staking or how randomly they're selected. If a validator behaves dishonestly—attempting to approve invalid transactions or manipulate the system—their stake can be *slashed*, meaning they lose some or all of their deposit.

The incentives are clear and aligned. Honest validators earn rewards; dishonest ones risk losing their capital. The cost of misbehaving is no longer computational—it's economic. This approach drastically reduces energy consumption, making the network more environmentally friendly and accessible. It also changes the game theoretics. While proof-of-work rewards sheer hardware power, proof-of-stake rewards capital commitment and honest participation. *You must have something to lose in order to be trusted.*

But proof-of-stake is not a perfect substitute. It introduces new concerns. Critics worry that it may lead to concentration of power, where those with the most capital gain disproportionate influence. In theory, a participant with enough stake could exert undue control over block validation, although most modern implementations include countermeasures—such as random selection, slashing risks, and governance limits—to mitigate this. Another tension lies in accessibility: while staking is less resource-intensive than mining, it still requires technical know-how and significant up-front capital, potentially centralising influence in the hands of exchanges or staking-as-a-service providers. In practice, the ecosystem is still grappling with how to balance accessibility, decentralisation, and security under proof-of-stake.

These two models—proof-of-work and proof-of-stake—represent different philosophies of trust and participation. Proof-of-work is battle-tested, adversarial, and rooted in thermodynamic cost. It says: "If you want to write to this ledger, you must prove that you spent real resources to earn the right." It's slow, deliberate, and difficult to compromise, which is precisely why Bitcoin's monetary policy is seen as credible and unchangeable. Proof-of-stake, by contrast, is agile, capital-efficient, and more sustainable. It says: "If you want to help secure this network, put your money where your mouth is." It relies on economic alignment rather than brute force. Both models have their merits, and both are evolving rapidly as developers experiment with hybrids and new variants.

There are also lesser-known consensus mechanisms being tested—delegated proof-of-stake (DPoS), used by networks like EOS and Tezos, which adds a layer of representative voting; proof-of-authority (PoA), often used in private or permissioned chains; and Byzantine Fault Tolerance (BFT) variants designed for fast finality. These systems often trade maximum decentralisation for speed or efficiency, and each comes with its own trade-offs. The choice of consensus mechanism is not just technical—it's political. It determines who gets to participate, how power is distributed, and what kinds of behaviour are rewarded or punished.

To make this tangible, consider an analogy. Imagine a giant communal spreadsheet that records every transaction ever made. You want to make sure that this spreadsheet is accurate, tamper-proof, and open to anyone to inspect. But you don't want just anyone scribbling on it—you need rules about who gets to write, how they gain that privilege, and what happens if someone tries to cheat. Proof-of-work says: *"You may write if you burn enough fuel to prove your seriousness."* Proof-of-stake says: *"You may write if you lock up your valuables as a promise of good behaviour."* Both models are trying to solve the same problem—how to coordinate strangers across the globe to agree on a single, shared history—without relying on a referee.

What makes this question urgent is that consensus mechanisms are not just technical architecture. They are foundational to how blockchains generate trust. A cryptocurrency's value proposition isn't only its supply cap, transaction speed, or brand recognition. It's the integrity of its consensus. A ledger that can be rewritten is not a ledger—it's a suggestion. A consensus mechanism that can be gamed is not neutral—it's an instrument of power. When people ask whether Bitcoin or Ethereum or any other network is "secure," they are really asking: *Can I trust this network to enforce its rules fairly, even under pressure?* Consensus is the answer.

Understanding mining and staking is therefore not about choosing sides, but about grasping the mechanics of digital trust. It allows you to ask better questions. Where are the incentives misaligned? Who controls the infrastructure? What happens in edge cases? How easy is it to participate? How difficult is it to cheat? These are the questions that separate informed observers from passive speculators.

Ultimately, the brilliance of consensus in crypto is that it decentralises not just record-keeping, but rule enforcement. It embeds integrity into the process itself, rather than relying on goodwill or oversight. And while no system is flawless, the ongoing evolution of consensus models is one of the most important—and least understood—frontiers in digital infrastructure. Whether you're an investor, a developer, or a curious onlooker, knowing how these mechanisms work is indispensable to understanding what crypto *is*, and what it can become.

Private Keys and Wallets Explained

Ownership in the traditional financial system is largely defined by trust in institutions. You hold money in a bank, and that bank is legally obliged to return it to you. You invest through a brokerage, and that brokerage maintains records on your behalf. Even your physical cash—notes and coins—is backed by central banks and their legal frameworks. In every case, your access to assets is mediated by third parties. Crypto ownership is fundamentally different. It doesn't rely on institutions to confirm or enforce your rights. It replaces institutional trust with mathematical certainty. In this world, access equals ownership. *You own a digital asset if—and only if—you control its corresponding private key.*

This insight cannot be overstated. The private key is not a metaphor, nor is it something vaguely symbolic of access. It is a cryptographic reality. A private key is a long, randomly generated number that gives you control over a specific crypto address. Lose it, and you lose access—permanently. Share it, and you invite theft. Forget it, and no one—not the network, not a company, not a court—can recover your funds. *Control over the private key is not just access; it is possession, it is power, it is identity.*

To understand this more concretely, imagine you've received some Bitcoin. That Bitcoin is recorded on a public ledger, the blockchain, as being associated with your address—a sort of digital mailbox. But to send that Bitcoin elsewhere—to spend it, transfer it, or trade it—you must sign the transaction with your private key. This is akin to having a unique, unforgeable signature that proves you are the rightful sender. Without it, nothing moves. The system doesn't care who you are, where you live, or what your story is. It only cares whether the cryptographic proof matches. *In crypto, identity is mathematical, not bureaucratic.*

This shift brings radical empowerment—but also unprecedented responsibility. Custody in crypto doesn't mean storing coins on a device like you'd store files on a hard drive. It means safeguarding the keys that allow you to prove control. That's where wallets come in. Despite the name, a crypto wallet doesn't hold your assets. It stores and manages your keys. It's more like a keyring than a purse. Some wallets are physical devices, like USB sticks with specialised firmware. Others are software applications, mobile apps, browser extensions, or even pieces of paper. What matters is how they generate, store, and protect your keys.

Wallets fall broadly into two categories: custodial and non-custodial. In a custodial wallet, a third party—often a centralised exchange—holds your private key on your behalf. This is convenient and familiar. It feels like using an online bank account. But it reintroduces a critical element of trust: *you must rely on the custodian to act in good faith, remain solvent, and maintain security.* If the exchange is hacked, collapses, or denies you access, your assets are at risk. The infamous collapse of Mt. Gox in 2014, where over 850,000 bitcoins were lost, remains a cautionary tale. More recently, the downfall of FTX in 2022 reminded everyone that centralised failures are not relics of crypto's early days—they remain a present danger.

Non-custodial wallets, by contrast, put you in full control. The private key never leaves your possession. This aligns with the foundational ethos of crypto—self-sovereignty, censorship resistance, and disintermediation. But it also places the burden of security entirely on your shoulders. *There is no password reset. No customer support line. No safety net.* A misplaced backup phrase—a string of 12 or 24 words used to recover your wallet—can result in irreversible loss. And indeed, billions of dollars in crypto have been permanently lost due to forgotten keys or poorly stored backups.

This tension—between empowerment and responsibility—is at the heart of crypto custody. It's not just a technical choice, but a philosophical one. Do you value convenience or autonomy? Do you trust yourself more than you trust an institution? Are you prepared to be your own bank?

The spectrum of wallet options reflects this trade-off. Hardware wallets like Ledger or Trezor offer high security by keeping keys offline, while still being user-friendly. They're ideal for long-term holders who don't need frequent access. Mobile wallets like Trust Wallet or MetaMask offer convenience and ease of use, but may be more vulnerable to phishing or malware. Paper wallets—literally printed keys—are highly secure if stored properly, but fragile and impractical for active use. Then there are multi-signature wallets, which require multiple keys to approve a transaction—useful for organisations or shared custody.

One of the most consequential developments in wallet technology is the rise of smart contract wallets, such as those built on Ethereum. These programmable wallets allow for features like transaction limits, account recovery mechanisms, and social guardianship—where trusted friends or devices can help restore access. This opens the door to more user-friendly custody without sacrificing control. But it also introduces complexity and new attack surfaces. *Smart wallets blur the line between custody and computation.*

It's tempting to assume that wallet choice is a matter of convenience. But in practice, it can become a matter of survival. For journalists in authoritarian regimes, dissidents, or vulnerable populations, having a non-custodial wallet can be the difference between financial agency and total loss. For wealth managers or institutions, balancing security with operational access is a sophisticated risk management exercise. Even for everyday users, losing access due to a device failure, upgrade mistake, or misplaced backup is a constant threat. The cautionary tales are legion: people digging through landfill sites for discarded hard drives, or locked out of fortunes worth millions due to forgotten passphrases.

Understanding wallets and private keys is thus foundational. It's not merely technical trivia—it's *the mechanism by which crypto enables trustless ownership.* In a system where there are no banks to call and no courts to appeal to, possession is not nine-tenths of the law—it is the law. That realisation is both exhilarating and sobering. It demands a mindset shift from passive consumer to active custodian.

This also explains why education around wallets is arguably more important than education around coin prices or market trends. Without secure custody, everything else—investment strategy, network choice, utility—becomes moot. The best encryption protocols and consensus algorithms in the world cannot protect someone who exposes or forgets their key.

The broader implications are profound. Crypto redefines what it means to "own" something in a digital world. In traditional finance, your access is provisional—granted by terms of service, revocable by institutions. In crypto, your access is intrinsic, unmediated, and final. This brings new freedoms, but also new risks. It challenges long-held assumptions about security, identity, and responsibility. And it forces each participant to reckon with an uncomfortable truth: *freedom without understanding is just another form of risk.*

If you're serious about engaging with crypto—whether casually or professionally—then understanding keys and wallets is non-negotiable. It's not an optional technical detail. It's the bedrock upon which every transaction, application, and innovation in this space is built. Master it, and you gain the full benefit of the system. Ignore it, and you remain vulnerable—regardless of your intentions, values, or expertise.

There is no such thing as partial control in crypto. Either you hold the key, or you don't. Either you own it, or someone else does. The question is not whether you trust crypto. It's whether you're ready to trust yoursel

Chapter 3
Why People Invest in Crypto

At first glance, the rush into cryptocurrency might seem like nothing more than speculative mania—a high-stakes playground for tech-savvy thrill-seekers chasing overnight fortunes in an unregulated digital frontier. Yet to reduce crypto adoption to mere greed or novelty is to overlook the intricate lattice of motivations beneath the surface. Crypto is more than a market; it is a mirror. It reflects our yearning for fairness, our scepticism of institutions, our desire for autonomy, and, most tellingly, our emotional relationship with money and meaning. Why people invest is as much about psychology, ideology, and social narrative as it is about economics.

To grasp the power of crypto as an investment narrative, one must acknowledge its dual identity. On one hand, it is technological—a decentralised infrastructure allowing peer-to-peer finance without intermediaries. On the other, it is socio-economic—a story of escape, empowerment, or enrichment, depending on who is telling it. Purchasers do not simply buy crypto; they buy into what it represents. For some, it is a rebellion against entrenched banking systems; for others, a hedge against inflation; for yet more, a chance to level a field that has long seemed skewed.

The early idealism animating crypto adopters was born from a critique of centralised authority. Bitcoin, for instance, was not a corporate invention or academic project. Emerging in 2009 in the aftermath of a global financial collapse, its genesis block contained a striking message: "The Times 03/Jan/2009 Chancellor on brink of second bailout for banks." That timestamp was a manifesto—a rejection of bailouts, opaque governance, and monetary policy decisions that had precipitated widespread economic turmoil. Bitcoin was deliberately unbailoutable.

This independence initially attracted libertarians, technologists, and critics of fiat currency. Over time, however, appeal broadened. As central banks engaged in repeated quantitative easing and inflation gnawed at savings worldwide, crypto began to be seen less as an anti-establishment experiment and more as a legitimate asset class. In nations facing currency crises or strict capital controls—Venezuela, Nigeria, Argentina—crypto became not a speculative venture, but a lifeline. It facilitated remittances, cross-border payments, and preserved financial dignity where traditional systems faltered.

Meanwhile, the financialisation of crypto in developed economies accelerated. Institutional investors entered the fray. Derivatives platforms and ETFs appeared. Wealth advisors were fielding questions from clients who had once dismissed digital coins outright. Crypto was leaving its countercultural niche, appearing in boardrooms, newspapers, and dinner table debates. Its volatility, lack of intrinsic value, and regulatory grey areas—once sources of alienation—were now selling points for risk-tolerant investors. For every person motivated by systemic critique, there were several hoping to multiply their portfolio tenfold.

Yet mainstreaming did not erase risk; it simply repackaged it. Crypto trades around the clock, creating an endless stream of price swings, notifications, and social chatter. Fear of missing out, or FOMO, looms constantly, nudging impulsive decisions. Dashboards are deliberately gamified, rewarding attention with colourful visual cues and real-time gains. Unlike regulated markets, crypto has few guardrails against manipulation, insider behaviour, or misinformation. Narrative often moves markets more than data.

This emotional dimension is further amplified by the culture of HODLing—a term that originated from a misspelt forum post in 2013. To HODL is to hold fast through market turbulence, placing faith in a coin's long-term trajectory. Behind the memes, however, lies psychology: investors often commit less because of rigorous analysis than emotional anchoring. Investment becomes entwined with identity. Crypto communities are not mere holders; they are tribes, movements, and occasionally, cults.

Despite the noise, tangible utility continues to grow. Cryptocurrencies facilitate faster, cheaper cross-border payments. In hyperinflationary regions, stablecoins help families preserve purchasing power. Freelancers bypass restrictive banking systems, and artists monetise digital work via NFTs. These examples are frequently overshadowed by headlines of dog-themed coins or celebrity-fuelled hype, yet they speak to crypto's long-term legitimacy, which will rest on utility as much as speculation.

Understanding crypto investment demands holding two truths simultaneously: the promise and the peril. It offers liberation for the financially excluded and temptation for the impulsive. It can inspire innovation or encourage gambling. It provides instruments for revolution and avenues for fraud. It seduces not only with logic, but with longing—for a fairer system, independence, generational wealth, or simply belonging.

The crypto market is as much psychological as it is financial. Behavioural finance illuminates why bubbles form, why people buy at peaks, cling to failing positions, and double down on flawed theses. Anchoring, confirmation bias, sunk cost fallacy, and herd mentality are all amplified in crypto, fuelled by social media echo chambers. Many believe they invest in technology, when in reality they respond to emotion—often amplified, reflected, and distorted by others.

As this chapter demonstrates, investing in crypto is not a binary of smart or foolish. It is a layered interplay of narratives, incentives, behaviours, and utility. Real people with real motivations navigate a volatile, misunderstood ecosystem. While some enter for gains and leave with losses, others find purpose, insight, or even meaningful profit.

What matters is not merely whether you invest, but why. Intentionality versus impulse, knowledge versus emotion, discernment versus delusion—these distinctions separate thoughtful participants from accidental casualties. Crypto will continue to attract attention, capital, and controversy. Understanding the human drivers behind the movement—freedom, fear, fairness, fortune—turns noise into insight.

This chapter seeks to deliver precisely that: a clear-eyed exploration of why people allocate money to this unusual asset class—not just to decipher the market, but to decode ourselves.

The Dream: Freedom, Fairness, and Fortune

There is something uniquely human about the way financial movements become philosophical ones. Money, in its most abstract form, is not merely a tool for exchange or a measure of wealth—it is a reflection of our values, ambitions, and societal structures. Cryptocurrency, in this sense, is not just a technological evolution in finance; it is a manifestation of an ongoing cultural and ideological shift. The crypto phenomenon has attracted attention not only because it promises financial returns, but because it taps into deeper yearnings for *freedom from control*, *fairness in systems*, and *fortune beyond reach*. To understand why millions across the globe have poured belief, time, and capital into crypto, we must begin not with the market charts but with the narratives that animate them.

At its ideological core, crypto speaks to a vision of *freedom*—not in the superficial sense of choosing one brand over another, but in the more profound sense of self-sovereignty. The original allure of Bitcoin, the first and still most symbolically important cryptocurrency, was not profit but principle. Emerging in the aftermath of the 2008 financial crisis, Bitcoin was conceived as a reaction against centralised power—against the idea that a handful of unelected officials could manipulate the money supply, debase currency through inflation, or rescue collapsing financial institutions while letting ordinary citizens bear the cost. In this context, Bitcoin was not merely a new kind of money; it was a protest. Its decentralised nature, capped supply, and transparent ledger represented an alternative to opaque central banking and unchecked monetary policy. *Owning Bitcoin was not just a financial choice—it was a political one.*

This philosophical stance drew its early adherents from the fringes: libertarians, cryptographers, anti-establishment thinkers. But it didn't take long for the vision to broaden. As traditional institutions lost public trust—amid data breaches, political scandals, rising inequality—crypto became a vessel for a growing sense that the system was rigged. Young people priced out of housing, workers locked out of equity markets, citizens in hyperinflationary economies—they all found in crypto a form of economic participation that didn't require institutional permission. *Crypto promised access without gatekeepers.*

The idea of *fairness* in the crypto context is subtle and often misunderstood. Critics point to the high volatility, the concentration of wealth among early adopters, and the proliferation of scams as evidence that crypto is anything but fair. And yet, proponents argue that the traditional financial system—rife with exclusion, fees, red tape, and discriminatory lending—is itself deeply unfair. They see crypto not as perfect, but as an *improvement in potential.* Consider the concept of "banking the unbanked." Across much of the developing world, millions of people are excluded from formal financial systems—not because they are unworthy, but because they lack paperwork, proximity, or institutional trust. With nothing more than a mobile phone and an internet connection, a person in rural Kenya or urban Lagos can now access decentralised finance protocols, stablecoins, and peer-to-peer transactions. This is not a speculative fantasy—it is already happening. *For the financially marginalised, crypto isn't a get-rich-quick scheme. It's a get-access-finally breakthrough.*

The fairness narrative also extends to creators. In the world of digital art, music, and writing, intermediaries have long dominated revenue flows. Record labels, publishers, and platforms often take the lion's share of income, while the creators themselves earn a fraction. Non-fungible tokens (NFTs), despite their hype-laden rollout, introduced a model in which creators could own and monetise their digital work directly—complete with automated royalties encoded into smart contracts. While the NFT market has seen its share of speculative excess, the core idea—of programmable ownership and direct patronage—remains a powerful reimagination of fairness in value creation.

And then, of course, there is *fortune.* No honest account of crypto adoption can ignore the financial motivations that drive it. From the early days of Bitcoin millionaires to the meme coin frenzies of recent years, crypto has become synonymous with windfall potential. The prospect of turning hundreds into thousands—or thousands into millions—has an undeniable gravitational pull. For many, especially those without access to traditional investment vehicles, crypto feels like a rare shot at upward mobility. It offers the kind of asymmetrical opportunity that Silicon Valley insiders and Wall Street players have long enjoyed—except, this time, the door appears open to the masses.

But fortune, in the crypto imagination, is not always personal. The dream of decentralised finance is also a dream of building systems that generate shared wealth rather than concentrated profit. Decentralised autonomous organisations (DAOs), yield farming protocols, and community-run blockchains represent attempts to *embed economic participation into the infrastructure itself.* Instead of passive consumption, participants become active stakeholders—governing platforms, proposing updates, and earning tokens in return. Whether these models are scalable or sustainable is still an open question. But they point to a redefinition of fortune: not just as individual gain, but as distributed upside.

Still, the pursuit of freedom, fairness, and fortune in the crypto space is not without its contradictions. *Not all dreams are equally achievable, and some come with costs.* The promise of freedom can become a burden of responsibility. Without central authorities, users must secure their own wallets, vet their own investments, and bear full liability for mistakes. The promise of fairness is often undercut by early access, unequal information, and insider advantage. The dream of fortune can lure people into high-risk behaviours, driven by hype, herd mentality, or outright deception. Crypto's architecture is neutral, but the outcomes it enables are shaped by human behaviour—and human behaviour is anything but rational or fair.

Moreover, the ideals espoused by crypto communities often conflict with their execution. For example, decentralisation is a rallying cry, yet many prominent crypto projects rely heavily on centralised exchanges or development teams. Transparency is championed, but many protocols operate with opaque governance and unclear incentives. The language of empowerment sometimes disguises schemes designed to extract capital from the uninformed. These tensions do not negate the dream, but they complicate it. They demand that we separate crypto's *potential* from its *performance*, its *promise* from its *practices*.

Even so, the narratives endure—because they tap into something elemental. When people talk about crypto, they are often really talking about their discontent with existing structures. They are talking about distrust in governments, banks, tech giants, or media institutions. They are expressing a desire to reclaim agency in a world that feels increasingly centralised, algorithmic, and unaccountable. Crypto, then, is not just a technology or an asset class—it is a story we tell about what might be possible if power were reimagined.

That story has real-world consequences. It influences policy debates about digital currencies, inspires entrepreneurs to build new systems, and informs the decisions of individuals moving their life savings into stablecoins or staking tokens. Whether those decisions lead to transformation or tragedy depends on more than belief—it depends on design, education, regulation, and community integrity. But without the dream, none of it would have started.

And so, the dream remains: *freedom from control, fairness in access, fortune for those left behind.* Whether crypto can deliver on all three is uncertain. But what is certain is that these aspirations are not going away—and any serious understanding of crypto must begin with them.

The Reality: Volatility and Vulnerability

It's easy to be seduced by headlines of overnight millionaires and life-changing gains. But for every tale of triumph in the crypto world, there are many more marked by chaos, confusion, and catastrophic loss. The crypto markets are not merely volatile in the way stocks or commodities might be—they are structurally unstable, deeply speculative, and largely unregulated. For many participants, particularly those without the technical savvy or emotional resilience to navigate this space, engaging with crypto is not a financial adventure—it is exposure to systemic risk. And unlike traditional finance, there is often no safety net.

Volatility in crypto is not incidental—it is architectural. Most crypto assets are not backed by physical commodities, government guarantees, or predictable revenue streams. Their price is determined by pure market sentiment—supply, demand, narrative, and attention. This creates an environment in which dramatic swings are normal. A coin might rise 40 percent in a single day on the back of a celebrity tweet, then lose 70 percent over the following week due to a regulatory rumour. Entire fortunes have been created and erased in the span of a long weekend. *To participate in crypto is to accept that the ground beneath your investment may shift without warning, logic, or recourse.*

Traditional markets have mechanisms to dampen this kind of turbulence—circuit breakers, oversight, institutional anchors. Crypto markets, by design, resist such controls. While this openness is celebrated as a feature, it comes with a cost: susceptibility to manipulation. Pump-and-dump schemes, coordinated buying groups, and influencer-driven hype cycles are rampant. Many tokens are launched with minimal disclosure, vague roadmaps, and no accountability. Retail investors often arrive late, lured by the illusion of momentum, only to find themselves exit liquidity for more informed actors.

But price volatility is only one part of the risk landscape. The emotional impact of such instability is profound, and it is underappreciated. Financial decisions, especially those involving significant personal capital, are never purely rational. They are coloured by fear, greed, shame, and euphoria. In crypto, where prices move with disorienting speed and social media reinforces every tick, the psychological strain can be severe. *Losses do not just erode wealth—they erode confidence, trust, and mental wellbeing.*

The culture of crypto trading often glamorises risk-taking and downplays caution. Online communities encourage participants to "HODL"—hold on for dear life—during downturns, dismissing rational exit strategies as weakness or betrayal. Others celebrate the thrill of "going all in," idolising figures who took massive bets and won. There is a persistent, almost cult-like belief that any hesitation or scepticism will cause you to miss "the next big thing." This creates a feedback loop in which newcomers, desperate not to be left behind, overexpose themselves in pursuit of unlikely gains. *The fear of missing out becomes a driver of reckless behaviour.*

Layered on top of this emotional volatility is the practical reality of fraud. Crypto has a scam problem—not as an incidental by-product of growth, but as a defining challenge of the ecosystem. Ponzi schemes, rug pulls, phishing attacks, fake exchanges, pump groups, and "airdrop" traps have cost investors billions. Because crypto transactions are irreversible and pseudonymous, once funds are lost, they are almost always unrecoverable. There is no central authority to appeal to, no call centre to request a reversal, no insurer to make you whole. *Self-custody means self-responsibility, and for many, it also means self-inflicted loss.*

Even those who avoid outright scams can fall victim to opaque risks. DeFi (decentralised finance) platforms often promise high yields—10%, 50%, even 1,000% APY—without clearly disclosing the mechanisms or risks involved. Many users deposit assets into smart contracts they don't understand, relying on the reputations of founders or influencers. These protocols may be vulnerable to coding errors, oracle manipulation, or governance attacks. In some cases, developers themselves exploit their control over the system, withdrawing funds or changing the rules after users have locked in their deposits. *The promise of decentralisation is undermined when power is not truly distributed.*

Custodial risk is another underacknowledged vulnerability. While many newcomers rely on centralised exchanges to store their crypto, these platforms are not banks. They are lightly regulated, often operate across jurisdictions, and may not offer meaningful consumer protection. If an exchange is hacked, freezes withdrawals, or disappears altogether—as has happened repeatedly—users may have little legal recourse. The collapse of FTX in 2022, once considered a blue-chip exchange, revealed just how fragile the facade of credibility can be. Users who believed they were holding assets discovered they held nothing but empty dashboards.

Technical failure is also a risk. Forgetting a password, misplacing a private key, sending coins to the wrong address—these errors can lead to permanent loss. Stories of people losing access to life-changing sums because of a misplaced USB stick or an outdated wallet file are not rare—they are emblematic. The very feature that makes crypto "trustless"—no intermediaries—is the same feature that makes it unforgiving. *In crypto, the line between ownership and oblivion is a string of characters. Lose it, and your assets are gone forever.*

Regulatory vulnerability further compounds the risk profile. Crypto operates in a legal grey zone in many jurisdictions. Rules change quickly, enforcement is uneven, and users often find themselves caught between inconsistent frameworks. A coin that is legal today may be banned tomorrow. A yield protocol that is accessible this week may be blocked by next. Entire categories of activity—staking, trading, privacy-enhancing tools—face potential restrictions depending on how regulators interpret them. This uncertainty affects not only prices but the viability of long-term strategies.

And yet, perhaps the most disorienting vulnerability is existential rather than technical. *Crypto does not guarantee a happy ending.* Many tokens have no intrinsic value. Many projects are abandoned. Many communities fracture. The idea that "number always goes up" is a myth constructed in bull markets and destroyed in bear ones. There are no fundamentals to fall back on, no earnings reports to anchor valuations, no central banks to intervene. What remains is narrative—and when belief fades, value evaporates.

For all its potential, crypto demands a new kind of literacy—one that blends technical understanding, emotional discipline, and sceptical inquiry. It requires users to think like engineers, act like risk managers, and learn from behavioural economists. It is not enough to read whitepapers or follow influencers. It is not enough to believe in the vision. *To participate in crypto responsibly is to acknowledge the ecosystem's fragility and to proceed with both eyes open.*

None of this negates crypto's promise. But it does contextualise it. The dream of decentralised finance, borderless assets, and economic inclusion cannot be realised if the ecosystem is riddled with fragility. Volatility and vulnerability are not footnotes—they are the terrain itself. Only by understanding them can we begin to navigate crypto with intelligence, caution, and integrity.

Beyond Speculation: Real Use Cases

Strip away the hype, memes, and moonshot fantasies, and a different picture of crypto emerges—one that is neither utopian nor hollow, but grounded in use. While the speculative frenzy has defined the headlines, what has quietly matured in the background is a decentralised financial infrastructure offering real utility to real people. *Crypto is not merely a playground for tech libertarians or get-rich-quick gamblers; it is a pragmatic toolset being wielded in some of the world's most volatile and underserved economic environments.*

Take remittances—arguably the most immediate and human use case. Migrant workers send over $800 billion globally each year, much of it through intermediaries that extract painful fees, delay transfers, and often exclude recipients without formal bank accounts. In countries like the Philippines, Mexico, and Nigeria, sending money through traditional remittance channels can cost anywhere from 5% to 15% in fees. Crypto dramatically reduces these frictions. A stablecoin transfer—such as one using USDC or USDT—can move value across borders in minutes, often at negligible cost, and without reliance on local banking infrastructure. For a mother in Lagos receiving money from her son in London, the difference is not abstract; it's food on the table, school fees paid on time, and dignity restored in the process.

This isn't hypothetical. In countries like El Salvador, crypto is being trialled at a national level. Despite the political and economic complexities surrounding its rollout, the experiment reveals something vital: *in contexts where trust in traditional financial systems is low, people are willing to try alternatives.* In Ukraine, amidst war and collapsing infrastructure, crypto donations have facilitated rapid, decentralised aid distribution in ways that conventional channels struggled to match. These are not crypto-native utopias—they are scenarios where legacy systems have failed, and decentralised ones are filling the vacuum.

Another sphere where crypto plays a critical role is inflation resistance. In places like Argentina, Venezuela, Zimbabwe, or Lebanon, inflation is not a concept buried in textbooks—it is an existential threat to savings. Local currencies can lose half their value within a year. Bank withdrawal limits, black-market exchange rates, and capital controls are common. In such environments, access to a censorship-resistant digital asset that holds value better than the national currency—even something as volatile as Bitcoin—can offer a meaningful hedge. For many, crypto is not an investment; it's an escape hatch.

Stablecoins—crypto tokens pegged to fiat currencies like the US dollar—extend this utility. While crypto critics often dismiss stablecoins as redundant or potentially dangerous, their on-the-ground use tells a different story. In Argentina, where the peso consistently devalues, workers increasingly request payment in USDT. In Nigeria, businesses accept stablecoins to shield revenues from sudden naira drops. In both cases, *stablecoins function as a parallel monetary system—not replacing local currencies entirely, but buffering against their dysfunction.*

Then there's the creator economy. NFTs, or non-fungible tokens, have been mostly caricatured in popular discourse—absurd monkey JPEGs selling for six figures, pump-and-dump art projects, speculative mania. But beneath the froth lies a powerful shift in how creators monetise their work and connect with audiences. Artists, musicians, and writers can now mint unique digital assets that represent ownership, access, or rights—and sell them directly to supporters without intermediaries. More importantly, many NFTs include programmable royalties, meaning that creators are paid automatically every time the asset is resold. *For the first time in digital history, creators have enforceable secondary income rights baked into the fabric of the internet itself.*

The broader implications of this are still unfolding. In a world where platforms like YouTube or Instagram control the terms of creative monetisation, NFTs offer an alternative architecture—one where creators retain control, visibility, and equity in their own outputs. Experimental projects are emerging that combine NFTs with membership models, patronage systems, and even co-operative governance. A digital cartoonist in São Paulo or a musician in Manila no longer needs a record label or publisher to reach global audiences or receive fair compensation. *Crypto rewrites the economic contract between artist and audience.*

Decentralised finance, or DeFi, offers another significant vector of real-world utility. At its best, DeFi replicates core functions of banking—lending, borrowing, saving, trading—without the traditional middlemen. This matters profoundly in underbanked regions. According to the World Bank, over 1.4 billion adults globally are unbanked. That number is not a reflection of laziness or ignorance—it reflects exclusion. Documentation requirements, geographic barriers, and discriminatory policies lock millions out of formal finance. DeFi tools, built on public blockchains, require only internet access and a crypto wallet to participate.

The sceptic's view is valid: DeFi can be fragile, experimental, and risky. But that critique is incomplete without acknowledging the risks of not having any access at all. *For those shut out of traditional systems, DeFi doesn't have to be perfect—it only has to be functional.* Yield farming protocols, liquidity pools, and algorithmic lending platforms may sound esoteric in London or New York, but in Lagos or Lahore, they represent new pathways to credit, savings, and opportunity. Even if imperfect, *they expand the financial map for people long written off it.*

There are other use cases still taking shape—blockchain-based identity systems, decentralised file storage, tokenised real estate, or micro-investing tools for emerging markets. Some will fail. Many already have. But that is true of any technological frontier. The early internet was full of clunky, overhyped projects too. What matters is not that every use case succeeds, but that enough of them do—and that their impact is not measured only in market capitalisation, but in lives improved.

Critically, what ties all these applications together is not speculation, but disintermediation. Crypto's value lies in its capacity to remove rent-seeking middlemen, reduce structural frictions, and widen access to systems previously gated by geography, privilege, or bureaucracy. Whether it's sending money to family, preserving wealth in a collapsing currency, funding creative work, or accessing credit, crypto is being used not just to bet on the future—but to fix the present.

This is not to ignore the contradictions. Crypto can reinforce inequality as easily as it disrupts it. Technical complexity still bars many users. Scam projects and predatory schemes often target the same vulnerable populations that crypto promises to serve. But those failures are not evidence of uselessness—they are evidence of *urgency. The fact that people reach for crypto in broken systems speaks not only to crypto's promise, but to the desperation of those systems themselves.*

What emerges, then, is not a binary story of scam or salvation, but a layered reality. *Crypto is not the answer to everything. But it is becoming an answer to more things than many assume.* As the infrastructure matures, regulation clarifies, and interfaces become more user-friendly, the shift from speculative asset to everyday tool will continue. Not because of ideology, but because of necessity.

If crypto's first chapter was defined by risk-takers and speculators, its next may be written by problem-solvers and pragmatists—people solving real issues, in real time, with tools that, for all their flaws, do something the old systems never did: *let them in.*

The Psychology of FOMO and "HODL"

In the midst of a market crash in December 2013, a misspelled word on a Bitcoin forum went viral. A frustrated user—possibly drunk, definitely distraught—typed "I AM HODLING" instead of "holding," referring to their refusal to sell during the downturn. That linguistic accident became a philosophy, a meme, and eventually a core identity in the crypto community. But beneath the humour lies something far more telling. *"HODL" is not simply about long-term investing; it's about emotional resistance in a market engineered to provoke irrationality.*

Crypto markets are uniquely wired to exploit human psychology. They operate 24/7, are globally accessible, and are flooded with volatility, tribalism, and social signalling. They reward impulsivity, punish hesitation, and blur the line between information and hype. To understand why people invest emotionally—and often destructively—in crypto, one must look not at blockchains or tokens, but at the architecture of the human mind.

FOMO, or Fear of Missing Out, is one of the most powerful psychological drivers in speculative environments. It's not new. Tulip mania in the 17th century, dot-com stocks in the 1990s, and meme stocks in 2021 all thrived on the same instinct. But crypto intensifies it through speed and visibility. You don't just hear that someone made a 10x return—you see it, in real time, on Twitter, Reddit, or Discord, complete with screenshots of gains and celebrations of "making it." The emotional signal is unambiguous: *You're being left behind.*

Behavioural economists have long studied this effect. In markets, people are not primarily motivated by rational risk-reward calculations; they're driven by *loss aversion.* The pain of missing a gain often outweighs the fear of enduring a loss. Daniel Kahneman's foundational work in *prospect theory* explains this bias: we irrationally weigh potential losses more heavily than equivalent gains, but in FOMO-driven contexts, perceived "social losses" (like not joining a mooning coin early) override that logic. We are not just afraid of financial loss—we fear *social exclusion from upside narratives.*

Crypto adds another layer: the "get-rich-while-you-sleep" mythology. You don't need to pitch investors, build a company, or clock in hours. You just need to buy early, HODL, and wait. This narrative seduces not because it's logical, but because it shortcuts years of psychological conditioning around effort and reward. It replaces delayed gratification with instant belonging in a success story. Every green candle validates the fantasy; every red one threatens to expose the illusion.

Ironically, the HODL mentality, born as a corrective to emotional selling, has itself evolved into a trap. It discourages critical thinking and encourages blind allegiance. What began as a rational commitment to long-term fundamentals now often becomes a refusal to re-evaluate positions. *The same emotional mechanisms that lead to panic buying also drive stubborn holding.* Confirmation bias—our tendency to seek out information that supports our existing beliefs—thrives in the echo chambers of Telegram chats and crypto Twitter threads. Once you've "gone all in," your identity becomes intertwined with the outcome.

Consider the psychological toll of riding crypto's volatility. When a coin surges 400% in a week, the dopamine hits hard. But when it plunges by 80%, it's not just a financial loss—it's an ego collapse.

Your judgment, your narrative, your optimism are all under siege. This emotional volatility mirrors the market's. Investors swing between euphoria and despair, not because of fundamentals, but because *their internal state is yoked to an external graph.* The market doesn't just move money; it moves identity.

Adding to the chaos is the performative nature of crypto investing. Gains are public. Losses are quiet. Leaderboards, badges, and meme-based status create a gamified environment in which investing feels like playing—not just financially, but socially. If you sell too early, you're mocked for lacking conviction. If you sell too late, you're ridiculed for being greedy. *The metrics for success are constantly shifting, which makes anchoring to rational goals extraordinarily difficult.*

This is not to say that all crypto investing is irrational—only that the surrounding environment rewards impulsive and emotional behaviours disproportionately. To invest wisely in crypto—or to avoid investing at all, if that's more appropriate—requires not just understanding markets, but understanding one's own psychological blind spots.

Behavioural strategies can help. *Pre-committing to exit points, using dollar-cost averaging, and maintaining written investment theses* can ground decisions in logic rather than emotion. Avoiding constant price-checking reduces exposure to short-term volatility-induced stress. Being sceptical of viral sentiment—especially when everyone seems to be getting rich—can preserve both capital and sanity. One of the most undervalued tools in crypto is simply boredom: the discipline to do nothing when there is nothing rational to do.

The social layer is equally critical. Crypto investors who surround themselves with rational peers tend to make better decisions than those immersed in high-emotion communities. Just as financial contagion spreads through networks, *emotional contagion does too.* The more a group reinforces urgency, hype, or tribal conviction, the harder it is to think independently. Building information hygiene—curating sources, limiting noise, and avoiding echo chambers—becomes a vital skill.

It's also important to question the narratives behind emotional investment. Why do people cling to projects with no traction? Why do they continue to buy into schemes despite red flags? Often, it's not about the project at all—it's about *what the project represents emotionally.* A small-cap altcoin might symbolise a chance to overcome systemic inequality. A failed NFT project might still carry the weight of one's creative aspirations. Emotional investments persist because they carry hopes, not just assets.

Crypto uniquely blurs the boundary between investing and identity. For some, buying into Bitcoin is a protest against fiat inflation; for others, it's an escape from economic exclusion. Ethereum represents not just a technology, but a vision of decentralised coordination. Meme coins become cultural artefacts. These identity layers complicate rational analysis. Once money is tied to meaning, the portfolio becomes a proxy for personal worldview.

To step back from these dynamics requires humility. It means recognising that *you are not immune to cognitive biases just because you understand them.* It means accepting that rationality is a practice, not a possession. And it means making peace with missed gains—because chasing every opportunity guarantees you'll eventually chase a disaster.

Ultimately, the antidote to FOMO is not cynicism—it is clarity. Not every opportunity is yours to take, and not every dip is yours to catch. The investors who survive and succeed in crypto are not the ones with the most conviction, but the ones with the most composure. They understand that while technology may change, *human nature doesn't.* The better you understand your own psychology, the less likely you are to become its victim—and the more likely you are to use the crypto markets, rather than be used by them.

Chapter 4
Wallets, Exchanges, and Custody—Where People Go Wrong

In the earliest days of Bitcoin, losing access to your funds might have meant misplacing a single sheet of paper. Today, the stakes are more immediate and complex: a misplaced click, a trusting tap on the wrong app, or a misjudged platform can erase wealth in moments. The tools for managing crypto have grown in sophistication, yet so have the pitfalls, blind spots, and seductive illusions of safety. Wallets are no longer mere digital folders. Exchanges have become far more than trading venues. And custody—the quiet, often overlooked art of safeguarding what is yours—has emerged as one of the most contested and misunderstood arenas in the entire crypto landscape. This chapter examines that infrastructure and the mistakes, both catastrophic and subtle, that shape how people interact with it.

At its core, cryptocurrency is about self-sovereign ownership. It makes a radical promise: you can hold, transfer, and access digital value without relying on a bank, a government, or any intermediary. Yet this promise is more delicate than many appreciate. Sovereignty is conditional, dependent on execution—on how private keys are stored, which platforms are trusted, and whether users even grasp the difference between control and mere access. And herein lies the common failure: convenience is mistaken for control, slick interfaces for security, and reputation for resilience.

Hot wallets and cold wallets are not mere technical distinctions—they embody choices about autonomy, risk, and responsibility. A hot wallet, connected to the internet, delivers convenience but exposes constant vulnerability. A cold wallet, kept offline, dramatically improves security, yet demands careful personal management. Neither is intrinsically superior; what matters is alignment. Does the storage method suit the user's habits, tolerance for risk, and intent? Too often, the easiest option is chosen over the safest.

Centralised exchanges occupy another crucial, paradoxical space. Platforms like Binance, Coinbase, and Kraken function as both gateway and middleman: they simplify trading and custody, but they reintroduce intermediaries that blockchain was designed to bypass. For casual users, this trade-off appears benign—until it is not. When exchanges fail, they do so spectacularly. The 2022 collapse of FTX was less a tale of market volatility than a cautionary lesson in misplaced trust, inadequate due diligence, and the illusion of decentralisation. Customers lost not because of price swings, but because their funds were never truly under their control.

Custody sits at the uncomfortable intersection of convenience and responsibility. The adage "Not your keys, not your coins" is more than rhetoric; it is a measure of genuine ownership. Without control of private keys, one has claims, not custody. This distinction becomes painfully clear when withdrawals are frozen, hacks occur, or companies go bankrupt. And yet, private key management remains poorly understood—rarely taught, often outsourced, and almost universally ignored until calamity strikes.

History offers cautionary tales. QuadrigaCX, the Canadian exchange whose founder allegedly held sole access to cold wallets before his death, left millions stranded. Mt. Gox, whose collapse in 2014 continues to reverberate, underscores the stakes. These failures are not isolated anomalies; they are symptomatic of a broader mismatch between decentralised assets and centralised habits. Users expect customer support, insurance, and recovery mechanisms in a system designed to dispense with such intermediaries.

Even those who assert control face another hurdle: complexity. Hardware wallets, seed phrases, multi-signature arrangements, and recovery protocols can feel like navigating a labyrinth without a map. The paradox is stark: those who trust too readily fall victim to third parties, while those attempting self-custody risk their own errors. Security in crypto is not merely technological; it is behavioural, contextual, and disciplined—and no amount of intelligence guarantees immunity.

Selecting an appropriate custody model is therefore not a matter of adopting the most advanced tool, but finding the right fit. A long-term investor with substantial holdings may require a cold wallet with geographical redundancy. A casual user holding a small sum in a meme token may be comfortable with a mobile wallet. A small enterprise accepting crypto payments may need multi-user access. The key is congruence: match the custody method to the threat model, and revisit that alignment as circumstances evolve.

Underlying all of this is a philosophical tension. Crypto promises personal freedom, yet freedom without literacy is perilous. Ownership implies responsibility: understanding how systems work, anticipating failure, and preparing for it. In conventional finance, the institution shields you; in crypto, you are the institution. That shift demands not only tools but a mindset.

This chapter aims to cultivate that mindset. It is not a technical manual but a strategic lens. We will unpack wallets, explore exchanges, dissect custody, and—above all—offer guidance for thinking clearly amid these choices. Principles will be grounded in real-world examples, myths surrounding "security" challenged, and frameworks provided for intelligent decision-making. In crypto, mistakes are seldom forgiven, but with knowledge, most are preventable.

Hot vs. Cold Wallets

Most people don't realise that when they "buy crypto," they're not really buying a coin or a token. What they are acquiring is a private key—a string of cryptographic information that gives them the exclusive right to move or spend that asset on a blockchain. That key is everything. If you hold it, you control the asset. If you lose it, no one can help you recover it. If someone else gets hold of it, they can empty your wallet without consequence, without trace, and without the possibility of reversal. *All digital ownership in crypto hinges on a single point of failure: your private key.* And that's why how you store that key—whether in a hot or cold wallet—is one of the most consequential decisions a crypto user will ever make.

Despite the seriousness of this decision, the language surrounding crypto wallets remains muddled by jargon and marketing. The terms "hot" and "cold" are widely used but poorly understood, often invoked without a clear explanation of what they actually mean in practice. At a high level, the distinction is simple: a **hot wallet** is connected to the internet, and a **cold wallet** is not. But the implications of that difference are profound. Connectivity introduces vulnerability. Air-gapped isolation introduces friction. Each trade-off matters.

A hot wallet is like a debit card in your back pocket. It gives you immediate access to your funds. You can send, receive, and interact with decentralised applications in real time. It's fast, user-friendly, and typically embedded in mobile apps, browser extensions, or desktop software. But the very features that make hot wallets convenient also make them dangerous. Because they are always online, they are always exposed—to malware, phishing attacks, rogue code libraries, and device compromise. Even the most careful user is only as secure as their operating system, browser integrity, and password hygiene.

Consider MetaMask, one of the most popular Ethereum wallets in the world. It lives in your browser, integrates seamlessly with decentralised apps, and allows you to interact with the world of DeFi, NFTs, and tokens with ease. But its ubiquity has made it a prime target. Fake MetaMask sites, malicious browser extensions, and phishing links designed to trick users into revealing their recovery phrases have all led to significant theft. *The more frictionless a wallet experience becomes, the more invisible the attack surface can be.*

Cold wallets, by contrast, are built on the principle of *deliberate inconvenience.* They prioritise safety over speed, redundancy over responsiveness. A cold wallet stores your private key offline—either on a specialised hardware device, an encrypted USB stick, or even written on paper and stored in a safe. Because it's disconnected from the internet, it cannot be hacked remotely. To authorise a transaction, you must physically connect the device and confirm the operation, often through a secure display and dedicated buttons that are isolated from your computer's operating system. This "air gap" protects against a vast array of digital threats.

The gold standard in this category is the hardware wallet. Products like Ledger Nano and Trezor have established themselves as the go-to solutions for long-term holders. These devices are not foolproof—nothing is—but they drastically reduce the attack vectors. They also shift the cognitive burden. Users must learn to manage seed phrases, secure backups, and recovery protocols. Mistakes can be costly. But *those mistakes are usually the user's*, not the result of third-party failure. Cold wallets demand responsibility—but they grant true custody in return.

This contrast raises a central tension in crypto security: *trusting yourself versus trusting the system.* A hot wallet trusts the infrastructure—your device, your software, your vigilance. A cold wallet trusts you. And many users, especially those new to crypto, overestimate both. They assume their phone is secure. They assume they'll remember their seed phrase. They assume they'll recognise a scam before it's too late. These assumptions persist until they fail—at which point, recovery is usually impossible.

There is no universal best choice. The right wallet setup depends on the use case. Traders who need constant access to funds may reasonably accept the risks of hot wallets, while long-term holders with significant assets should lean heavily toward cold storage. Some users maintain a hybrid approach—keeping small amounts in a hot wallet for daily use, while safeguarding the bulk of their holdings in cold storage. *Risk should be proportional to exposure.* But very few users consciously calculate that risk. They default to convenience.

Real-world consequences make these distinctions painfully clear. In 2022, the Ronin Network—a blockchain used by the popular play-to-earn game Axie Infinity—was compromised due to lax security practices tied to its validator nodes. Over $600 million was drained, largely because keys were managed in hot environments with inadequate multi-signature protocols. Contrast this with institutional-grade custody solutions like those offered by Anchorage or Fireblocks, where assets are stored with bank-grade protocols, requiring multiple approvals and physical security infrastructure. One model is frictionless; the other is fortified. The trade-offs aren't theoretical—they're quantifiable.

And then there's the human element. Some of the most damaging losses in crypto history didn't stem from hacking at all. They came from carelessness: users misplacing their recovery phrases, accidentally resetting their wallets, or throwing away old hardware devices that contained irreplaceable access. The most famous example remains James Howells, the British IT worker who accidentally discarded a hard drive containing 8,000 bitcoins—now worth hundreds of millions of pounds—into a landfill. His story is extreme, but the principle applies to everyone: *ownership in crypto is fragile not because of technology, but because of human error.*

To navigate this landscape, users must first shift how they think about wallets. A wallet isn't a place that stores coins. It's a cryptographic interface that manages private keys. The assets themselves are always on the blockchain; what your wallet controls is the authority to move them. Lose that key, and the blockchain doesn't care who you are. There is no reset button, no helpline, no undo. This reality demands a new kind of digital literacy—one that values redundancy, planning, and clear-sighted risk management over blind trust in UX or convenience.

This is not to suggest that hot wallets are inherently irresponsible. For many legitimate use cases, they are indispensable. But they must be used with awareness, restraint, and context. Keeping large sums in a browser wallet is like walking through a crowded city with your life savings in your back pocket. You might be fine. You might not. The point is not to fear the street—but to know what you're carrying and why.

Ultimately, the question users must ask is not "which wallet is safest?" but "which wallet is safest for what I need to do?" Cold wallets shine in static, high-value, long-horizon scenarios. Hot wallets excel in dynamic, interactive, low-friction environments. The challenge is to match the tool to the context—and to do so before something goes wrong. Because in crypto, *loss is often permanent.* And preparation is the only antidote to regret.

How Exchanges Work (and When They Fail)

The vast majority of crypto users do not interact with blockchains directly. They rely on centralised platforms—exchanges like Binance, Coinbase, or previously, FTX—to convert fiat currency into digital assets and to trade those assets with other users. These exchanges are not merely middlemen. They are infrastructure providers, liquidity engines, custodians, and marketing machines rolled into one. They shape user experience, market behaviour, and public perception. And when they work, they make crypto feel safe, accessible, and almost normal. But when they fail—as FTX did catastrophically in 2022—they expose one of the central paradoxes of crypto: *the promise of decentralisation often depends on deeply centralised institutions.*

A centralised crypto exchange operates much like a traditional brokerage or trading platform. Users sign up with an email address, undergo identity verification, deposit fiat currency via bank transfer or card, and begin trading digital assets. The platform handles all the complexity: it stores the private keys, matches orders, settles transactions, and displays balances. This convenience is underpinned by *custodial architecture.* The exchange holds users' funds in pooled wallets and manages those funds internally. Trades happen off-chain in the platform's database and are only occasionally settled on the blockchain. This model allows for speed, scalability, and efficiency. But it also demands trust.

That trust is not purely technical—it is institutional. When a user deposits money on Coinbase, they are not in control of the private keys. They are trusting Coinbase to keep those keys safe, to honour withdrawals, to maintain solvency, and to act with integrity. For most users, this trust is tacit. They treat their exchange balance as if it were a bank account, assuming that withdrawals will work as expected. And most of the time, they do. But *unlike a bank, a crypto exchange is not subject to the same regulatory oversight, capital requirements, or deposit insurance.* This makes their stability more opaque and their failures more devastating.

FTX, at its peak, was the second-largest crypto exchange in the world. It processed billions in daily volume, operated globally, and was backed by major venture capital firms. Its founder, Sam Bankman-Fried, was a media darling and political donor, hailed as a wunderkind of responsible crypto innovation. But behind the scenes, FTX was funnelling user funds to its sister hedge fund, Alameda Research, to make speculative bets. When those bets went sour—and when a leaked balance sheet revealed the house of cards—confidence evaporated almost overnight. Within days, withdrawal requests overwhelmed the platform. FTX froze accounts, declared bankruptcy, and left users with billions in frozen assets. *The very custodian entrusted with safeguarding crypto wealth had repurposed it for its own trading strategy without consent or disclosure.*

What made FTX particularly dangerous was how normal it looked. Its interface was polished. Its branding was clean. It had sports sponsorships, celebrity endorsements, and glowing press coverage. But underneath the facade, it lacked the fundamental controls—auditable books, clear separation of funds, coherent governance—that any institution holding customer assets should have. It was not a technical failure. It was a human one, wrapped in the language of innovation. *The collapse was not a warning about crypto itself—it was a cautionary tale about where crypto still behaves like traditional finance at its worst.*

Yet even among exchanges that haven't collapsed, the risks remain non-trivial. In 2014, Mt. Gox—then the world's largest Bitcoin exchange—lost over 850,000 BTC to hacking and mismanagement. In 2018, Canada's QuadrigaCX revealed that its founder had died without sharing the exchange's wallet passwords, freezing over $100 million in customer funds. More recently, smaller platforms have suffered breaches, exit scams, and liquidity crises. The central pattern is unmistakable: *when users entrust their assets to a single point of failure, they inherit the consequences of its decisions, good or bad.*

The solution is not to demonise exchanges wholesale. Platforms like Coinbase and Binance have become critical on-ramps for global adoption. They offer user-friendly interfaces, deep liquidity, institutional custody partnerships, and compliance with evolving regulatory frameworks. For many users, especially beginners, exchanges provide a manageable first experience with crypto. The key is *to recognise what these platforms are, and more importantly, what they are not.* They are not decentralised. They are not transparent by default. And they are not immune to governance risk.

Part of the confusion stems from crypto's branding. Many users assume that because they are "using crypto," they are somehow protected by the principles of decentralisation. But when you hold assets on an exchange, you are not using crypto—you are using a database controlled by a company. Your coins exist as entries on a ledger you cannot audit, held in wallets you do not control, subject to rules you did not write. This is why the adage "not your keys, not your coins" remains one of the most enduring truths in the space. *Exchanges are convenient, but they are not neutral terrain.*

At a technical level, decentralised exchanges (DEXs) like Uniswap or dYdX offer a different model. Trades are executed directly on-chain using smart contracts. There is no custody, no intermediary, and no pooled fund. Users connect their wallets, sign transactions, and retain full control over their assets. But these platforms require a higher degree of user sophistication. They lack fiat on-ramps, have steeper learning curves, and depend on the user's ability to manage their own security. As a result, most trading volume still flows through centralised exchanges.

The regulatory picture adds another layer of complexity. Different jurisdictions treat crypto exchanges with varying degrees of scrutiny. Some require full compliance with anti-money laundering laws and customer verification. Others operate in legal grey zones, exploiting jurisdictional arbitrage to avoid oversight. This regulatory fragmentation creates uneven standards and patchy consumer protection. It also incentivises risky behaviour, as firms compete for market share without uniform accountability. *The illusion of professionalism is easy to manufacture in a digital interface—but regulation and governance are harder to fake when it matters most.*

Ultimately, users must move beyond brand loyalty and interface polish. The core questions should be: Who controls the keys? What happens if withdrawals are paused? What legal protections exist if the platform becomes insolvent? Is the company registered, audited, and accountable? If the answers to those questions are vague or hidden behind marketing language, that is a red flag—not a philosophical dilemma.

Exchanges remain essential to the crypto economy. They provide access, liquidity, and infrastructure. But they also introduce centralised risk into a decentralised vision. Their failures—whether through fraud, incompetence, or misaligned incentives—serve as reminders that *technology does not eliminate trust; it simply reassigns it.* And when that trust is misplaced, the consequences are not theoretical—they are measurable in frozen assets, lost savings, and shattered confidence. Understanding how exchanges really work is not optional for the informed user. It is a necessary form of self-defence.

Custody: Not Your Keys, Not Your Coins

There is a foundational truth in crypto that's often learned too late: *if you don't control your private keys, you don't control your crypto.* This axiom, distilled into the slogan "Not your keys, not your coins," is not a technicality—it is a hard-won lesson echoing through the failures, frauds, and forgotten passwords that litter crypto's short history. Custody—the question of who holds the keys—sits at the heart of digital asset ownership. And yet, it remains one of the most misunderstood, neglected, and consequential aspects of crypto participation.

To understand custody in crypto, one must first grasp the nature of ownership in a blockchain-based system. Unlike traditional finance, where assets are held in custodial accounts under the oversight of banks or brokers, crypto is built on decentralised trust. Ownership is determined cryptographically through possession of a private key—a string of characters known only to the holder, which serves as the password to a specific wallet address on the blockchain. Whoever controls the key controls the funds. There is no "forgot password" button. No customer service line. *Custody is not metaphorical; it is literal, absolute, and unforgiving.*

In practice, this creates a tension. On one hand, users are drawn to crypto for its promise of self-sovereignty—the ability to own assets outright, free from intermediaries. On the other, managing private keys securely is non-trivial. Hardware wallets must be stored safely. Recovery phrases must be written down and hidden with care. The consequences of error are severe: a lost key is a lost fortune. There is no central authority to reverse a mistake. This makes self-custody both empowering and perilous. *It grants the user full control, but with it, full responsibility.*

Because of this complexity, many users opt for convenience. They leave their crypto on exchanges, trusting third-party platforms like Binance, Coinbase, or Kraken to manage custody on their behalf. These platforms provide an experience that feels familiar—usernames and passwords, withdrawal options, account dashboards. But behind the interface lies a centralised architecture. User funds are pooled into custodial wallets, managed by the platform's internal systems. Users do not hold the keys. They hold a claim on the platform's promise to honour redemptions.

When that promise holds, the model works. But history shows how fragile that trust can be. In 2014, Mt. Gox—then the largest Bitcoin exchange—imploded after losing 850,000 BTC, most of which was never recovered. In 2019, QuadrigaCX collapsed when its founder, Gerald Cotten, reportedly died with sole access to the platform's private keys. In 2022, FTX melted down in spectacular fashion after revelations that customer funds were secretly funnelled to affiliated trading firms. These are not isolated mishaps—they are manifestations of a deeper systemic flaw: *centralised custody reintroduces the very risks crypto was designed to eliminate.*

What makes these failures so devastating is their opacity. When users leave funds on an exchange, they forfeit transparency. They cannot verify solvency, track fund flows, or confirm that their assets are segregated from operational capital. They rely on faith in corporate governance, compliance, and integrity. And too often, those pillars are weaker than they appear. *In a decentralised world, centralisation becomes the blind spot where the most egregious abuses can occur.*

Yet the alternative—self-custody—requires more than ideological conviction. It demands operational competence. Consider the cautionary tale of Stefan Thomas, a programmer who lost access to over 7,000 BTC because he forgot the password to his encrypted

IronKey device. Or the thousands of users who fall victim to phishing attacks, malware, or social engineering that compromises their seed phrases. The crypto landscape is littered with wallets whose contents are permanently inaccessible—digital treasure locked away by human error. *The promise of absolute ownership cuts both ways: it liberates the individual from dependence, but it also isolates them from recourse.*

To navigate this tension, users must think critically about custody as a spectrum, not a binary. There are gradations of control and trade-offs at every level. Hardware wallets like Ledger or Trezor offer cold storage—offline, self-controlled, and highly secure against digital attack. But they require careful handling, backup, and physical security. Mobile wallets like MetaMask offer a balance of usability and control but remain vulnerable to malware or compromised devices. Multi-signature wallets, which require multiple parties to authorise transactions, provide enhanced security and shared custody, often used by businesses or high-net-worth individuals. *Each solution carries its own operational risk, and no setup is foolproof.*

Institutional custody is evolving in parallel. Regulated custodians such as BitGo, Anchorage, and Fidelity Digital Assets offer services tailored to funds, family offices, and corporate treasuries, combining cold storage with insurance, compliance, and auditability. These players blur the lines between traditional finance and decentralised assets, attempting to professionalise crypto custody without abandoning its foundational principles. For individuals, the emergence of hybrid models—like Ledger Recover or collaborative custody with trusted partners—signals a growing awareness that usability must coexist with security.

Still, *the decision to delegate custody should never be made blindly.* Users must ask hard questions: Who holds the keys? What legal protections exist if the custodian fails? Is there insurance? What happens in the event of regulatory action, insolvency, or internal fraud? Can I verify the custodian's practices? These are not mere technicalities—they are existential inquiries that determine whether ownership is real or imagined.

The phrase "Not your keys, not your coins" endures because it articulates a core philosophical truth: *digital assets invert the default assumptions of ownership*. In the traditional world, assets are held by institutions on your behalf, and your rights are enforced by legal systems. In crypto, assets exist on a public ledger, and your rights are enforced by mathematics. The legal system is secondary, and intermediaries are optional. But the clarity of this model only holds if users understand the implications. If you trust someone else to hold your keys, you have returned to the old paradigm—with fewer protections and more fragility.

The irony is that crypto, in trying to eliminate trust, redistributes it in new forms. Trust in software, in one's own competence, in hardware devices, in institutional custodians. There is no escape from trust—only a reshaping of where it resides. And so the question is not whether to trust, but *who*, *how*, and *with what safeguards*.

Crypto does not demand that everyone become a self-custody purist. But it does require that every user understand the cost of convenience. Custody is not a backend technical detail. It is the frontline of responsibility. It is where ideology meets pragmatism, where freedom meets risk. And it is often the difference between holding wealth and hoping someone else gives it back.

How to Choose the Right Setup

The right wallet setup is not the one with the highest security, nor the one with the slickest interface, nor the most decentralised credentials—it is the one that fits your threat model, use case, and tolerance for complexity. In crypto, the question of how to store your assets is not merely logistical. It is philosophical, operational, and deeply personal. It reflects what kind of user you are, what you fear most—loss, theft, inconvenience—and how much responsibility you are prepared to accept. A secure setup for a venture fund is not appropriate for a university student exploring DeFi. A frequent trader's needs diverge sharply from those of a long-term holder in a politically unstable region. Yet far too often, people copy someone else's solution without considering whether it suits their context. *Security begins with self-awareness.*

Consider the casual user who holds a few hundred pounds' worth of crypto, acquired through curiosity more than conviction. This person may not need a hardware wallet or air-gapped cold storage. The cost and friction of such a setup would exceed the value at risk. A reputable mobile wallet with client-side encryption, such as Trust Wallet or Exodus, offers an appropriate balance. The user must still back up their seed phrase and avoid phishing attempts, but the trade-off is practical. For many beginners, *overengineering security becomes a barrier to participation.* The goal is not to simulate institutional-grade defences for trivial sums; it is to build good habits without discouragement.

Contrast this with a professional investor holding six-figure positions or more. Here, the stakes demand a different posture. A hardware wallet becomes essential, not optional. Devices like Ledger or Trezor store private keys offline, isolating them from malware and browser-based attacks. The seed phrase should be split, encrypted, or stored in tamper-evident metal backups. Some choose to add a passphrase—a 25th word that unlocks a hidden wallet—while others use Shamir's Secret Sharing to distribute key fragments across trusted parties. Complexity rises with the amount of capital at risk, but so does the need for operational discipline. *Paranoia becomes rational when the consequences of failure are life-altering.*

Then there are users in high-risk environments—journalists, dissidents, refugees—who rely on crypto not for speculation, but survival. For them, the ability to memorise a seed phrase and cross borders without physical luggage is not a novelty—it is existential. Cold wallets may not be practical if discovered during a search. Centralised exchanges may freeze accounts under government pressure. In these scenarios, mental custody—knowing one's seed phrase by heart—offers radical mobility, but at the cost of fragility. A moment of cognitive lapse can result in permanent loss. *There is no universal best practice—only a contextually best-fit model based on the adversaries you face.*

Now consider an active trader who moves funds frequently between exchanges, wallets, and decentralised protocols. Speed, interoperability, and interface design matter more than absolute cold storage. Hot wallets—like MetaMask or Rabby—integrated with browsers, offer essential functionality but also expose attack surfaces. In this case, isolating a portion of assets for daily operations, while keeping the majority in cold storage, becomes prudent. This tiered approach balances usability with resilience. A similar model applies to those involved in NFTs or DAO participation, where regular signing of transactions is needed. *Security must not cripple functionality; it must adapt to how the user actually behaves.*

Family offices and institutions face yet another equation. They must contend with internal controls, compliance, and auditability. Here, multi-signature wallets—such as those offered by Gnosis Safe or Casa—enable shared custody, requiring multiple parties to authorise withdrawals. This prevents a single rogue actor or compromised device from draining funds. Key ceremonies can be performed with geographic separation, documented procedures, and failover mechanisms. Insurance policies may also be relevant, provided the custodian meets regulatory standards. The challenge lies in designing controls that protect against internal malfeasance without paralysing operational agility. *Institutional custody is not just about keys—it is about governance, accountability, and continuity planning.*

Some setups defy clean categorisation. Consider a DAO treasury governed by token-weighted voting. Its "wallet" is smart contract-based, with on-chain logic dictating asset flows. Or a Lightning Network user holding Bitcoin in a custodial mobile app to send microtransactions across borders. Or an artist selling generative NFTs via smart contracts that auto-split royalties. These use cases introduce application-specific trade-offs. Sometimes, trusting a managed service is necessary because the protocol or infrastructure demands it. Other times, the value lies in the workflow, not the asset held. *The purpose should shape the custody—not the other way around.*

It is also critical to revisit setups as circumstances evolve. A setup that made sense when holding £1,000 may become dangerously insufficient at £100,000. Conversely, obsessing over cold storage when holding volatile tokens on experimental blockchains may lead to false security. Security theatre is not security. Nor is doing nothing a safe default. *Crypto's immutability punishes passivity just as harshly as recklessness.* Many users only act after a close call—a hacked hot wallet, a rug pull, a friend's loss. But waiting for failure is not strategy. It is denial.

Choosing the right setup also means understanding the ecosystem's moving parts. Exchanges offer convenience but expose users to solvency and governance risk. Wallets vary in their implementation quality, UX, and support for different blockchains. Bridges between chains can be exploit vectors. Browser extensions may leak data or be hijacked. Air-gapped systems resist remote attack but invite physical risk. No layer is perfectly secure. But when these layers are composed intelligently, with awareness of the underlying assumptions, they can produce resilient systems. *Security is never absolute; it is adversarial, adaptive, and contextual.*

There are also trade-offs between recoverability and privacy. Seed phrase backups written in plaintext are vulnerable if discovered, but encrypted ones are inaccessible without the decryption key. Storing phrases with cloud services adds convenience but introduces surveillance exposure. Social recovery schemes, where trusted individuals hold fragments, mitigate single points of failure but require deep interpersonal trust. Custodial services offer recovery options but may be compelled by legal orders. *Every backup method assumes a threat model, even if unconsciously.* The job of the user is to make those assumptions explicit and choose accordingly.

Ultimately, the best setup is the one that reflects a conscious alignment between goals, risks, and behaviour. It requires a frank audit of one's threat model: Who or what am I protecting against? What are my operational capabilities? How much loss can I tolerate? What does success look like if something goes wrong? These are not technical questions—they are strategic ones. Crypto rewards those who think rigorously and act deliberately. It punishes those who treat custody as an afterthought or defer it indefinitely. *Ownership in crypto is not given—it is maintained through vigilance.*

There is no one-size-fits-all answer to custody. But there is a one-size-fits-all imperative: to make the decision deliberately, not by default. Whether you are a student holding your first £200, a startup managing a protocol treasury, or a retired engineer diversifying into digital assets, the principle is the same. Understand the tools, know your vulnerabilities, and align your custody model with your reality. In crypto, your keys are not just a security detail. *They are the dividing line between asset and access, freedom and fragility, promise and peril.*

Chapter 5
The Language Barrier—Jargon, Memes, and Hype

No revolution comes without its own language, and crypto has crafted one of the most bewildering. The vocabulary is dense, self-referential, and sometimes deliberately obscure—a mash-up of programmer shorthand, financial engineering, internet meme culture, and techno-utopian branding. It is not merely a collection of tricky terms, but a network of social signals, conceptual shortcuts, and status markers that determine who can meaningfully participate. Words like "gas," "layer 2," "wrapped tokens," "liquidity pool," and "staking APY" may sound innocuous, yet they conceal complex mechanisms with real-world consequences. Misunderstand them, and money can vanish; fail to grasp them entirely, and entry may be blocked altogether. For many bright and curious newcomers, this linguistic barrier is often the first—and sometimes last—obstacle. But crypto's language is more than just vocabulary; it reflects the culture's contradictions, ambitions, and illusions.

Much of the lexicon borrows authority from traditional finance. Terms such as yield, leverage, collateral, and arbitrage are redeployed in ways that resemble their original use just enough to mislead. "Decentralised finance" evokes images of democratised banking, yet often refers to a lattice of smart contracts replicating Wall Street functions without regulatory oversight. "Stablecoin" implies reliability, though it may rest on opaque reserves, algorithmic stabilisation, or little backing at all. "Consensus" suggests agreement, yet in practice it is a probabilistic process that can still fracture into forks or reversions. This is not merely imprecise; it is marketing by association. Ambiguity invites belief—and sometimes exploitation.

Then there are the memes: "to the moon," "HODL," "buy the dip," "NGMI," "rekt," "wagmi." These function less as language than as ritual. They signal in-group membership, cushion risk with humour, and convert individual financial decisions into communal narratives. To outsiders, they may seem frivolous; to insiders, they communicate conviction, cynicism, or both. Yet memes do more than entertain—they distort perception, amplify emotion, and sometimes drive price independently of utility. Dogecoin did not rise because it was useful; it rose because a meme became self-fulfilling. In lightly regulated markets, mood often moves capital more than fundamentals.

For newcomers, this mix of opaque terminology and performative culture can be a trap. Faced with torrents of unfamiliar words and a community that prizes speed over comprehension, many adopt a posture of forced confidence. They repeat phrases they only half-understand, imitate strategies seen online, and rush to avoid missing out. Jargon replaces clarity. In a market where genuine expertise is scarce but feigned authority abundant, language becomes a vehicle through which risk is disguised and transferred. A "yield farm" may sound like passive income; in reality, it is a high-volatility product bundling leverage, derivatives, and smart contract exposure. Airdrops appear as gifts, but often mask attempts to manufacture demand or shift liability. Words frame risk—and in crypto, that framing is rarely neutral.

Opacity is rarely accidental. Complexity often aligns with incentives: developers, founders, influencers, and investors benefit from a system that discourages scrutiny. If a concept cannot be explained in plain terms, it is less likely to be questioned, regulated, or responsibly used. Yet complexity also alienates capable participants who lack the time to decode it. Confronted with immersion or ignorance, most choose the latter. Worse, those who ask "naive" questions risk ridicule, while those who admit confusion are told to "ape in" and learn by loss. The culture punishes curiosity rather than nurturing literacy.

Still, understanding is possible. Every concept—from validator slashing to gas optimisation to impermanent loss—follows a discernible logic if framed correctly. Gas fees are not magic; they are a bidding mechanism to process transactions on a network with limited capacity. Liquidity pools are not black boxes; they are smart contracts holding token pairs to enable automated swaps. When explanation prioritises usefulness over posturing, the fog begins to lift. Once language shifts from signalling to sense-making, decisions can be grounded in understanding rather than imitation.

Not all jargon is malicious. Some serves as shorthand in a fast-moving field—repeating "zero-knowledge rollups" every time would be unwieldy. But necessity should never excuse opacity, nor should insider language exclude others. If crypto is to fulfil its promise of openness and decentralisation, comprehension itself must be decentralised. A system that cannot be explained cannot be trusted. A financial product designed so the buyer cannot understand it is not innovation—it is predation.

This chapter unpacks the crypto lexicon with intellectual honesty, cultural fluency, and functional clarity. It will not read as a glossary or meme decoder. Instead, it illuminates how language shapes risk, invites hype, and distorts perception. It examines how memes and narrative engineering drive the creation—and destruction—of value in digital markets. And it offers practical frameworks for distinguishing substance from speculation, empowerment from exclusion. You will not become fluent in every acronym, but you will learn to remain grounded, ask sharper questions, and filter signal from noise. In crypto, the first thing purchased is the story—and if you do not understand the story, you cannot understand the risk.

Decoding the Crypto Lexicon

The language of crypto isn't merely technical—it's territorial. Knowing how to navigate it signals belonging, fluency, and confidence. For the uninitiated, however, it often feels like walking into a financial cockpit covered in blinking acronyms, insider slang, and philosophical buzzwords. Yet these terms shape how users perceive risk, assess opportunity, and make decisions with real financial consequences. Clarity isn't a luxury—it's a prerequisite for agency. Misunderstanding a single concept like "gas," "layer 2," or "yield farming" can lead to poor strategy, missed opportunity, or outright loss. Worse, the crypto lexicon often blends technical precision with cultural shorthand, creating a dual language that rewards insiders and confuses everyone else. Disentangling these layers requires more than definitions; it demands intellectual honesty, functional clarity, and cultural decoding.

Consider "gas fees." In Ethereum and similar blockchain systems, gas is the cost of computing power, measured in units that reflect how much effort a network must exert to process a transaction. But gas is not priced in dollars. It's priced in the native cryptocurrency of the network (e.g. ETH), and the cost fluctuates based on real-time network demand—much like surge pricing for taxis. A basic transaction might cost a few cents during periods of low activity, or $50 or more during network congestion. The concept is simple at heart: you're paying miners or validators to prioritise your action. But the presentation is often obscured by unfamiliar units, changing metrics, and poorly designed interfaces. The term "gas" itself, borrowed from everyday life, disguises the fact that this is a fee market subject to volatility, inefficiency, and strategic manipulation. *When fees are opaque, so is value.*

Now shift to "DeFi," or decentralised finance. The term suggests an open, autonomous financial system built on blockchain protocols rather than banks or brokers. In theory, DeFi removes the need for intermediaries. In practice, it introduces new forms of complexity and risk. Platforms like Uniswap, Aave, and Compound allow users to lend, borrow, swap, and speculate—often without revealing their identity. But they rely on smart contracts, which are only as secure as the code and audits behind them. When these contracts fail—or are exploited—the losses are instant and irreversible. Users participate with tokens that represent other tokens, wrapped assets, synthetic instruments, or governance rights. Many users don't fully understand what they hold, let alone the layered exposure they've assumed. DeFi's language is built to signal innovation and openness, but often masks fragility and concentration of power among a small group of developers or liquidity providers. *Calling it "decentralised" doesn't make it democratic.*

"Layer 2" is another term that sounds deceptively benign. It refers to scaling solutions built on top of existing blockchains, designed to reduce congestion and lower fees. Ethereum, for instance, has become notoriously expensive for routine transactions. Layer 2 platforms like Arbitrum, Optimism, and zkSync aim to fix this by processing batches of transactions off-chain and then settling them back on the main chain. It's a sensible idea, and a crucial one for crypto's usability. But the technical complexity of these systems is significant, and the trust assumptions vary. Some rely on optimistic models that assume honesty unless challenged. Others use cryptographic proofs that require rigorous validation. The average user, however, often has no idea which system they're using or what the trade-offs are. What matters is that it's "faster" and "cheaper." Yet if a bridge between a layer 2 and its parent chain fails—as has happened repeatedly—assets can become stranded, or worse, stolen. *The abstraction of "layer" simplifies the conversation while deepening the technical dependence.*

Then there's "yield farming," a phrase that evokes pastoral imagery of growth and patience. In reality, it refers to the practice of moving capital across DeFi platforms to capture high returns from incentives, liquidity provision, and token emissions. It is often complex, fast-moving, and deeply speculative. Investors may stake one token to earn another, provide liquidity to pools that automatically rebalance, or participate in systems where interest is paid out in volatile assets with no clear utility. The yields advertised—sometimes hundreds or even thousands of percent—are almost never sustainable. Many "farms" rely on Ponzi-like dynamics: new users fund returns for old ones until the scheme collapses or the incentives run out. Yet the language of farming implies slow, natural reward, masking the speed and fragility of what's actually occurring. *When financial products are sold like metaphors, the metaphors often win—and the participants lose.*

Language doesn't merely confuse—it shapes behaviour. The phrase "smart contract" implies autonomy and reliability, but in truth, these are just pieces of code. They cannot think, adapt, or interpret intention. If a smart contract contains a bug—or if a user makes a mistake—the results are permanent. "Tokenomics" sounds like a science, but often reflects arbitrary supply schedules, manufactured scarcity, and community hype rather than sound monetary policy. Even "wallet" is a misleading term; most crypto wallets don't actually hold anything. They store keys—access credentials—while the assets themselves live on-chain. If you lose the keys, you lose the assets. That's not like losing your leather wallet; that's like burning your bank vault key with no chance of recovery. *Each familiar term obscures an unfamiliar truth.*

The lexicon becomes even more treacherous when marketing blurs with engineering. "Governance token" implies democratic control, but often confers disproportionate influence to large holders. "Stablecoin" suggests reliability, but algorithmic stablecoins like TerraUSD proved catastrophically fragile. "Community-led" may describe a small group of insiders coordinating in Telegram chats. *The problem is not simply that these words are inaccurate—it's that they are used to build trust where trust should be earned through transparency.* In traditional finance, misrepresenting risk carries legal consequences. In crypto, the boundary between optimism and obfuscation is far thinner, and the burden of understanding falls entirely on the user.

Still, the solution is not to reject the lexicon but to reclaim it. Each term in crypto carries a kernel of insight, often embedded in a genuinely novel mechanism. Gas fees reflect the economics of decentralised computation. DeFi reimagines what financial services could look like in a peer-to-peer world. Layer 2s represent an evolving response to real scalability bottlenecks. Yield farming, for all its risk, is an expression of open market experimentation. The key is to separate *what the term hopes to mean* from *how it functions in practice.* And that requires a willingness to slow down, ask hard questions, and prioritise understanding over participation.

The crypto conversation is often dominated by speed—of transactions, of hype cycles, of language itself. But comprehension cannot be rushed. As the space continues to evolve, new terms will emerge, old ones will fade, and meanings will shift. Users must develop not just fluency but literacy—a capacity to interrogate language, connect it to mechanisms, and see beyond the surface. Because in crypto, as in law or medicine, *terminology is not neutral—it's architecture. It builds assumptions, expectations, and systems of accountability.* The question is whether those systems serve the user, or merely the issuer.

To decode the crypto lexicon is not to memorise definitions. It is to build an internal compass for navigating ambiguity, filtering noise, and thinking critically about what words are doing—not just what they say. In a domain where understanding drives autonomy and confusion invites exploitation, *language is the first battleground for trust.* Get it right, and everything else becomes clearer. Get it wrong, and every step becomes a risk you can't even name.

Meme Culture and Market Psychology

When Dogecoin, a cryptocurrency originally created as a parody of Bitcoin, surged in market capitalisation to over $80 billion in 2021, it did so not because of any underlying technological innovation or financial utility, but because of a collective wink—an internet meme that snowballed into a speculative frenzy. A coin based on a Shiba Inu dog, pushed by online forums and fuelled by celebrity tweets, became one of the most talked-about financial assets on Earth. It is tempting to dismiss this as an anomaly or an internet joke taken too far. But it was neither. Dogecoin's rise, and the countless other meme-fuelled surges in crypto markets, reveal something far more profound: *memes are not marginal to crypto—they are central to how it moves, feels, and functions.*

Memes are the grammar of online culture—concise, emotionally charged, and infinitely replicable. They distil complex ideas into digestible signals and, crucially, *they bypass rational filters.* In the traditional investment world, sentiment is studied, modelled, and cautiously integrated into decision-making frameworks. In crypto, sentiment frequently overwhelms those frameworks entirely. Phrases like "to the moon," "HODL," and "diamond hands" are more than punchlines. They encode narratives of identity, loyalty, defiance, and belief—ideas that can rapidly galvanise millions of people to act, often in synchronised irrationality. The meme is the mechanism by which a decentralised crowd becomes a coordinated force.

This phenomenon has precedents. Behavioural economics has long studied the impact of social proof, herd behaviour, and narrative contagion in markets. But crypto intensifies these forces through platforms where investors don't just react to news—they produce it. On Reddit, Twitter, Discord, and TikTok, financial ideas are memefied in real-time, turning investment decisions into social rituals. A user who says, "I'm going all in on DOGE," is not merely disclosing a financial position; they are expressing group affiliation, humour, and rebellion against traditional financial gatekeepers. In such an environment, *truth becomes a function of virality*, and financial value becomes indistinguishable from narrative momentum.

Consider the phrase "to the moon." It originated as a way to express optimism about price appreciation, but quickly evolved into a cultural motif—one that implied not only belief in a particular asset but also allegiance to the ethos of defiance against Wall Street, cynicism toward institutional expertise, and unshakable faith in collective action. The success of a token becomes a kind of prophecy fulfilled by enthusiasm, not fundamentals. This dynamic reverses the usual order of investing: instead of assessing risk and return, participants chase conviction and confirmation. *The meme supplies the conviction. The market follows the meme.*

This dynamic is particularly potent in environments where technical knowledge is scarce and volatility is high. Unlike equities or bonds, most cryptocurrencies do not have traditional valuation anchors—no earnings, dividends, or cash flows. That informational vacuum leaves space for alternative signals. When people cannot grasp the fundamentals, they grasp for meaning, and memes fill that void with astonishing efficiency. A picture, a phrase, or a TikTok trend can drive millions in capital flows. *Narrative becomes proxy for analysis.*

Of course, not all meme activity is naive or irrational. Some traders ride meme waves strategically, leveraging short-term sentiment spikes for rapid gains. Others view meme coins as community experiments or protest instruments—a way to challenge the seriousness and gatekeeping of conventional finance. There is a subversive intelligence in the meme economy, a recognition that financial systems are themselves built on stories, symbols, and confidence games. From central bank credibility to stock ticker popularity, belief has always mattered in finance. Crypto simply strips away the formalities and exposes belief as the main event.

However, the consequences of meme-driven psychology are far from trivial. The same emotional energy that drives euphoric buying can just as easily turn into panic selling. The volatility of meme coins is not merely technical—it is emotional. Rapid narrative reversals, sudden shifts in sentiment, and the withdrawal of influencer support can collapse market capitalisation in hours. The faster the rise, the more fragile the foundation. *When people invest based on memes, they tend to exit based on memes too.*

Moreover, meme dynamics can create profound distortions in perceived legitimacy. A coin with a strong meme presence may attract more attention, liquidity, and developer activity than a technically superior but less culturally resonant project. In some cases, memes have obscured outright frauds—schemes that used ironic branding, charismatic mascots, or "fun" marketing to conceal malicious intent. The line between satire and scam is often blurred in crypto, and many users, eager to join the next big wave, fail to distinguish between cleverness and deceit.

This is where psychology meets responsibility. Understanding meme culture is not just about recognising market trends—it's about *understanding how our brains respond to novelty, belonging, and emotion under financial stress*. FOMO (fear of missing out) is a meme unto itself, one that hijacks rational process and replaces it with a desperate urgency to participate. The logic becomes circular: everyone is buying because everyone is buying. Each successive meme reinforces the illusion of inevitability.

Yet the solution is not cynicism or disengagement. It is discernment. Memes can be powerful tools for onboarding new users, spreading awareness, and critiquing stale financial orthodoxies. They can challenge elitism, promote accessibility, and build genuine community. But they are also volatile instruments of hype, and their energy must be contextualised. *A meme can be an invitation to explore—or a trapdoor to manipulation.*

Investors and observers alike must develop a kind of "meme literacy"—a capacity to read, interpret, and assess cultural signals with the same seriousness they would apply to a balance sheet or a white paper. That means recognising when a meme reflects genuine grassroots enthusiasm, and when it's being artificially inflated by marketing budgets or bot armies. It means asking what psychological need the meme is fulfilling: is it providing comfort, identity, distraction, or a scapegoat? And most importantly, it means separating the aesthetic of momentum from the mechanics of sustainability.

As the crypto ecosystem matures, meme culture will not disappear. If anything, it will deepen—evolving in form, sophistication, and influence. But maturity demands nuance. A well-informed participant must be able to enjoy the meme without being governed by it, to appreciate the community without outsourcing critical thinking. In that balance lies the difference between engagement and exploitation.

Ultimately, meme culture in crypto is not a sideshow—it is the show. It is where users first encounter ideas, where narratives are born, and where sentiment is moulded. To ignore it is to miss the emotional engine that drives much of the market. But to submit uncritically to it is to forfeit autonomy. *The challenge is to stay aware in a system designed for emotional acceleration—to be fluent in the language of memes without being swept away by their momentum.* That is what makes the modern crypto participant not just an investor, but a translator of culture and psychology in a market that trades on belief as much as on bytes.

How Language Obscures Risk

In crypto, complexity is often mistaken for credibility. A project described as "an optimised layer 2 rollup for asynchronous cross-chain liquidity aggregation" sounds impressive—until you pause to ask what any of those words actually mean. And more importantly, what they might be hiding. Language in crypto is not just a communication tool; it is a gatekeeping mechanism, a marketing shield, and at times, a smokescreen. Risk is not always downplayed directly. More often, it is obscured behind the fog of technical vocabulary, grandiose ambition, and linguistic sleight of hand. *When the language becomes more elaborate than the product, it is often the risk that's being buried.*

This is not a new trick. Jargon has long served as a filter in elite institutions—whether in finance, academia, or law—where specialised language establishes credibility, asserts authority, and excludes outsiders. But in the crypto world, which claims to be decentralised and inclusive, the irony is stark: *the very people crypto was meant to empower are often silenced or confused by its vocabulary.* What should be a democratising technology becomes a domain for linguistic domination.

Consider the proliferation of terms like "DeFi," "staking," "slippage," "impermanent loss," "gas wars," and "yield farming." Each term, in isolation, may have a technical justification. But in aggregate, they create a semantic haze through which risk is not only hard to identify—it is actively disguised. Investors may be lured into providing liquidity to a protocol promising "triple-digit APYs" without understanding the volatile mechanics that underpin those returns. What's described as "automated market-making" may in practice expose users to a blend of smart contract risk, platform risk, and price volatility they are ill-equipped to evaluate. *The language seduces before it educates.*

This phenomenon is particularly dangerous in environments where trust is scarce and due diligence is thin. White papers—often more performative than informative—mimic the structure of academic research while offering none of its rigour. Glossaries on project websites serve not to clarify, but to overwhelm. A user may walk away with the vague sense that something "feels legit" without being able to articulate why. That feeling is the product of language architecture, not evidence.

The problem intensifies when technobabble is weaponised by marketing teams. Words like "decentralised," "trustless," or "immutable" are routinely deployed to invoke a kind of moral superiority. But these terms are rarely explained with the precision they demand. A "decentralised exchange" might, in fact, rely on a single development team with unilateral control over key updates. A "trustless system" may still require users to trust the people who wrote the code, the people who audited the contracts (if they were audited at all), or the platform hosting the interface. *The illusion of security often rests on semantic ambiguity.*

There is also a subtler danger at play: the conflation of complexity with inevitability. If a project's technical description is impenetrable, some users assume that it must be advanced—perhaps even the future of finance. This assumption is not just intellectually lazy; it is perilous. The 2022 collapse of the Terra ecosystem was a case study in how obfuscation can amplify systemic fragility. The term "algorithmic stablecoin" sounded cutting-edge. But beneath the language was a mechanism dependent on circular logic and reflexive confidence. As soon as that confidence broke, so did the peg. Billions vanished. The risk was not hidden in the code; it was hidden in the language used to explain the code.

Contrast this with how traditional finance, for all its faults, handles similar concepts. A mutual fund may disclose its "net asset value," "expense ratio," or "benchmark index," but these terms are codified, regulated, and standardised. In crypto, where regulatory clarity is still emerging, the linguistic terrain is fluid, opportunistic, and largely unaccountable. Projects invent their own definitions, stretch familiar words into unfamiliar shapes, and rebrand risks as features. An unsustainably high return becomes "hyper-yield." A lack of liquidity becomes "low float for early access." A lock-up period becomes "vesting designed to align incentives." *Euphemism is not a glitch in crypto—it is a design pattern.*

One might argue that all new technologies come with their own learning curve. But there is a difference between complexity born of innovation and complexity deployed as camouflage. The former challenges the learner; the latter deceives them. And the consequences are not merely semantic. They affect how capital is allocated, how reputations are built, and how disasters unfold. When investors cannot understand what they are buying, they cannot assess risk. And when risk is obscured, so too is accountability.

This obfuscation extends beyond technical terms to the very metaphors and narratives that drive market enthusiasm. Tokens are "burned," "minted," or "farmed"—words borrowed from physical processes that evoke scarcity, creation, or effort. Yet these metaphors often bear no relationship to the actual function of the protocol. They are designed to create intuitive associations where none exist. A token burn may sound like a deflationary move, but if the supply is simultaneously being increased elsewhere, the net effect may be neutral or inflationary. The metaphor distracts from the mechanics. *The language flatters the ear while concealing the truth.*

To be clear, language in crypto is not inherently dishonest. But it is deeply performative. Projects must signal innovation, technical prowess, and community momentum all at once. Language becomes the theatre in which that performance unfolds. And like all theatre, it relies on suspension of disbelief. The problem is that many participants don't realise they're watching a play.

How, then, should a thoughtful participant respond? Not with cynicism, but with inquiry. *Ask what every word means—not just technically, but practically.* What risk is being renamed? What mechanism is being dressed up? What assumption is being passed off as fact? Replace adjectives with questions. When a protocol is described as "bulletproof," ask, "According to whom?" When something is called "the future of finance," ask, "For whom, and why?" Push past the surface fluency and demand functional clarity.

Language should not be a barrier to participation in the crypto ecosystem. It should be a bridge. But that bridge must be built on precision, honesty, and intellectual humility. Projects that explain themselves clearly signal confidence. Those that hide behind jargon often signal fear—fear that transparency will reveal weakness, that simplicity will expose limitations, that truth will slow adoption. *But clarity is not a weakness. It is a filter for truth.*

Ultimately, the burden is shared. Builders must speak with integrity. Analysts must translate with care. And participants must read with scepticism—not because they expect to be misled, but because *they understand that words are never neutral.* Every term encodes a perspective. Every phrase implies a trade-off. Every explanation reveals—or conceals—risk.

The crypto ecosystem, if it is to mature, must treat language not as ornamentation but as infrastructure. Just as we audit code, we must audit speech. Just as we value open-source protocols, we must value open-access understanding. The goal is not to flatten complexity, but to *expose it to the light*—to make risk visible, describable, and therefore manageable.

If crypto truly intends to reshape financial systems, it must also reshape how those systems are described. That begins not with new terms, but with a renewed commitment to clarity. Because where language obscures risk, truth becomes a casualty—and trust is the price.

How to Stay Smart Without Getting Overwhelmed

The crypto ecosystem is not merely fast-paced—it is strategically overwhelming. Unlike traditional finance, where news cycles and regulatory calendars establish some cadence, crypto exists in a perpetual state of narrative acceleration. There is always a new protocol, a new airdrop, a new partnership, a new hack, a new layer 2, a new meme coin. Blink, and the landscape appears to have shifted. The result is a psychological environment designed to provoke urgency while eroding clarity. *The challenge is not only to understand the space—but to resist being consumed by it.*

Most intelligent readers approaching crypto are not short on cognitive capacity. What they lack is not intellect, but a filtration mechanism. The information overload is not just a matter of volume—it is also structurally engineered. Crypto communities reward constant engagement: Discord channels run 24/7, influencers post in bursts of hyperbolic urgency, and Twitter feeds conflate speculation with news. Each new development is positioned as pivotal. Every token's white paper is supposedly paradigm-shifting. Each market correction is either the end or a generational buying opportunity. *In this context, discernment becomes more valuable than knowledge.*

To stay smart without being overwhelmed, one must first recognise that the crypto conversation is not neutral—it is skewed by incentives. Content creators monetise attention. Projects craft narratives. Analysts optimise for engagement. Even self-professed educators are often token holders with vested interests. Therefore, *the first mental filter must be scepticism—not cynicism, but a commitment to interrogating the incentives behind each claim.* Ask: who benefits if I believe this?

A second filter is time sensitivity. Crypto information has a half-life. What is true today may be irrelevant next month—not because it was wrong, but because the system evolves so rapidly. This makes it tempting to overconsume, to chase currency in all senses of the word. But very little information in crypto is truly urgent. Most of it can be examined with the same calm reasoning we apply to any other discipline. *The urgency is performative; the value lies in reflection.*

Building a reliable signal-to-noise filter means learning to distinguish between the *form* of authority and its *substance.* A YouTube thumbnail with neon graphics and an all-caps title is not a warning of imminent collapse—it's a marketing strategy. A tweet thread that starts with "This will change everything" is rarely predictive—it is bait. High production value does not equal high epistemic value. *Substance often speaks softly, while hype shouts.* Seek out voices that explain more than they predict, that frame complexity without simplifying it into slogans.

Another effective strategy is to choose your sources with surgical precision and commit to a narrow set. Information hygiene is not about consuming more—it's about consuming better. A well-curated newsletter, a podcast with thoughtful guests, or a transparent researcher's Substack can often outperform an endless scroll of feeds. Focus on thinkers who show their reasoning, cite their sources, and openly declare their uncertainties. *Expertise in crypto is not demonstrated by certainty, but by intellectual humility.*

At a conceptual level, it is also useful to develop a taxonomy of noise. Much of the daily discourse in crypto falls into repeating archetypes: hype cycles ("X is the next Ethereum"), fear cycles ("regulators are about to ban Y"), recovery narratives ("bull market returning soon"), and ideological crusades ("true decentralisation or bust"). These tropes are not always false—but they follow predictable patterns. Once recognised, they become less hypnotic. *A framework for recognising rhetorical patterns protects your mental bandwidth.*

Technical terms also deserve careful handling. Some signal genuine innovation; others are camouflage. Learn to pause on the unfamiliar. You don't need to master every protocol architecture or consensus algorithm—but you do need to know when to ask, "What does this actually do?" Language that obfuscates should be flagged. As explored earlier, the manipulation of vocabulary often serves to sell risk as innovation. *Understanding begins with the refusal to be dazzled.*

The fear of missing out—so pervasive in crypto—is rooted in a misunderstanding of the time horizon. Most transformative technologies play out over decades, not days. Missing a trade is not the same as missing the future. Therefore, slow thinking is a strategic advantage. Instead of chasing every opportunity, define your own lens. Are you drawn to the philosophical implications of decentralisation? The financial architecture of DeFi? The sociocultural dynamics of NFTs and DAOs? Clarity of interest reduces cognitive noise. *Specialisation is not limiting—it's liberating.*

Another overlooked strategy is temporal distancing. Step back from real-time feeds. Read materials not designed to be consumed instantly: long-form essays, protocol documentation, technical audits. The signal-to-noise ratio increases dramatically when you shift your input toward structured thought. Historical parallels can also serve as an antidote to short-termism. Technologies such as the internet, mobile computing, and cloud infrastructure were all subject to hype, crash, consolidation, and maturity. *Crypto is not immune to these rhythms—it is simply louder about them.*

It is also worth acknowledging the role of emotion. Overwhelm is not just intellectual; it is physiological. The constant stimuli, price charts, notifications, and opinion cascades trigger stress responses. This depletes the very faculties we need to stay sharp: attention, patience, and memory. For this reason, any practice of staying smart must also involve stepping away. Schedule disengagement. Set limits on screen time. Avoid decision-making in states of emotional agitation. *Mental clarity is a precondition for meaningful learning.*

For professionals and researchers navigating the space, the question becomes one of filtering for relevance. Not all developments are equally pertinent to every inquiry. If you're studying governance models, you can ignore meme coin dynamics. If your focus is on Layer 1 scalability, celebrity NFT launches are a distraction. *Discipline begins with knowing what to ignore.* Map your intellectual terrain and apply that map to your media consumption.

One useful cognitive habit is to constantly test your understanding. Can you explain what you've learned in plain language, without jargon? Can you articulate the assumptions behind a project's claims? Can you map its incentives? The Feynman Technique—explaining a concept as if teaching it to a novice—is particularly useful here. When clarity breaks down, that's a sign to pause and investigate. *Comprehension is the antidote to overwhelm.*

In practical terms, this means taking notes—not just collecting information, but processing it. Summarise protocols in your own words. Keep a running list of key concepts. Track your own questions. This internal knowledge base becomes a scaffolding that allows you to place new information in context rather than reacting to it in isolation. *Curation is a form of intellectual self-respect.*

Above all, the most effective filter is your own epistemic stance. Cultivate a mindset that prizes truth over novelty, precision over performance, and understanding over participation. Crypto, for all its noise, is a genuine frontier. But it is a noisy frontier—one where distraction is profitable and confusion is commonplace. *Your job is not to keep up, but to think clearly.*

The most seasoned participants in crypto are not those who speak the most, trade the fastest, or read the widest range of sources. They are those who have constructed mental frameworks that absorb new information without being distorted by it. They have developed immune systems for hype, antibodies for jargon, and filters for risk. And they understand that staying smart is not about being early—it's about being wise.

Chapter 6
Scams, Traps, and Red Flags

The mythology of crypto is stitched together from two contrasting threads: liberation and deception. For every tale of fortunes won through foresight or innovation, there exists another—quieter, often obscured—of capital lost to schemes dressed in the trappings of technical sophistication. Within this space, the very tools that empower peer-to-peer finance can just as easily be repurposed to exploit the curious, the trusting, or the unprepared. Crypto is indifferent to understanding; it functions whether or not you consent. And that is why grasping its darker mechanisms is not merely useful—it is essential.

Unlike traditional finance, which offers some semblance of recourse—regulatory oversight, customer service desks, central banks—crypto operates on radically different principles. Decentralisation is not just a design choice; it is a challenge to conventional safeguards. In many instances, once a transaction is signed and broadcast to the blockchain, it is final. That technical elegance is unforgiving for the uninformed. Scams do not require advanced cryptography; they only need to outpace comprehension.

The scams themselves are rarely original; what changes is their delivery. Pump-and-dump schemes—where token prices are artificially inflated through coordinated hype and then dumped on the unwary—are as old as the markets themselves. But in crypto, they unfold at digital velocity, fuelled by social media and automated bots. Rug pulls, a close cousin to exit scams, see liquidity or leadership vanish abruptly after funds are amassed from hopeful participants. Such operations succeed not merely through greed but through ambiguity, often shrouded behind polished websites, clever branding, and the haze of collective optimism.

Intelligence offers no immunity. Some of the sharpest, most experienced actors in the space have surrendered millions to schemes that, in hindsight, appear glaringly flawed. The vulnerability lies not in stupidity, but in narrative manipulation. Crypto projects are storytellers par excellence, appealing to visions of the future, injustice, opportunity, or FOMO. White papers read like manifestos. Discord servers double as secretive clubs for early believers. Tokenomics charts promise certainty under the guise of data. Deception is rarely outright falsehood; it is selective truth arranged for maximum effect.

Consider the ICO boom of 2017: over $20 billion poured into token launches, many lacking working products, legal grounding, or realistic roadmaps. Some, like Ethereum, established infrastructure foundational to the ecosystem. Others, like BitConnect, collapsed spectacularly, erasing retail savings and trust. Even now, new "innovations" repackage similar patterns—IDOs, IEOs, algorithmic stablecoins—but the underlying structure remains familiar: stories of promise veiled in opacity and urgency.

Blockchain's decentralised nature introduces further complication: anonymity. Privacy is legitimate, yet it shields malefactors. Developers can vanish behind pseudonyms. Founders may rebrand under new identities. Smart contracts may harbour subtle backdoors, overlooked even by auditors. In such an environment, trust must be earned deliberately.

Deception is not only technical; it is social. The so-called "community" often becomes a mechanism of influence. Telegram groups, Discord channels, Twitter threads, Reddit forums—all can turn into echo chambers where doubt is mocked, scepticism dismissed, and herd mentality rewarded. The rhetoric of early adoption, tribal identity, and perceived closeness to developers constructs a psychological container that replaces rational analysis with emotional allegiance. People invest not merely in tokens but in movements—and movements discourage dissent.

Communities can be weaponised. Developers may orchestrate raids to suppress criticism, employ moderators to silence dissent, or incentivise social amplification. Token prices are cited as validation, creating self-reinforcing loops of perception over fundamentals. By the time clarity emerges, exit doors are closed. Often, participants are both victims and unwitting agents, propagating the very scams they will later regret.

The antidote is not paranoia; it is methodical scrutiny. Evaluating legitimacy requires no esoteric knowledge, only disciplined questioning. Does the team have verifiable identities and track records? Is the code open source and audited? Are token incentives aligned with long-term value creation or short-term extraction? Is the community receptive to critique or cult-like in tone? Are roadmaps realistic or merely rhetorical? Suspicion is prudent; structure is protective.

Protection does not necessitate retreat. Crypto hosts remarkable builders, pioneering technologists, and ethical thinkers. Yet signal is often drowned in noise. Navigating confidently demands a shift—from reactive consumer to proactive evaluator. Think less like a gambler, more like a researcher. Fewer clicks, more reading. Less hype, more verification.

As the ecosystem matures, scams will evolve. AI-generated endorsements may mislead. Smart contract platforms may host automated exploit networks. DAOs could facilitate collective fraud. Regulation may intervene, but always belatedly. Individual literacy remains the lasting safeguard—not just technical understanding, but psychological resilience: a capacity to separate enthusiasm from due diligence, discern flattery from fact, and recognise the traps that appeal to intellect as much as to greed.

This chapter provides not a manual for cynicism, but a compass for discernment. It cannot catalogue every scam—new ones will continually appear—but it offers frameworks to detect patterns, interrogate narratives, and make decisions grounded in reason rather than fear. To participate in crypto is to embrace risk. Risk without awareness is not ambition; it is exposure. And it is in that unexamined exposure that the harshest lessons are learned.

Pump-and-Dumps and Rug Pulls

A financial market without friction—open 24/7, globally accessible, and largely unregulated—sounds like a libertarian dream. But in practice, it also becomes a playground for manipulation. Crypto's decentralised ethos, while empowering in principle, strips away many of the safeguards that traditional markets developed precisely to deter bad actors. *In such a vacuum, old scams find new efficiency.* Among the most pernicious are pump-and-dumps and rug pulls, two of the most common methods used to extract wealth from unsuspecting investors under the guise of innovation.

What makes these schemes particularly insidious is that they often don't masquerade as crimes. Instead, they present themselves as excitement. A new coin "about to moon." A "once-in-a-generation" presale. A Telegram group buzzing with activity. The language of community and momentum is weaponised not to inform but to entice. And for those who miss the early warning signs, by the time prices begin to collapse, the damage is irreversible.

Pump-and-dumps are not new—they have long histories in penny stocks and thinly traded securities. What crypto has done is remove the structural barriers that once slowed their spread. A token can be created in minutes, given a polished website and meme-worthy name, and listed on decentralised exchanges without any need for vetting. Influencers—some paid, others acting out of self-interest—can promote these tokens to thousands or millions of followers, creating the illusion of organic interest. *At the core of every successful pump is not technology—it's narrative control.*

The mechanics are brutally simple. Insiders accumulate a large position in a low-liquidity asset. They then initiate a wave of publicity—sometimes through coordinated tweets, sometimes through insider channels—designed to spark fear of missing out. Prices spike as retail traders rush in. Volume surges. And then, just as quickly, the orchestrators sell their holdings into the rally, crashing the price and exiting with profits. Those who arrived late are left holding worthless tokens, often without understanding what happened.

What complicates detection is that pumps often look like genuine market movements—at least at first. Volatility is endemic in crypto, and sharp price increases are not inherently suspicious. But *it is the source and sequence of that activity that matters.* Are there sudden, unexplained surges in volume? Has a dormant project suddenly returned to life without any code updates or development activity?

Is the buzz concentrated in a few insular social groups, or does it reflect genuine interest from a diverse base of users and analysts? These questions matter. They are not mere red flags—they are thermometers of legitimacy.

Rug pulls, meanwhile, tend to be more abrupt and final. While pump-and-dumps rely on external buyers to absorb insiders' sales, rug pulls often involve the direct withdrawal of liquidity or abandonment of a project by its founders. They come in different forms. Sometimes a decentralised exchange (DEX) token is paired with a liquidity pool that the creators can unilaterally drain. Other times, developers retain admin privileges over smart contracts, enabling them to redirect funds or disable user access with a single transaction. In either case, trust is manufactured to build deposits—and then violated at scale.

One of the most well-known cases was the collapse of "AnubisDAO," a DeFi project that attracted nearly $60 million in ETH overnight, only to have the funds vanish within 24 hours. The project had no clear roadmap, no audits, and no known team. But its branding, combined with the frenzy around "dog coins" at the time, gave it just enough credibility to convince thousands of participants to deposit capital. The lesson was not just that scams exist—but that *they often don't need to hide. They only need to appear momentarily legitimate.*

Indeed, part of what enables rug pulls to proliferate is the way many crypto investors misunderstand decentralisation. They assume that because a project is on-chain or open source, it is trustless. But decentralisation is not binary; it is a spectrum. Many so-called decentralised applications rely on centralised infrastructure or privileged access. A truly decentralised protocol should be resistant to unilateral change, have transparent governance, and limit admin rights. Yet time and again, we see projects that are technically decentralised but practically vulnerable to centralised abuse.

The psychology that makes these scams effective is also worth examining. First, there is *asymmetric information.* Founders or insiders always know more than retail participants. They know the limitations of their code, the true size of their treasury, the reality of their roadmap. When they speak confidently on podcasts or livestreams, many listeners mistake that polish for credibility. But *confidence is not competence. And certainty is not truth.* A healthy investor posture is one of measured scepticism, not passive belief.

Second, there is *herd behaviour.* In fast-moving markets, few participants want to be contrarian. If everyone appears excited about a new token, questioning its fundamentals can feel socially costly. This effect is amplified in closed groups—Telegram channels, Discord communities—where the majority of conversation is bullish by default. Critical voices are often drowned out, banned, or mocked. The result is a vacuum of independent thinking, replaced by reinforcement loops of enthusiasm and speculation.

Third, there is *the illusion of control.* Crypto tools empower users to move quickly: buy tokens, connect wallets, stake funds—all with a few clicks. But this frictionless experience can disguise the risks beneath it. People confuse user agency with safety. Just because you can buy something easily does not mean it is a good idea. *Technology lowers barriers to entry, but not the need for judgement.*

What makes all of this even more dangerous is that these schemes often begin with real capital and real users. Not all rug pulls are premeditated. Some begin as earnest projects that fail, with founders choosing to exit unethically once momentum stalls. Others begin as experiments that spiral out of control. In either case, the result is the same: losses for late entrants, disillusionment for early adopters, and a reputational stain on the entire ecosystem.

So how can one identify scams early? There is no single checklist, but patterns do emerge. Watch for anonymous teams unwilling to reveal identities or past experience. Examine tokenomics carefully: are there large pre-mines, unlocked allocations for founders, or reward structures that incentivise hype over sustainability? Look at GitHub or development logs: is there real engineering work happening, or just cosmetic updates? Question narratives that rely heavily on memes, emotion, or vague references to "disruption" without clear technical underpinnings.

Also, interrogate how the community behaves. Does it welcome hard questions, or dismiss them as "FUD"? Are critics engaged with respectfully, or banned outright? Is the project timeline realistic, or filled with jargon and moonshot promises? *A good project is not afraid of scrutiny. A scam thrives on deflection.*

The uncomfortable truth is that crypto, like any financial frontier, attracts opportunists alongside pioneers. But the burden of discernment rests with the individual. There is no substitute for deep reading, cross-referencing sources, and slowing down the decision cycle. Scammers rely on urgency—limited-time offers, countdown timers, private sale windows. The antidote is patience. Not paralysis, but pause. Long enough to verify claims, cross-check identities, and consider second-order effects.

In traditional finance, due diligence is institutionalised. In crypto, it must be internalised. No regulator will protect you from a bad click. No customer service rep will reverse an on-chain transfer. And no influencer—no matter how compelling—will take responsibility for your loss. This is not meant to frighten; it is meant to clarify. *Self-custody begins with self-responsibility.*

Pump-and-dumps and rug pulls are not inevitable, but they are persistent. They will evolve in form but remain consistent in goal: the extraction of wealth from those who don't ask enough questions. But the very same tools that enable fraud—open data, immutable ledgers, transparent smart contracts—also empower due diligence. The line between victim and participant is often drawn not by intention, but by attention. In crypto, clarity is not given—it is earned.

Fake Coins, Fake Promises

In a marketplace flooded with jargon, volatility, and unchecked enthusiasm, few dynamics reveal the risks of crypto investing more starkly than the proliferation of illegitimate tokens. Beneath the surface of technical whitepapers and flashy Twitter promotions lies a fundamental asymmetry: while legitimate projects aim to solve real problems, many tokens exist solely to exploit the belief that scarcity equals value. This conflation of speculative excitement with substantive innovation has birthed an ecosystem where illusion is often indistinguishable from integrity—until it's too late. Understanding how to evaluate the legitimacy of a cryptocurrency project or initial coin offering (ICO) is not just a useful skill—it is a critical safeguard against losing everything in a market designed to reward discernment and punish naivety.

The initial coin offering boom of 2017 introduced a flood of projects with lofty claims and barely functioning prototypes. Billions were raised on little more than websites, pseudonymous teams, and roadmaps that read like startup science fiction. Yet despite the collapse of countless ICO-funded ventures, the same psychological machinery that fuelled that era remains at work. New waves of fake coins—sometimes built on forked contracts or indistinguishable copycats—continue to re-emerge with each cycle, cloaked in the language of disruption and decentralisation. Their promise is rarely innovation; it is *excitement*—a manufactured narrative engineered to extract capital before vanishing.

Assessing a cryptocurrency's legitimacy requires more than technical literacy. It demands pattern recognition, scepticism, and an appreciation for the human incentives driving project founders, influencers, and speculative investors alike. A token's design can be cloned, its name can be a near match to a legitimate coin, and its code may even be open source. But the *intent* behind a project—what it seeks to deliver and whether that goal is coherent and technically feasible—is where the real analysis begins.

One early tell is the mismatch between narrative and substance. Promoters of fake projects frequently focus on the price of the token rather than the product it powers. They boast about potential returns, future exchange listings, or celebrity endorsements—diverting attention from whether the protocol actually works or even exists. The more emphasis placed on tokenomics over technological utility, the greater the chance the offering is more marketing than mechanism. A legitimate project might describe its market fit, developer traction, or governance model. A fraudulent one recycles buzzwords: Web3, AI, scalability, metaverse, yield-generating NFT infrastructure. The language is impressive; the substance is often vapour.

Even in ostensibly serious ICOs, look closely at the team. Anonymous developers are not necessarily suspect—Bitcoin's creator is famously unknown—but projects that rely on this anonymity while seeking millions from the public deserve added scrutiny. Evaluate team credentials: have they shipped code, led credible ventures, or worked in the relevant domain? Do they respond to tough questions, or is dissent discouraged through social media bans and aggressive moderation?

A key red flag lies in token distribution. If insiders control a disproportionate share of the supply—with minimal lock-up periods or no clear vesting schedule—investors risk being exit liquidity for the core team. Many rug pulls unfold precisely this way: insiders dump their tokens on the open market after building hype, often with liquidity pools configured to favour early sellers. While decentralisation is marketed, the power structure remains entirely centralised behind the scenes. True decentralisation, whether in token supply or project governance, is measurable and verifiable.

Another dimension worth dissecting is the promise of *use cases* that defy economic logic. Projects will sometimes propose multi-billion-dollar markets that they plan to disrupt despite having no customers, no partnerships, and no working product. They advertise technical whitepapers that recycle terminology without detailing how the underlying infrastructure will be built, secured, or scaled. If a project claims it will "replace banks," "disrupt Amazon," or "democratise real estate" with a few thousand lines of smart contract code and zero regulatory plan, scepticism is not cynicism—it's sanity.

The visual polish of a token's website or social media presence can be misleading. High-quality branding is cheap; substance is not. A well-funded scam may look indistinguishable from a serious startup. Legitimate projects welcome scrutiny and often undergo public code audits, with results posted transparently. They publish GitHub repositories, disclose tokenomics in clear terms, and outline both short-term milestones and long-term vision. Fraudulent projects tend to obscure these elements behind marketing hype and complexity. When technical documentation is unavailable, vague, or plagiarised, it's worth assuming the project cannot withstand serious inspection.

Even endorsements can be weaponised. Celebrity backing, viral TikToks, or high-profile Twitter threads are often taken as signals of legitimacy. But crypto history is littered with cases where public figures endorsed products they didn't understand, or worse, were paid to promote without disclosing conflicts. The SEC's enforcement actions against figures like Floyd Mayweather and DJ Khaled over unregistered ICOs are not anomalies—they are warnings. *Attention is not validation.* And in crypto, attention is cheap to manufacture.

Evaluating a coin's legitimacy also requires understanding its *economic model*. Is the coin inflationary or deflationary? What incentivises users, validators, or liquidity providers? How does value accrue to token holders? Many fake coins obfuscate these questions by creating tokenomics that sound impressive but collapse under scrutiny. A common tactic is to promise unrealistic yield percentages (e.g., 10,000% APY) through mechanisms like rebasing or unsustainable liquidity incentives. These projects thrive on rapid inflows of new capital—essentially Ponzi dynamics wrapped in DeFi language.

This is not to suggest that every project with an ambitious roadmap or anonymous founder is a scam. Innovation often comes from the fringes, and early-stage ventures naturally involve risk. But there is a clear difference between uncertainty born of experimentation and deception rooted in falsehood. The former is a risk you can choose to manage; the latter is a trap designed to exploit.

The ICO era may be fading, but the same psychological levers—greed, urgency, FOMO—have simply evolved into new forms: meme tokens, algorithmic stablecoins, generative NFT drops. What binds them is not necessarily malice, but the strategic leveraging of narrative over clarity. For a legitimate project, the product is the pitch. For a scam, the pitch *is* the product.

Ultimately, the best defence against fake coins and fake promises is intellectual patience. The willingness to *not* act immediately, to verify before trusting, and to embrace the boring discipline of due diligence. Legitimate opportunities in crypto do not need to rush you. They don't hide behind complexity. They invite questions—and survive them.

The Dark Side of "Communities"

One of the most seductive promises of the crypto world is that of belonging. In a digital economy fuelled by anonymity and borderless participation, communities have emerged not just as support networks but as primary engines of adoption, evangelism, and collective belief. Telegram channels, Reddit forums, Discord servers, and Twitter Spaces—these are not ancillary features of blockchain culture; they are its core infrastructure. But while the concept of a decentralised, grassroots collective sounds ideal in theory, the practical execution often reveals something more precarious: tightly wound echo chambers that reward conformity, punish dissent, and weaponise enthusiasm against critical thinking. In many cases, these self-described "communities" evolve into mechanisms of persuasion, hype, and emotional control—pressuring individuals into financial decisions that, in retrospect, defy rationality.

The psychological dynamics underpinning these online collectives are not new. The phenomenon of groupthink—first defined by psychologist Irving Janis in the 1970s—describes the process by which groups suppress dissent and self-censor in pursuit of harmony. Crypto communities, especially those formed around specific coins or tokens, exemplify this tendency to an extraordinary degree. The dominant attitude in many spaces is one of unwavering optimism, often framed in moralistic or tribal language: holders are "strong," sellers are "weak," and outsiders are "FUD-spreaders" (fear, uncertainty, and doubt). This binary framing leaves little room for nuanced discussion. Once a token is embraced, any attempt to question its legitimacy, value, or long-term viability is interpreted not as curiosity but as betrayal.

This rhetorical rigidity serves a function: it sustains price momentum. In small-cap coins or illiquid tokens, perception is often more important than fundamentals. If the community can maintain a shared illusion of confidence, it may attract new buyers and push prices higher—at least temporarily. What appears as grassroots support is, in many cases, a performative loop: early investors hyping the asset to attract later buyers who, in turn, amplify the hype. The project itself may not be malicious, but the feedback loop of reinforced belief creates an environment where scrutiny becomes dangerous—not to the protocol, but to the portfolio of those invested in it.

A particularly vivid illustration of this dynamic was the rise of the "SafeMoon Army," a loosely organised group of holders who patrolled social media with zealous intensity during the token's early surge. Dissenting voices—whether from sceptical analysts, rival projects, or former insiders—were swiftly labelled as enemies, bots, or covert operatives from "centralised finance." The mission was to defend the community, but in practice, it became an exercise in insulating the group from reality. As the token's value eventually declined and liquidity evaporated, many newcomers found themselves financially trapped, emotionally manipulated, and socially isolated—all under the guise of belonging to something revolutionary.

What makes these dynamics so potent is that they often operate under the language of empowerment. Community members are told they are early adopters, visionary thinkers, part of a financial revolution. These messages flatter the ego while bonding the individual to the group's identity. But this sense of empowerment is frequently illusory. The real power often lies with the developers, influencers, or administrators who manage the flow of information, curate the community narrative, and in some cases, orchestrate price manipulation. While the average member is staking tokens or buying dips based on collective sentiment, those in control are executing exit strategies with a quiet precision.

The structure of online engagement further amplifies these distortions. Algorithms on platforms like Twitter or Reddit promote content that receives high engagement—likes, retweets, upvotes. In crypto communities, this translates to a visibility advantage for content that aligns with the prevailing group narrative. Thoughtful critiques or cautious analysis are drowned out by memes, moon emojis, and declarations of inevitable wealth. Over time, this creates a distorted sense of consensus, where the loudest opinion is mistaken for the majority view. For a newcomer, the constant stream of bullish content can be overwhelming. The repetition of slogans like "just HODL," "WAGMI" (we're all gonna make it), or "buy the dip" presents a facade of certainty in a domain characterised by risk.

Another layer of complexity is the role of moderators and admins, who often function as both enforcers and gatekeepers. In theory, their role is to maintain order and protect members from spam or scams. In practice, they may also shape discourse in subtle or overt ways—removing sceptical posts, banning users who challenge the project, or even disseminating misinformation to sustain morale. While some moderation is necessary, unchecked control over dialogue can turn community spaces into propaganda machines. The result is an illusion of grassroots enthusiasm that masks a curated and often manipulated consensus.

This is not to suggest that all communities are inherently toxic or malicious. Many projects benefit from engaged, thoughtful user bases who contribute meaningfully—by writing code, helping with translations, educating newcomers, or stress-testing the protocol. These are examples of communities at their best: decentralised, constructive, and transparent. The danger arises when participation becomes conditional on belief—when loyalty to the community replaces critical judgment, and disagreement is treated as disloyalty rather than debate.

The distinction is subtle but important: *a healthy community encourages questions; a harmful one silences them.* In evaluating whether a crypto community is a valuable resource or a risky echo chamber, consider how it handles dissent. Are difficult questions met with thoughtful responses or with sarcasm and dismissal? Are users encouraged to do their own research or to trust unnamed insiders and anonymous admins? Are contrarian views permitted, or do they result in exclusion? The answers to these questions often reveal more about the underlying project than the token's technical whitepaper ever could.

There is also an emotional toll to participating in these communities. The constant stream of price updates, speculative predictions, and peer pressure can create a psychologically destabilising environment—especially for those with real money on the line. The euphoric highs of a token's rise are often matched by crushing lows during drawdowns. Within these cycles, members may feel guilt for selling, shame for doubting, or fear of missing out. These emotional currents are not accidental; they are reinforced by the group's internal norms, its leaders' tone, and the feedback loops of social validation.

The broader implication is that crypto communities, while often framed as liberatory or democratising, can recreate the very hierarchies and psychological traps that decentralisation was meant to dissolve. Charismatic leaders, unaccountable gatekeepers, and groupthink dynamics—these are not just relics of traditional finance or legacy institutions. They thrive in the unregulated and emotionally charged spaces of digital finance unless actively challenged.

Understanding the dark side of communities is not an argument against participation; it is a call for awareness. The most powerful communities are those that foster critical thinking, tolerate disagreement, and allow members to evolve their views without penalty. If crypto is to fulfil its potential as a tool for individual empowerment, then its communities must mature beyond tribalism. Loyalty must never come at the cost of discernment. And enthusiasm must always leave room for inquiry.

Protecting Yourself Without Paranoia

The most dangerous misconception in crypto is not that it's risky—it's the belief that risk can be outsourced entirely. Newcomers often enter the ecosystem under the impression that someone else has already figured out how to navigate it safely. Influencers, platforms, exchanges, and self-declared experts offer simple, confident answers to complex, fluid problems. But while there are principles that can meaningfully reduce exposure to loss or deception, *no single person or product can fully protect you from the nature of a decentralised, unregulated, and rapidly evolving environment.* The burden of discernment remains with the participant. And yet, that responsibility need not feel paralysing.

There is a way to engage intelligently without succumbing to cynicism or fear.

Security in crypto is not binary—it is not a matter of being either totally exposed or totally protected. Rather, it is a set of gradients: levels of care, decision-making, and configuration that depend heavily on your goals, profile, and behaviour. The key is not to memorise a list of fixed rules, but to develop the habits of caution and pattern recognition that allow you to make informed trade-offs in real time. *Security is not an end state; it is a way of thinking.*

Much of the paranoia around crypto safety arises from media coverage that favours drama over detail. Multi-million dollar exploits, high-profile exchange failures, and dramatic token collapses make for excellent headlines. But what rarely gets reported is how many of these losses could have been avoided with fairly modest precautions. Not heroic levels of technical sophistication—just a few well-placed questions asked at the right time. Was the smart contract audited? Is the founder verifiable? Are the funds stored in cold wallets? Is the yield model mathematically sound or economically absurd? These are not questions of paranoia; they are questions of competence.

Perhaps the most fundamental principle for protecting yourself is understanding *what you are actually doing when you interact with crypto assets.* For example, when you approve a smart contract in your wallet, you are not merely "buying a coin." You may be granting that contract the right to transfer assets out of your wallet without further approval—sometimes indefinitely. That distinction is invisible to those who see crypto purely through the lens of trading screens. It becomes legible only when you realise that you are not investing *in* crypto, you are interacting *with* it. And like any interaction, it carries assumptions and consequences that you are responsible for parsing.

Many crypto losses are not the result of malicious attacks but of inattentive behaviour—sending tokens to the wrong address, clicking a phishing link, reusing passwords, or skipping two-factor authentication. These are human vulnerabilities, not technological ones. And they can be addressed with habits rather than hardware. Use a password manager. Segment funds across wallets. Bookmark trusted sites and avoid clicking through from social media. If something feels rushed, confusing, or emotionally charged, pause. *Scams depend on urgency; safety thrives on clarity.*

The importance of digital hygiene becomes even more obvious in light of the platforms we rely on. Major centralised exchanges like Binance or Coinbase offer convenience and liquidity, but they are still custodians. If you leave your assets on their platform, they control the private keys—not you. This is not inherently unsafe, but it does introduce dependencies. If the exchange goes down, gets hacked, or freezes accounts, your access is compromised. Cold storage, hardware wallets, and self-custody tools offer more control but demand more responsibility. The goal is not to eliminate risk, but to understand *where it lives*—and to ensure that it lives in a place you're prepared to monitor.

Yet there is a deeper challenge that often goes unaddressed in safety discussions: *the emotional psychology of risk*. Crypto markets move quickly, and price swings can trigger powerful cognitive biases—FOMO (fear of missing out), loss aversion, anchoring, and herd behaviour. These emotional triggers can override even the best security setups. A person who stores their funds in a hardware wallet can still lose everything by falling for a token with no intrinsic value, promoted by a charismatic YouTube personality. Emotional discipline is part of operational security. *Security is not just about where your keys are stored; it's about how your attention is manipulated.*

This is why safety must be reframed not as a checklist of tools but as a posture of engagement. It means asking whether a project's claims make sense within basic economic logic. It means tracing incentives: who benefits if this product succeeds, and who gets hurt if it fails? It means recognising that decentralisation does not always mean equality—and that some actors will always have more information, more liquidity, or more exit options than you do. Accepting this doesn't mean retreating; it means adjusting your expectations and calibrating your exposure accordingly.

Even the most credible projects can harbour vulnerabilities. Consider the DAO hack in 2016, which led to the loss of $60 million in ETH despite the project being seen as a bold, well-regarded experiment in decentralised governance. The code had been audited. The idea was compelling. The community was active and thoughtful. And still, an attacker found a way to manipulate the logic of the smart contract to siphon funds. The takeaway is not to avoid all experimentation, but to remember that *transparency does not guarantee robustness*, and popularity does not equal safety.

This is also why diversification in crypto is not simply about holding different coins—it's about diversifying *risk types*. If you hold only tokens on centralised exchanges, you are exposed to custodial risk. If you use only DeFi protocols, you are exposed to contract risk. If your entire portfolio is in a single asset class—say NFTs, or memecoins—you are exposed to narrative risk. A robust setup spreads exposure across layers of control: custody, liquidity, volatility, and technical complexity. This is how sophisticated investors operate, and newcomers would do well to emulate the underlying reasoning, if not the specific configurations.

Importantly, protection does not mean isolation. The best way to stay safe in crypto is not to retreat from participation but to *cultivate discernment within it.* This includes learning how to read a whitepaper without being dazzled by jargon, how to follow on-chain activity using basic blockchain explorers, and how to interpret the difference between marketing and substance. It also means knowing when to stop researching and take action—or when to hold back because the data is inconclusive. Confidence in crypto does not come from certainty. It comes from *knowing what you know, and knowing where your blind spots are.*

Above all, avoid adopting a fear-based approach to crypto participation. Suspicion is not the same as sophistication. There is no virtue in assuming everything is a scam. That attitude not only distorts perception but leads to missed opportunities and intellectual laziness. The point is not to be paranoid—it is to be precise. Most scams are not successful because they are cleverly engineered; they are successful because they are tailored to people who want shortcuts, who want guarantees, who want magic. If you let go of those desires, the scams lose their grip.

Paranoia is paralysing, but precision is liberating. Protecting yourself in crypto does not require becoming a security maximalist or a techno-sceptic. It requires staying engaged, asking difficult questions, and taking responsibility for your decisions. That is the price of participation. But it is also its reward. Because the same mindset that keeps you safe is the one that makes you smarter—and that, ultimately, is the most powerful form of protection.

Chapter 7
Risk, Timing, and Strategy for First-Time Investors

Advice for first-time crypto investors is abundant—often loud, occasionally lucrative, and sometimes dangerously incomplete. What is seldom offered, however, is a coherent framework. Not a string of tips or rules of thumb, but a structured approach to engaging with an asset class that defies conventional categories, operates beyond business hours, and feeds as much on narrative momentum as on data. New entrants frequently oscillate between urgency and uncertainty: the fear of missing out on generational gains collides with the apprehension of wandering blindly into a digital casino. Both instincts are valid, yet neither should dictate action. What is required is not perfect foresight but grounded judgement—a mindset that acknowledges volatility without succumbing to it.

The challenge is not that crypto is inherently incomprehensible. It is that it is simultaneously too many things. Is it currency, speculative asset, social movement, software protocol, regulatory puzzle? The answer is yes—depending on timing and perspective. This ambiguity is intrinsic, not transient. Investors, therefore, must first clarify their role. Are you trading, holding, experimenting, hedging, or learning? Without this understanding, capital—whether £50 or £50,000—floats unmoored. And unmoored capital rarely acts rationally.

The often-overlooked starting point is not which token to buy, but how much to allocate. Allocation seems straightforward, yet most newcomers rely on instinct: investing only what they are "willing to lose." Pragmatic at first glance, this approach skips a crucial step. What is the goal? Is it a 1% portfolio exposure, asymmetric upside, diversification of a thesis, or a speculative bet? "Willing to lose" is not strategy; it is an emotional placeholder for decisions insufficiently interrogated.

A more rigorous approach begins by recognising crypto as a high-volatility, low-maturity asset class, still loosely correlated with traditional markets. Exposure must be contextualised within a broader financial plan. No professional certification is required, but clarity of purpose is essential. Saving for a house in twelve months? Crypto likely has no place. Investing with a ten-year horizon and comfort with double-digit drawdowns? A modest allocation may be appropriate. Missteps arise not from participation but from failing to situate that participation within personal circumstances.

Timing, too, is often misunderstood. Many obsess over the "perfect" moment, scrutinising charts, sentiment, and macroeconomic cues as if predictability were possible. In truth, even professionals with sophisticated tools cannot consistently forecast short-term movements. Consistency outweighs timing. Dollar-cost averaging (DCA) exemplifies disciplined response: it spreads exposure, reduces the emotional rollercoaster, and cultivates process-oriented thinking—a vital skill in markets engineered to provoke impulsivity.

Yet consistency does not equate to passivity. Strategic investors interrogate the ecosystem: What problem does the token solve? Who is building it? Is the code open-source and audited? Is the community active or stagnant? Where does liquidity originate? Does the token accrue intrinsic value, or is it hype dressed as opportunity? These are not technical queries—they are investment questions reframed for a digital context. Due diligence is not the preserve of developers; it is the duty of every capital deployer.

The capacity to ask meaningful questions depends on mental models. Traditional finance offers many transferable tools. Consider expected value: a high potential return is enticing only if the probability and consequences are favourable. Or opportunity cost: each pound spent on a memecoin is a pound not compounding elsewhere. Behavioural finance offers further insight—loss aversion, confirmation bias, recency effects—all magnified in a 24/7 ecosystem with instantaneous feedback loops.

Diversification, too, translates. While crypto lacks a true broad-market index, carefully curated portfolios—comprising major layer-1 protocols, infrastructure tokens, and stablecoins—can emulate indexing's benefits: mitigating idiosyncratic risk while capturing general market growth. The insight persists: diversification protects against what you do not know, not merely against what you anticipate.

This assumes, however, that one is not distracted by noise. Crypto excels at manufacturing urgency. Discord groups, Telegram channels, Twitter threads, and YouTube influencers weaponise immediacy, turning attention into impulsive action. Emotional content spreads fastest, distorting perception and compressing decision cycles. Novices react—they buy late, sell early, freeze altogether. Strategic investors cultivate filters: prioritising data over opinion, on-chain metrics over hype, signal over noise.

Risk is often defined as volatility—but that is superficial. The deeper risk is misunderstanding exposure: token mechanics, flawed sources, market structure, regulatory pressure. Timing alone cannot shield from this. Nor does diversification if misapplied. Strategy must extend beyond allocation into disciplined interrogation of assumptions within a shifting ecosystem.

None of this is intended to intimidate. On the contrary: crypto rewards curiosity and self-education over credentialism. No insider access, advanced degrees, or decades of experience are required. What matters is process: grounding each decision in principle rather than emotion. Knowing why you invest, how much you can bear to lose, what success looks like, and how to respond when markets turn—as they invariably will.

First-time investors who embrace this mindset will not escape losses. But they will escape surprise. And in a world defined by asymmetry, being prepared may be the most strategic position of all.

How Much (If Any) Should You Invest?

The most consequential decision a first-time crypto investor makes is not which coin to buy, nor when to buy it. It's *how much to invest in the first place*. This question appears deceptively simple but reveals more about the investor's psychology, risk posture, and financial literacy than any other variable. The crypto markets, notorious for their volatility and unpredictability, tempt even cautious participants with visions of exponential returns. But enthusiasm is not a strategy. What's needed is a personal framework—one that links investment size to life goals, financial capacity, and psychological resilience.

Unlike traditional asset classes, crypto exists in a zone of probabilistic extremes: outcomes swing from windfalls to wipeouts without warning, and the asset's fundamental value often lags behind price action by several years—if it exists at all. This is not a defect. It's a structural feature of emerging markets, where narratives outrun models and investor behaviour moves faster than regulation. As such, any decision about allocation must begin with a premise both obvious and overlooked: *you are not buying a financial product—you are buying into a volatile experiment.*

The central challenge is one of calibration. Many newcomers attempt to "dip their toes in," but do so without clear thresholds. They invest an amount they think they can afford to lose—but fail to define what *losing* actually entails. Is it a numerical figure? A drawdown percentage? A level of stress that begins to disrupt their thinking? Treating risk as an abstract notion rather than a measurable variable leaves the investor exposed—not just financially, but emotionally. Once the market turns (and it always does), that undefined tolerance is tested. More often than not, it fails.

It is more productive to invert the question: *how much can I invest in crypto while remaining indifferent to the outcome?* This doesn't mean apathy; it means psychological insulation. The right allocation is not one that excites you, but one that leaves you unshaken—able to carry on with your life, your goals, your other investments, whether your crypto bet goes up tenfold or drops by 90%. If either scenario causes sleeplessness, the allocation is misaligned.

To construct such an allocation, start with first principles. Every investment exists in the context of a broader financial landscape. What are your fixed obligations? Your liquid reserves? Your retirement strategy? Your income stability? Crypto cannot be evaluated in isolation. The proper amount to invest is not a static number but a *percentage of a diversified, intentioned portfolio.* For some, that may be 1–2%; for others, up to 5–10%. Beyond those ranges, the investor enters speculative territory—a valid choice, but one that must be made consciously, not impulsively.

Historical data provides further perspective. While the price history of Bitcoin or Ethereum is often used as a justification for large allocations ("if you had just bought and held since 2015…"), such backtested hindsight ignores survivorship bias and underestimates emotional volatility. Even those who held through major drawdowns did not do so in a vacuum. They were not just resisting market dips; they were navigating public ridicule, media attacks, exit scams, and regulatory uncertainty. The point is not that holding through adversity is impossible—it's that *few are psychologically prepared to do so at large scale.* This is why modest exposure, combined with long-term discipline, outperforms oversized bets made in euphoric moments.

Importantly, allocation must also reflect *investment intent.* Are you here to learn or to earn? If your aim is educational—understanding how wallets work, participating in governance, experimenting with decentralised apps—then a small, "tuition-fee" investment may be enough. This aligns capital with curiosity. On the other hand, if your goal is to seek non-correlated returns, hedge against fiat debasement, or speculate on emerging infrastructure, then your allocation should reflect conviction. But that conviction must be evidence-based, not emotionally driven.

Conviction, in this context, is not a feeling. It is the result of research, reflection, and a clear understanding of trade-offs. A responsible investor should be able to articulate not just why they're buying an asset, but what would cause them to exit. They should also understand what role the asset plays in their portfolio: is it a core holding or a satellite? A hedge or a thesis? These are questions borrowed from institutional portfolio management, but they are just as relevant to individuals—perhaps even more so, given the lack of guardrails.

Another essential consideration is *liquidity.* Crypto assets are highly liquid in market mechanics but illiquid in behavioural terms. Many investors are reluctant to sell after a 200% gain, fearing further upside. Others panic-sell at a 50% drop, despite a long-term thesis.

This gap between theory and practice means that any investment should be mentally treated as "locked" for a defined time horizon. If you can't stomach that lock-in—if you might need the funds in six months for rent, tuition, or emergencies—then the asset is misallocated. Short-term funds do not belong in long-volatility instruments.

Taxation also plays an underrated role in deciding how much to invest. In many jurisdictions, crypto gains are taxed as capital gains, and losses may not be deductible in meaningful ways. This asymmetry increases the effective risk: you may bear full downside but only partial upside. Additionally, frequent trading can trigger complex tax events that create paperwork, penalties, or legal ambiguity. All of this should feed back into the initial question—not as a deterrent, but as a context. *A good allocation is not just affordable in cash terms; it is affordable in time, complexity, and compliance.*

What about age and life stage? Young investors often assume they can afford to be more aggressive because they have time to recover. This is partially true. But it overlooks the fact that early capital—if well managed—has compound effects far greater than later windfalls. Losing £5,000 at age 25 may seem harmless, but that amount properly invested in diversified assets could be worth £50,000 by retirement. Conversely, older investors may feel pressure to "catch up" by chasing returns. This often backfires, leading to misallocation, poor timing, and regret. The more useful lens is not age but *financial trajectory*: are you on track for your goals, or compensating for past gaps?

The myth that crypto must be "all or nothing" is especially harmful. You do not need to go all-in to benefit from crypto exposure. Even small allocations—1–3% of a portfolio—have historically had outsized effects on returns, while keeping risk manageable. This is the principle behind *convexity*: the idea that a small input can produce large, asymmetrical outcomes. But convexity only works if it is not compromised by overexposure. Once the bet becomes large enough to threaten your financial foundation, its asymmetry disappears.

None of this is meant to dissuade participation. Rather, it is an invitation to *intentional participation*. Crypto is not just about technology; it's about design—of systems, incentives, and identities. Your portfolio should be no different. Designed, not defaulted. Anchored in principles, not vibes. Every pound you allocate is a vote—not just for a protocol, but for your own future orientation: how you navigate uncertainty, how you absorb risk, how you express curiosity without self-sabotage.

So how much should you invest? Enough to care. Not so much that you panic. And never so much that a market downturn becomes a personal crisis. The real test of an allocation is not whether it captures upside, but whether it leaves you *empowered*—clear-minded, adaptable, and still focused on the rest of your life. In that sense, the right amount is the one that lets you walk away, whenever needed, without regret.

Understanding Timing Without Time-Travelling

The idea of "perfect timing" in investing is a seductive illusion. It appeals to our instinct for control, our hindsight bias, and our longing to outwit uncertainty. Nowhere is this more potent—or more misleading—than in the world of cryptocurrency. In an ecosystem defined by volatility, hype cycles, and emotional trading, the myth of the ideal entry point exerts a psychological pull that is both powerful and perilous. The belief that one must catch the next Bitcoin or Ethereum "at the bottom" in order to make meaningful gains often drives erratic behaviour, fuels market anxiety, and clouds rational judgment. Yet, the truth is less glamorous and more empowering: sustainable investing is far more about consistency than clairvoyance.

This chapter invites the reader to dismantle the notion that timing the crypto market is either feasible or necessary for long-term success. It offers a reframing—one rooted in discipline, data, and decades of behavioural finance research. It draws from both traditional and decentralised finance to show how intelligent exposure doesn't require a crystal ball. It requires a framework.

The overwhelming appeal of timing stems from two assumptions: that markets are "beatable" in the short term by individuals, and that missing out on the "next big thing" is an unforgivable error. The first assumption has been thoroughly dismantled in traditional finance. Active fund managers rarely outperform the market over long periods, despite extensive tools, teams, and data. The second assumption—fear of missing out—has become crypto's emotional backbone. Its memes, community narratives, and viral headlines tend to exalt those who "got in early" and disparage those who "missed it," even though the lifecycle of viable assets spans years, not news cycles. What this chapter emphasises is not how to chase a price dip, but how to build a resilient entry strategy regardless of market phase.

One of the most effective antidotes to timing anxiety is *dollar-cost averaging* (DCA). The premise is elegant in its simplicity: invest a fixed amount at regular intervals, irrespective of the asset's price. Over time, this approach smooths out volatility and reduces the impact of short-term price fluctuations. It protects the investor from the twin traps of overconfidence and hesitation—jumping in too aggressively when euphoric, or staying paralysed when fearful. In a market as emotionally charged as crypto, this kind of mechanical discipline offers not just mathematical benefit but psychological stability. It shifts the investor's identity from a reactive speculator to a consistent participant.

Critics of dollar-cost averaging often point to opportunity cost—arguing that lump sum investing can outperform DCA in bull markets. Statistically, they are correct, assuming a strong upward trend from the start. But this critique misses the point for most first-time investors. The purpose of DCA is not to maximise theoretical gains in optimal market conditions; it is to reduce regret in suboptimal ones. *The value of DCA lies not just in its returns, but in its emotional survivability.* It allows a person to stay invested without being consumed by anxiety over daily moves, tweets, or technical patterns they barely understand.

Diversification adds another critical dimension to timing-resilience. In traditional finance, the principle is almost sacred: spread risk across asset classes, sectors, and geographies. In crypto, diversification requires more nuance. Diversifying between Bitcoin, Ethereum, and a handful of carefully vetted Layer 1 or Layer 2 projects is not the same as blindly holding a dozen obscure tokens in the hope one "moons." Real diversification in this space means exposure across different functional types of assets—such as store-of-value coins, smart contract platforms, stablecoins, and governance tokens—*with a clear understanding of what each is for.* The aim is not just to spread bets, but to hedge structural risks.

Timing also becomes far less intimidating when one adopts a *long-term mental frame.* Many crypto newcomers enter the space with a mindset borrowed from gambling or gaming: high stakes, rapid moves, and a constant sense of urgency. Yet, most of the foundational growth in this sector—protocol adoption, infrastructure development, regulatory clarity—unfolds over years, not weeks. Bitcoin took over a decade to go from fringe curiosity to institutional asset. Ethereum's transition from proof-of-work to proof-of-stake required years of coordinated technical development and still continues to evolve. If the investor can emotionally detach from the 24-hour candle and instead anchor their expectations to a 5- to 10-year horizon, the appeal of precise timing diminishes dramatically.

Another overlooked factor in resisting the timing fallacy is *liquidity planning.* Crypto is often treated as a high-risk, high-reward asset class—but what amplifies the risk is not just the volatility, but poor integration into the investor's broader financial life. If a person commits money they cannot afford to lose, or funds they may need to access in the near term, the stakes of every market fluctuation become existential. This leads to panic selling, emotional decisions, and unnecessary stress. A more rational approach treats crypto as a satellite holding—*a meaningful but measured part of a broader portfolio*—funded with capital that is consciously allocated for longer-term exposure. Such an approach transforms volatility from a threat into a strategic opportunity.

None of this is to say that the timing of entry is irrelevant. It's simply to say that it's unknowable, and therefore ungameable. What can be known, however, is one's tolerance for volatility, their actual investment goals, and the structure of their financial life. These are the levers that matter most. They are also the most neglected, especially in a culture that rewards hot takes over thoughtful strategy.

A first-time investor may enter in a bear market and see losses on paper for years—but if their capital was allocated wisely, their conviction based on sound principles, and their timeline appropriately long, the entry point becomes a footnote, not a headline.

There is a deeper philosophical point here. The obsession with perfect timing is ultimately rooted in a desire to eliminate uncertainty—to master the future through precision. But investing, like life, is shaped more by adaptability than accuracy. Those who survive and thrive are not the ones who guessed right; they are the ones who kept showing up, adjusted with context, and stayed clear-headed when others lost perspective.

As this chapter will show, entering the crypto space doesn't require foresight so much as foresight's humbler cousin: preparation. Dollar-cost averaging and diversification are not clever tricks—they are timeless tools. Tools that empower investors to participate meaningfully without becoming overwhelmed, reactive, or disillusioned. They create a structure in which intelligence can express itself without requiring perfection.

And most importantly, they shift the question from "When should I buy?" to "How should I build?" That is a question far more worthy of serious attention—and far more within your control.

Smart Questions to Ask Before You Buy

The most dangerous thing a new investor can bring to the crypto markets isn't ignorance—it's unexamined confidence. Confidence, when rooted in curiosity and supported by thoughtful questions, is a strength. But confidence borrowed from influencers, momentum trends, or peer pressure is merely disguised vulnerability. The investor who asks the right questions—not to impress, but to understand—builds an internal compass that becomes more valuable than any price chart or newsletter recommendation. Especially in crypto, where innovation and speculation coexist in tension, asking the right questions is not a formality. It is a survival skill.

The challenge for non-technical investors is not just access to information; it's knowing *which* information matters. Crypto project websites are often dense with jargon, animated roadmaps, and buzzwords like "decentralised," "scalable," or "interoperable." Whitepapers may present themselves with academic formatting but often mask vague or unprovable claims. Even well-meaning communities can create a false sense of consensus. In this climate, asking structured, well-phrased questions becomes an act of intellectual self-defence—and the first step in transforming from a passive consumer of hype into a discerning participant.

Start with *What does this project actually do—and for whom?* It's remarkable how often this foundational question goes unasked. A token is not inherently valuable just because it exists, is listed on a popular exchange, or has a clever name. Is the token linked to a functioning product? If so, what problem does the product solve? Who are its users? In traditional investing, companies are evaluated based on customers, revenue, and competitive edge. Crypto investing should be no different in spirit, even if the metrics vary. A blockchain designed to handle supply chain verification, for instance, should offer a demonstrable advantage over existing systems—not just claim it. Ask yourself whether the project is addressing a real, painful, and scalable problem, or merely recycling a popular idea with new branding.

Another critical filter: *Why does this need a token at all?* A surprising number of projects introduce tokens not as a necessary part of their architecture but as a means to raise capital. In some cases, the token's only function is to be traded. That's not utility; that's speculation. True utility tokens serve a function within a network: to pay for computation, reward validators, enable governance, or facilitate transactions. If the project would still make sense without the token, then the token may be superfluous—and your investment may be tied to a gimmick rather than a system. This question helps clarify whether you are investing in infrastructure or in noise.

Then consider: *Who is behind this project, and what is their track record?* In crypto, pseudonymity is common, but that does not excuse opacity. Reputable founders may use pseudonyms, but they typically have established credibility—via previous projects, published work, or verifiable contributions. Anonymous founders are not necessarily red flags, but total invisibility is. If a project's team cannot be identified, if its GitHub repository is inactive, or if its leadership communicates only through meme accounts and anonymous forums, your trust should not come easily. Look for evidence of competence, commitment, and accountability.

Ask also: *How is this project funded, and where is the money going?* Many investors skip this question because they assume early-stage crypto projects operate outside the norms of traditional financial transparency. But this is precisely why the question matters. Has the project raised money through a public ICO, private seed round, or via venture capital? How much was allocated to the founding team, developers, or community treasury? What is the token release schedule (commonly referred to as a vesting schedule), and when will large amounts of supply enter circulation? A token with low float and a looming supply unlock is structurally prone to price suppression. Understanding tokenomics is not a technical indulgence—it is a lens into future incentives and potential dilution.

Equally essential: *Where does the yield or promised return come from?* If a project offers high yields—especially fixed or guaranteed ones—it must be able to explain, clearly and credibly, how those returns are generated. Are rewards coming from protocol revenue, transaction fees, or lending activity? Or are they being paid out from newly minted tokens, which dilutes existing holders? If a yield depends primarily on new user inflows, it bears disturbing resemblance to a pyramid scheme. Sustainable yield is hard-earned, not air-dropped. If the answer to "Where does the money come from?" sounds like circular logic, step away.

Next, ask: *How is security handled, and what happens when things go wrong?* Audits, bug bounties, and open-source code are positive signs, but not guarantees. Was the protocol audited by a reputable third-party firm? Has the team responded promptly and transparently to past issues? In the event of an exploit, what protections are in place for users—insurance funds, protocol-level safeguards, or clear governance mechanisms? DeFi platforms, especially, operate without traditional customer service or regulatory recourse. If a bridge is hacked or a smart contract fails, your funds could be irrecoverable. A serious project anticipates this risk and communicates mitigation strategies upfront.

Another overlooked question: *What is the community like, and how does it behave under stress?* A healthy crypto community is not just enthusiastic—it is intellectually honest. If dissent is silenced, if criticism is ridiculed, or if every market dip is explained away as market manipulation, this is not community—it is cultism. Join Telegram groups, Discord servers, or subreddit threads not just to observe sentiment, but to study tone. Are questions answered with patience or sarcasm? Is transparency encouraged or deflected? Market euphoria attracts followers, but true resilience is shown during corrections. A project whose backers can engage constructively with scepticism is likelier to have staying power.

Finally, ask yourself: *What role will this asset play in my portfolio, and am I emotionally prepared to hold it?* Many investors neglect self-questioning in their due diligence process. But introspection is as critical as research. Are you buying because you believe in the technology, or because someone on social media said it would "10x"? Is your time horizon consistent with the asset's developmental stage? Are you prepared to endure sharp drawdowns without panic-selling? Crypto investing tests emotional discipline more than most asset classes. The better you understand your own motivations and limits, the more effectively you can filter opportunities through a lens of personal integrity.

This is not about creating a checklist of correct answers—it's about cultivating intellectual posture. *The questions you ask determine the quality of your investment experience.* Good questions keep you humble when the market tempts arrogance. They keep you focused when the crowd shouts in multiple directions. They help you distinguish between what is merely possible, what is probable, and what is proven.

In an environment saturated with noise, sharp questions are your only defence against regret. They require no advanced technical knowledge—just clarity of thought, curiosity, and the willingness to pause before acting. They transform crypto from a casino of chaos into a landscape of possibilities. And perhaps most critically, they remind you that you are not here to follow the smartest person in the room. You are here to think clearly for yourself.

Mental Models from Traditional Investing

The cryptocurrency markets, despite their branding as disruptive, permissionless, and decentralised, continue to reflect many of the same psychological and structural patterns that have shaped traditional investing for decades. Speculative bubbles, momentum trading, narrative-driven assets, and overconfidence in novelty are not new phenomena; they simply wear different digital clothing. For first-time investors entering crypto, the key to developing clarity in a volatile, overhyped space lies not in reinventing how to think about investing, but in rediscovering the time-tested mental models that have governed prudent financial decision-making across generations.

One of the most powerful mental anchors borrowed from traditional finance is the idea of *opportunity cost*. Every unit of capital committed to a crypto asset is capital that cannot simultaneously earn compound interest elsewhere, whether in a savings account, bond fund, or low-cost index. When euphoria dominates sentiment, this basic truth is often ignored. The possibility of outsized returns can lead to distorted comparisons: investors begin to treat 10% annual returns from a diversified portfolio as "boring" when crypto Twitter is full of screenshots showing 10x returns in a week. But those screenshots rarely mention the corresponding losses, or the actual timelines. Seasoned investors understand that money is not only a tool for speculation—it is also a reservoir of optionality. Preserving optionality is an underappreciated form of risk management.

Another foundational lens is that of *asset allocation*. In traditional finance, portfolios are diversified across asset classes—equities, bonds, real estate, commodities—not because diversification guarantees returns, but because it reduces idiosyncratic risk. Crypto, by contrast, is often treated monolithically. Newcomers speak of "investing in crypto" as if Bitcoin, a decentralised digital store of value, and a newly launched DeFi protocol with a 25-page whitepaper are equivalent instruments. They are not. Mental discipline requires asking: within the category of crypto, how am I diversified? Am I overexposed to tokens with high correlation? Do I understand the distinction between infrastructure-layer assets (like Ethereum), governance tokens (like Compound), and speculative meme assets (like Dogecoin)? Simply holding a basket of different coins does not constitute true diversification if they all rise and fall on the same narrative wave.

The principle of *expected value* is equally critical. At its core, investing is probabilistic, not deterministic. This means decisions should not be judged solely by their outcomes but by the quality of reasoning and risk-adjusted reward at the time they were made. In traditional portfolio theory, an investment that fails may still have been the correct decision if the process was sound. Crypto investing tends to encourage outcome-chasing. Investors who doubled their money on a random token may believe this confirms their foresight. But unless the thesis was based on coherent fundamentals, it is indistinguishable from gambling. When you apply an expected value framework, the question shifts from "What could I make?" to "What is the likelihood-weighted value of this outcome, and is the downside manageable?" This mental model encourages intellectual humility and mitigates overconfidence in luck masquerading as skill.

Reversion to the mean is another bedrock principle that often vanishes from crypto discourse. Traditional markets recognise that extreme outperformance is usually unsustainable. Funds that produce stellar returns in one year often underperform in subsequent years, particularly when their strategies attract an influx of capital. In crypto, the psychological effect is amplified: assets that surge 200% in a month often become magnets for retail investors precisely when their probability of correction is highest. Those who assume past performance implies future trajectory are not misinformed—they are mistaking noise for signal. Reversion to the mean reminds us to contextualise returns and be sceptical of anything that appears to defy gravity.

In tandem with market mechanisms, behavioural finance contributes critical models. *Loss aversion*, for instance, explains why investors feel the pain of a 10% loss more intensely than the pleasure of a 10% gain. In crypto, where price volatility is extreme and corrections of

30–50% are routine, this can lead to counterproductive behaviours: panic-selling at the bottom, chasing rebounds out of desperation, or holding deteriorating assets in the hope of emotional redemption. A clear-eyed understanding of loss aversion doesn't remove the discomfort, but it helps investors anticipate and resist their own impulses. Knowing that your future self will likely regret emotion-driven trades is the first step toward overriding them.

Closely related is the model of *confirmation bias*. Investors tend to seek information that reinforces their existing beliefs, particularly in noisy or ambiguous environments. Online crypto communities—whether on Reddit, Telegram, or Discord—can become echo chambers that reward bullish narratives and downvote caution. Traditional investors learn to triangulate their thesis against opposing views. They ask: "What evidence would disprove my thesis?" or "Who are the smartest people who disagree with me?" This is not pessimism; it is discipline. Transferring that habit into crypto means resisting the urge to only follow influencers who confirm your enthusiasm, and instead cultivating intellectual diversity in your sources.

Another vital model is *time horizon alignment*. In traditional investing, the mismatch between an investor's goals and their asset's behaviour can produce needless stress. An individual saving for a house in two years has no business holding a volatile small-cap equity. Similarly, someone who needs liquidity in the short term should think twice before locking up assets in illiquid DeFi protocols or betting on pre-product tokens. Time horizon clarity affects not just *what* you invest in, but *how* you behave when markets test your patience. If you've allocated crypto as part of a long-term "moonshot" segment of your portfolio, daily price swings become less relevant. But if you've placed your emergency fund into a meme coin hoping for a 10x, you've confused gambling for strategy. Traditional finance offers the corrective: investment choices should be matched to the timeline and purpose of the capital deployed.

Finally, no discussion of mental models is complete without reference to *the power of compounding*. Albert Einstein reputedly called compounding the eighth wonder of the world—not because it is complex, but because it is easily neglected. In crypto, where gains can be spectacular, the temptation to frequently rotate between positions, chase trends, or "take profits" too early is strong. But compounding works best when friction is minimised. In traditional investing, a well-structured portfolio—often with simple index funds—can double over time without constant tinkering. The lesson for crypto is not to buy and forget, but to avoid confusing activity with productivity. Sometimes the best move is to let high-conviction, well-researched assets grow over time while managing risk intelligently. Chasing short-term excitement can destroy long-term compounding through poor entries, tax inefficiencies, and cognitive fatigue.

In sum, the models that govern traditional investing are not artefacts of a bygone system. They are intellectual tools forged through the hard lessons of history. They help investors navigate noise, resist impulsive behaviour, and build frameworks that are portable across asset classes. Applying these models to crypto does not make you conservative—it makes you coherent. It enables you to separate genuine innovation from engineered hype, to position your capital with intention, and to engage with this emerging asset class as a serious investor rather than a speculative tourist. The future of crypto is uncertain. But the discipline to think well, evaluate risk, and respect reality is timeless.

Chapter 8
Stablecoins and the Illusion of Safety

There is an undeniable allure to the word "stable" in a landscape defined by relentless volatility. For newcomers overwhelmed by flashing charts, speculative jargon, and the incessant hum of price movement, stablecoins offer a promise of steadiness. Marketed as digital assets immune to chaos, pegged to fiat currencies like the US dollar or the euro, they present themselves as reliable mediums of exchange, stores of value, or entry points into the blockchain economy. The narrative is compelling: all the speed, programmability, and accessibility of crypto, yet without the stomach-churning swings. A digital dollar that refuses to tumble at midnight. Yet, as with so many elegant stories in crypto, the reality lies in the mechanics—and the marketing rarely tells the full truth.

To appreciate why stablecoins have become both a cornerstone of crypto infrastructure and one of its most precarious pillars, it is necessary to look beyond the promises and examine the methods employed to maintain them. The term "stablecoin" may evoke reliability, but the underlying architectures differ dramatically. Some are collateralised by reserves held in banks and subject to audit; others rely on algorithms, game theory, and assumptions about human behaviour—assumptions that falter the instant market participants act unpredictably. The distinction is not semantic; it is existential. Misunderstanding it is not merely academic—it carries real financial consequences.

The collapse of TerraUSD (UST) in 2022 offered a harsh lesson. This widely used algorithmic stablecoin unraveled in days, obliterating billions in paper wealth and demonstrating the fragility of engineered stability when not underpinned by robust collateral. The failure was not merely technical; it was a collapse of confidence, design, and transparency. It also highlighted a persistent misconception: that all stablecoins are created equal, and that a $1 peg guarantees safety. Countless users continue to make decisions based on this assumption, often hastily, on mobile apps, or under the sway of bullish communities and sleek interfaces.

Part of the problem is linguistic. "Stablecoin" functions as a catch-all, masking meaningful differences in structure and risk. A fiat-backed token like USDC, issued by Circle and theoretically backed by audited cash and Treasuries, carries a vastly different risk profile from an algorithmic asset such as UST or its imitators. Yet in daily conversation—on exchanges, dashboards, and wallets—they are often treated as interchangeable digital dollars. This simplification is not merely misleading; it is hazardous. It encourages the assumption that a dollar-pegged token is inherently safe, ignoring the engineering that maintains, or threatens, that peg.

User interfaces and marketing exacerbate this illusion. Platforms typically display stablecoins with a neat $1.00 label, a comforting visual cue that conceals fragility. The screen rarely reminds users that value is not legally guaranteed, that collateral may be overstated or illiquid, or that redemption mechanisms can fail under stress. Contrast this with traditional finance: a money market fund prospectus meticulously details conditions under which principal may be lost. In crypto, promises are implied by branding and silence; the lack of friction in the user experience quietly reinforces the belief in absolute stability.

Yet stability in crypto is never absolute—it is engineered, contingent, and sometimes performative. The peg exists because confidence, mechanisms, and liquidity sustain it. Remove any of these, and the peg can snap. The story of stablecoins is therefore one of design trade-offs. Fiat-backed tokens rely on banking relationships, introducing regulatory and custodial dependencies. Crypto-backed coins such as DAI require overcollateralisation, efficient yet vulnerable to market shocks. Algorithmic stablecoins promise elegance and decentralisation, but frequently overestimate the predictability of human behaviour. Each model embodies distinct philosophical commitments and systemic exposures, and understanding these differences is essential for anyone hoping to use stablecoins wisely.

The appeal extends beyond investment strategy. In emerging markets, stablecoins can preserve value in inflationary economies, facilitate cross-border transfers, or grant access to dollar-denominated assets without relying on fragile banking systems. In this context, they are genuinely empowering. Yet empowerment without comprehension is precarious. Without clarity on function, governance, and backing, users risk misplaced confidence. The question is not whether stablecoins are useful—they clearly are—but whether reliance on them is informed rather than naive.

This chapter does not vilify stablecoins nor declare a single model superior. Its aim is to sharpen critical judgement. What does "backed" truly mean? Who audits reserves? Can the token be redeemed at par, in real time, and by whom? Is the peg algorithmic, or dependent on identifiable counterparties? How does it behave under liquidity stress? These are practical, not abstract, questions—ones responsible users must ask before committing capital in a system where code and narrative often outpace regulation.

Equally important is discerning when and why to deploy stablecoins. They are tools, not magical internet dollars: instruments to enhance liquidity, reduce exposure to volatility, or facilitate cross-border transactions. But they carry risks, dependencies, and the danger of fostering false security. A trader may use them to hold between positions; a remittance worker to bypass local currency volatility; an NFT collector for price consistency. Each context carries its own risk envelope, and the decision to trust a stablecoin must match that specificity, not rest on broad assumptions.

As regulators, developers, and users continue to negotiate the place of stablecoins in global finance, one truth remains: no peg is inviolable. Stability is an achievement, not an inherent property. Recognising this distinction is the first step toward intelligent engagement—using stablecoins as informed participants, not hopeful passengers. This chapter equips readers with the frameworks, distinctions, and case studies necessary to cut through the illusion of safety and approach stablecoins with strategic clarity and scepticism. In crypto, as in all investing, what you assume is safe can be far more dangerous than what you do not know.

What Are Stablecoins Supposed to Do?

In the fragmented, fast-moving world of cryptocurrencies—where volatility is the norm and price swings are measured not in percentage points but in double digits—stablecoins emerged with a singular, stabilising promise: to bring predictability into an otherwise chaotic landscape. The concept is deceptively simple yet conceptually profound. A stablecoin is a type of cryptocurrency that pegs its value to a stable asset—typically a national fiat currency like the US dollar, euro, or Japanese yen—so that one unit of the coin should, in theory, always be worth one unit of the asset it mirrors. The implication is that, unlike Bitcoin or Ether, which fluctuate wildly and can lose or gain substantial value in hours, stablecoins offer a digital alternative that behaves more like cash—reliable, consistent, and calm amidst the storms of speculation.

This promise of constancy is more than a technical feature; it is a psychological bridge. Stablecoins are designed to give users a sense of control in a domain otherwise defined by unpredictability. For early adopters, they served as a safe haven between trades. For DeFi participants, they became the lubricants of liquidity pools. For cross-border users, they offered a workaround to capital controls or unstable local currencies. And for the vast cohort of crypto-curious newcomers, stablecoins became the familiar face in an alien crowd—digital tokens that behaved like money they already understood. *The utility of stablecoins lies not merely in what they are, but in what they prevent: unnecessary exposure to volatility, conversion friction, and transactional uncertainty.*

Yet this function—stability—is not a feature granted by divine architecture. It is engineered, often imperfectly, through one of several mechanisms, each with its own trade-offs. The simplest and most intuitively trustworthy model is the fiat-backed stablecoin, exemplified by USD Coin (USDC) and Tether (USDT), which claim to be backed one-to-one by reserves held in traditional financial institutions. These reserves are typically a mix of cash and cash-equivalents, such as short-term government bonds. The promise is clear: for every digital coin in circulation, there is an equivalent unit of fiat money held in custody, theoretically redeemable at any time. This model benefits from conceptual familiarity and can feel "safer" to users, particularly when backed by transparent audits and credible custodians. However, it introduces regulatory, custodial, and centralisation risks, and depends heavily on the trustworthiness of the issuing entity.

More complex and more ideologically aligned with the decentralised ethos of crypto are crypto-backed stablecoins. These are not backed by fiat but by overcollateralised digital assets such as Ether or wrapped Bitcoin, held in smart contracts. DAI, issued by the MakerDAO protocol, is the most prominent example. Because the underlying assets are volatile, they must be held in excess to maintain the peg. If the value of the collateral drops too sharply, automated liquidation mechanisms kick in to preserve solvency. This model trades off simplicity for autonomy: there's no need to trust a centralised entity, but it requires users to trust code, governance, and market behaviour. *It is stable in function, but fragile in architecture.*

Then there is the most speculative—and now widely discredited—class of algorithmic stablecoins. These tokens rely on supply-demand algorithms and paired token dynamics to maintain their peg. The idea is that when the price of the stablecoin drifts from its peg, incentives will nudge market participants to bring it back in line. TerraUSD (UST) was the poster child of this model, using a burn-and-mint mechanism tied to its sister token, Luna. The entire structure collapsed catastrophically in May 2022 when the confidence loop broke, destroying over $40 billion in value and shattering the illusion that algorithmic stability could operate reliably at scale. That event was a sobering reminder: *engineering a peg is not the same as guaranteeing it.*

So, what are stablecoins supposed to do? At their most functional, they offer three primary utilities. First, they act as a medium of exchange, particularly in decentralised applications where fiat banking rails are absent. Second, they serve as a store of value, albeit one whose "value" is linked to an external reference point—usually the dollar. Third, they function as a unit of account, enabling contracts, lending platforms, and payment systems to denominate obligations in a predictable currency. These roles are not trivial. In fact, they are foundational to the long-term viability of crypto-based financial systems. But the execution of these roles is not consistent across all stablecoins. Understanding what a stablecoin is *meant* to do requires unpacking how it actually operates—and whether it can be expected to succeed under stress.

Stablecoins also play a critical role in market infrastructure. They are used extensively on centralised exchanges for trading pairs, especially where fiat onramps are limited or subject to regulation. They provide collateral for lending protocols in decentralised finance. They underpin liquidity pools in automated market makers. In many ways, they have become the invisible scaffolding of the crypto economy—a sort of monetary connective tissue linking speculative assets, real-world use cases, and user psychology. But this also means that when a stablecoin fails, the damage is systemic, not isolated. It reverberates through DeFi protocols, triggers cascading liquidations, and erodes trust across the entire ecosystem.

It is important to note that stability itself is a contextual concept. A coin may appear stable under normal market conditions but become unstable when liquidity dries up, when redemption pressure intensifies, or when the underlying collateral proves insufficient. The perception of stability can create a dangerous complacency. Users may park funds in a stablecoin believing it to be as safe as cash, without fully understanding the mechanics that sustain its price. This is particularly risky in algorithmic or low-transparency models, where the line between "stable" and "illusory" is easily crossed.

Moreover, the term "pegged" implies a fixed relationship, but that relationship is never absolute. It is conditional. Fiat-backed coins depend on access to bank accounts and regulatory compliance. Crypto-backed coins depend on collateral value and liquid markets. Algorithmic coins depend on game theory working under pressure. Each of these is a moving part in a machine that must keep running smoothly to avoid a breakdown. And yet, despite these complexities, the simplicity of the user interface often masks them. To the average user, a stablecoin appears as a $1 balance on an app, devoid of nuance or caveat. *The simplicity of presentation should not be mistaken for simplicity of design.*

Despite these risks, the appeal of stablecoins remains compelling—particularly in contexts where traditional financial infrastructure is broken, exclusionary, or inefficient. For users in countries with high inflation, capital controls, or weak currencies, stablecoins provide an escape valve, a way to store and move value that bypasses local constraints. For remittance corridors, they offer speed and cost advantages over legacy systems. For institutional actors exploring blockchain-based settlement, they provide a testbed for programmable money. But in each of these use cases, the question of *which* stablecoin to use—and under what conditions—remains paramount. Not all stablecoins are created equal, and not all should be treated as functionally equivalent.

The core value proposition of stablecoins lies in their ability to simulate fiat money in digital form, while operating on decentralised infrastructure. But that simulation is only as robust as the model behind it. Users, developers, and policymakers alike must understand that the word "stable" in stablecoin is not a guarantee; it is an aspiration. And like all aspirations, it must be constantly tested, maintained, and evaluated. *The future of stablecoins depends not just on adoption, but on a deeper collective literacy about how and why they work—or fail to.*

When Stablecoins Fail

The collapse of a system that was explicitly designed *not* to collapse sends a far more potent signal than the failure of one expected to take risks. Stablecoins, by definition, promise predictability in a realm dominated by speculation. Their job is simple: maintain parity with a reference currency, usually the US dollar. Yet the history of crypto is already littered with high-profile implosions of so-called stablecoins—tokens that failed to do the one thing they were created to ensure. These failures were not mere technical glitches; they were structural unravelings of designs that presumed more than they could deliver. Understanding how and why these failures occur is central to grasping the real nature of risk in decentralised finance.

The most infamous case is that of TerraUSD (UST), a stablecoin that in May 2022 went from being the third-largest in market capitalisation to essentially worthless in a matter of days. Before its collapse, UST had attracted billions in user deposits, often through high-yield decentralised protocols like Anchor, which promised up to 20% annual returns on UST holdings—returns that were neither sustainable nor organically generated. UST's claim to stability rested not on fiat reserves or crypto collateral, but on an algorithmic design: it was paired with another token, Luna, through a mint-and-burn mechanism. When demand for UST rose, users could burn $1 worth of Luna to mint 1 UST; when demand dropped, they could redeem 1 UST for $1 of Luna, which would be burned, tightening supply.

This mechanism worked until it didn't. When market confidence faltered—triggered in part by large withdrawals and a lack of sufficient reserves—UST began to lose its peg. The supposed arbitrage incentives failed to restore equilibrium because the system assumed infinite market appetite for Luna and infinite faith in its redemption logic. As UST fell below $1, more and more Luna was minted to compensate for redemptions, creating a hyperinflationary spiral that collapsed the value of both tokens. Within days, $40 billion of paper wealth was erased. Thousands of investors lost life savings. Ecosystems built on top of UST, from lending protocols to NFTs, were devastated. *The system didn't just fail—it disintegrated in plain view, taking trust with it.*

What made the TerraUSD failure so profound was not just the monetary loss, but the exposure of fundamental design flaws masquerading as innovation. The assumption that market participants would behave rationally under stress, that algorithmic incentives would always rebalance supply and demand, and that speculative demand could permanently anchor a stablecoin—all of these were revealed to be dangerously fragile. There were no guardrails, no circuit breakers, no hard collateral. There was only belief, code, and liquidity—three pillars that proved insufficient when pressure mounted. *Stability, it turned out, had been an illusion made plausible by good times.*

TerraUSD is not alone. Other algorithmic stablecoins have similarly crumbled under scrutiny. Iron Finance, a lesser-known example, saw its TITAN token go to zero in 2021 in what its own creators described as a "bank run." The mechanics were not dissimilar: a two-token system, incentives to maintain a peg, and the hope that arbitrage would do the rest. But hope is not architecture. When users panic, when redemptions spike, or when the economic logic breaks down under stress, these systems have no external anchor. They implode.

Contrast this with fiat-backed stablecoins like USDC, which maintain reserves in the form of short-term US Treasury bills and cash equivalents, and which undergo third-party attestations to verify backing. While these are not without their own vulnerabilities—regulatory risk, centralisation, dependence on traditional banking—they at least provide a concrete, redeemable backing. Users know that, at least in principle, they can exchange one USDC for one dollar. The risk shifts from algorithmic collapse to institutional reliability. That is not a trivial trade-off, but it is one that's far easier to assess for most users. *A system can survive loss of faith if it retains a fallback asset. It cannot survive if the only collateral is its own momentum.*

Crypto-backed stablecoins like DAI attempt to strike a balance between autonomy and backing. Collateralised by digital assets held in smart contracts, they employ overcollateralisation and liquidation thresholds to protect the peg. DAI survived the TerraUSD crisis without losing its peg, though not without stress. Its relative resilience stemmed from its conservative design, transparent governance, and mechanisms that forcibly unwind risk when market conditions deteriorate. However, even DAI has had to evolve—incorporating fiat-based collateral such as USDC into its backing—to ensure reliability. The irony is stark: even decentralised protocols have leaned into centralised assets to stabilise themselves. *Purity of design gives way to pragmatism when the alternative is existential failure.*

The lesson across these cases is sobering but clear: not all stablecoins are stable, and not all failures are created equal. When assessing a stablecoin, the critical questions are not what it *promises*, but what it *depends on.* Does it have redeemable reserves? Is it overcollateralised or undercollateralised? Does its stability depend on perpetual demand or external institutions? What happens in the event of a market shock, a liquidity crunch, or a loss of confidence? Systems that rely on reflexive belief without hard backing are particularly vulnerable to sudden collapse because, in a digital environment, capital exits can be instantaneous and irreversible.

Failures also expose the social and regulatory implications of stablecoins. TerraUSD's collapse caught the attention of policymakers around the world. In the United States, Treasury Secretary Janet Yellen cited UST's fall as evidence for stablecoin regulation. In South Korea, the aftermath triggered investigations and lawsuits. Regulators are beginning to recognise that a failed stablecoin is not just a crypto problem—it's a financial stability problem, a consumer protection problem, and a systemic trust problem. *The very thing that makes stablecoins attractive—their role as a bridge between crypto and the real economy—is also what makes their failure consequential beyond crypto's borders.*

Moreover, failures change the behavioural map of the ecosystem. After TerraUSD, trust in algorithmic models evaporated overnight. Investors, developers, and exchanges became more cautious. Projects scrambled to reduce exposure. Users migrated to more conservative instruments. The ecosystem, in effect, recalibrated its appetite for experimental stability. This behavioural shift is not merely emotional—it is structural. Market participants began to favour transparency, auditability, and real-world backing over abstraction and elegance.

None of this is to say that stablecoins are inherently flawed. Rather, they are inherently precarious unless their design aligns with realistic assumptions about human behaviour, market dynamics, and system stress. The desire to create a truly decentralised, scalable, and trust-minimised stablecoin remains alive—but it must be approached with humility. The history of failure is not a reason to give up; it is a reason to learn. *Stability is not a design choice—it is a performance standard that must hold under pressure.*

To treat all stablecoins as equivalent is to misread the most critical variable in their construction: their fragility. Understanding which ones are built on hard collateral, which rely on code and incentives, and which are fuelled mostly by speculative belief is essential to using them responsibly. It is not enough to see "USD" in the name. One must ask: *what stands behind that dollar?* If the answer is nothing more than faith and good intentions, then one is not holding a digital dollar—they are holding a digital IOU that could vanish with the next wave of doubt.

How to Spot a Reliable Stablecoin

A stablecoin's name is its promise: stability. Yet, as with any financial instrument, the critical question is not what it claims but *how* it attempts to deliver. In a landscape where marketing language often masquerades as architecture, understanding the underlying mechanism of a stablecoin is not just academic—it is essential. The public's confusion is understandable. At first glance, USDT, USDC, DAI, and formerly TerraUSD may all seem like interchangeable vehicles for parking value, transferring funds, or hedging against volatility. But beneath the surface, their foundations diverge in ways that are anything but trivial. The category "stablecoin" is deceptively uniform; reliability is not. What distinguishes a durable protocol from a ticking time bomb is not visibility or popularity but *design fidelity under stress*. The most critical thing an investor, trader, or developer can do is understand what stabilises the coin when markets destabilise.

At the heart of stablecoin analysis lies a taxonomy: algorithmic, crypto-backed, and fiat-backed. Each operates on different assumptions about trust, incentives, and economic logic. Algorithmic stablecoins are perhaps the most seductive and the most dangerous. These are not backed by any tangible reserve—neither fiat currency in a bank account nor collateralised crypto assets in a smart contract. Instead, they rely on code-driven incentive systems that aim to balance supply and demand through market behaviour. TerraUSD (UST) exemplified this model, pairing its coin with a volatile asset (LUNA) in a mint-and-burn feedback loop. When confidence was high and user demand grew, the peg held. When cracks emerged and withdrawals surged, the feedback loop inverted into a death spiral. No collateral meant no anchor. The system depended entirely on belief and reflexivity—market players believing that others would continue to participate, which in turn stabilised the price. Once that belief cracked, the cascade was unstoppable. This is not a criticism of code, but a caution about *the brittleness of designs built purely on behavioural incentives with no external safeguards.*

Crypto-backed stablecoins offer a more grounded alternative. These coins are typically overcollateralised with digital assets—often Ethereum, sometimes diversified with additional tokens—locked in smart contracts. DAI, the most prominent example, requires users to deposit collateral worth more than the stablecoins they mint. This overcollateralisation is not just a cushion but a dynamic mechanism: if the collateral's value falls below a set threshold, it is liquidated automatically to restore solvency. In theory, this creates a system that self-corrects through enforced economic discipline. In practice, it introduces exposure to crypto market volatility. When Ethereum's price crashes, the entire system faces stress tests: can liquidations occur fast enough, are there enough bidders, is oracle data accurate and timely? DAI has proven resilient through several major market downturns, not because it is immune to volatility but because its architects accounted for it. Still, crypto-backed stablecoins are not plug-and-play money—they require a high degree of technical fluency to navigate responsibly. For the average user, the reliability of such systems may hinge less on comprehension and more on the integrity of the code and the governance that steers it.

Fiat-backed stablecoins are the simplest to understand and, for many users, the most intuitively trustworthy. These are digital representations of real-world dollars (or other fiat currencies) held in custody by a centralised issuer. USDC, issued by Circle, maintains a fully-backed reserve—primarily in US Treasury bills and cash equivalents—and publishes regular attestation reports verified by third-party auditors. USDT, or Tether, historically suffered from opacity regarding its backing but has recently moved towards increased transparency, albeit under continued regulatory scrutiny. What makes these tokens reliable is not decentralisation or algorithmic elegance but *auditable reserves* and a redemption mechanism. Users can, at least in principle, exchange 1 USDC for 1 US dollar, anchored by assets held in traditional financial institutions. However, fiat-backed models are only as strong as their custodians. If the underlying reserve is mismanaged, seized, or frozen, the peg is compromised. Moreover, users must trust that the issuer is honest, solvent, and legally compliant. These are not minor assumptions. For all their technical simplicity, fiat-backed stablecoins represent a return to centralised trust—a necessary trade-off for stability, but a trade-off nonetheless.

Determining whether a stablecoin is reliable therefore requires a layered approach—*not just what it is called, but what it holds, how it is governed, and how it behaves under pressure.* The following criteria, while not exhaustive, provide a pragmatic lens:

Reserve composition: What assets back the stablecoin? Are they liquid, high-quality, and independently verified?

Redemption mechanism: Can users redeem the stablecoin for its underlying value? Under what conditions, and with what limitations?

Transparency: Are regular audits or attestations available? Is the collateral composition disclosed in detail, and is it updated frequently?

Peg history: Has the coin maintained its peg during periods of extreme market volatility? Did it ever trade below or above parity for extended periods?

Governance and risk controls: Who controls the parameters of the system? Are there mechanisms in place to respond to market shocks, oracle failures, or liquidity crunches?

Case studies sharpen the distinctions. USDC briefly depegged in March 2023 after the collapse of Silicon Valley Bank, where part of its reserves were held. While the coin traded as low as $0.88 on some exchanges, the peg quickly recovered once it became clear that federal regulators would backstop deposits. The episode revealed both a vulnerability—exposure to traditional banking—and a strength: a transparent reserve model that allowed users to assess the risk in real time. Contrast this with UST, where the reserve model was opaque and synthetic. No matter how fast users reacted, they could not recover what had already evaporated.

The philosophical tension here is not just about technology; it's about the nature of trust. Algorithmic stablecoins ask users to trust in logic and game theory. Crypto-backed models invite trust in code and collateral. Fiat-backed tokens ask users to trust institutions. Each model reflects a different theory of money and risk. None is without fault. The key is alignment between the mechanism and the user's expectations. A system designed to protect value should not rely on the same volatility it claims to hedge against. A coin marketed as "stable" must demonstrate stability not only in calm waters but in chaos. Otherwise, its name is a brand, not a benchmark.

A final consideration, often overlooked, is legal and regulatory standing. The difference between a reliable stablecoin and a high-risk token may ultimately come down to compliance. If an issuer is subject to regulatory oversight, adheres to anti-money laundering standards, and maintains proper banking relationships, the coin is more likely to hold up under scrutiny. If the issuer is based in a jurisdiction with no financial transparency and publishes no attestation, confidence becomes speculative at best. *Reliability is not just about backing—it's about recourse.*

In an ecosystem obsessed with innovation, it is easy to forget that boring is often better. A reliable stablecoin should be boring: predictable, transparent, slow to change. It should operate like a well-run financial utility, not a high-risk speculative instrument. For users seeking to preserve value, execute trades, or bridge between crypto and fiat, reliability is not a technical feature—it is a foundational requirement. The true mark of a reliable stablecoin is not how fast it grows during bull markets, but how little drama it causes during bear markets. That kind of quiet performance is hard to engineer, even harder to maintain—and worth every bit of scrutiny it demands.

When (and When Not) to Use Them

To the uninitiated, stablecoins can feel like the safest corner of a volatile world—a digital sanctuary in a sea of crypto chaos. Pegged to traditional fiat currencies like the US dollar or the euro, they appear to offer the best of both worlds: the programmability and speed of blockchain with the predictability of fiat. But this sense of safety is often overstated. *Stablecoins are tools, not truths. Used wisely, they can bring remarkable utility; used blindly, they can become liabilities disguised as security.* Knowing when—and when not—to use them is not a matter of mastering technical specifications, but of understanding their real-world function, fragility, and fit for purpose.

Stablecoins shine in contexts where speed, interoperability, and fiat equivalence are needed simultaneously. For example, a freelance designer in Buenos Aires might accept USDC as payment from a client in London, bypassing wire fees, currency controls, and bank delays. That designer could receive the funds in minutes, then hold or convert them depending on local exchange access. Here, stablecoins act as a bridge between geographies, banking systems, and value systems. They also facilitate rapid settlement in decentralised finance (DeFi) applications. In yield farming, lending protocols, or automated trading strategies, the need for a stable base currency is constant. Users don't want to hold volatile tokens when evaluating returns or rebalancing portfolios. A stablecoin offers a neutral denominator—a crypto-native cash equivalent that supports complex transactions while anchoring perceived value.

For international businesses, stablecoins can reduce reliance on intermediaries. A supplier in Vietnam can invoice in USDT, receive funds without going through SWIFT, and choose when or whether to convert to local currency. For companies operating in high-inflation economies or jurisdictions with capital controls, stablecoins offer something rare: *monetary optionality*. The ability to hold value in a widely accepted denomination without engaging with a local banking system grants agency in environments where financial autonomy is limited. In humanitarian work or emergency relief, organisations have used stablecoins to deliver direct aid to individuals in countries where infrastructure is compromised or government surveillance is a concern. The speed, traceability, and lack of intermediaries can improve both transparency and delivery.

However, these advantages only hold when the underlying asset behaves as expected. The word "stable" implies consistency, but as previous failures have shown, this can be dangerously misleading. Not all stablecoins are created equal. Algorithmic models that use game-theoretic incentives instead of reserves—such as the infamous TerraUSD—offer no tangible backstop when demand collapses. Even fiat-backed coins, which are generally considered the safest variety, have shown moments of vulnerability. In March 2023, USDC briefly lost its peg due to temporary uncertainty about its banking reserves. Though it recovered, the event was a stark reminder that even "fully backed" assets are exposed to counterparty risk, market panic, and information asymmetry. *Trust in a stablecoin should never exceed understanding of what actually backs it.*

So when should non-technical users consider using stablecoins? First, when a transaction requires speed and cost-efficiency across borders. Second, when they need a consistent unit of account within a crypto-native platform or DeFi ecosystem. Third, when access to traditional banking is limited, obstructive, or politically compromised. In each of these contexts, stablecoins offer unique capabilities that traditional systems do not. Their programmability allows for conditional transfers, automated distributions, and round-the-clock availability. Their decentralised architecture (in some models) offers resistance to censorship and systemic outages.

But this utility must be balanced with discernment. Holding significant value in stablecoins long-term is not always prudent. The user cedes control to the coin's issuer, whose reserves, governance, and compliance posture may not be transparent or legally robust. Fiat-backed stablecoins may be subject to regulatory intervention, blacklisting of addresses, or unilateral account freezes. Crypto-backed coins require users to understand the mechanics of liquidation, overcollateralisation, and smart contract risk. And algorithmic models, for all their innovation, should be treated with deep scepticism unless proven under extreme stress. *Stability is not a label; it is an empirical quality observed over time and under pressure.*

There are also psychological risks that come with stablecoin use. For many newcomers, the perception of safety becomes a gateway into riskier behaviour. Having once parked funds in a stablecoin, users may be tempted by adjacent opportunities—staking yields, high-return lending protocols, leveraged trades denominated in "stable" units. The stablecoin becomes not a destination but a launchpad, often without users realising they've crossed a line from preservation to speculation. This is where stablecoins become dangerous—not because of their code or mechanics, but because of the false sense of security they confer. They are not digital equivalents of a savings account or a vault. They are financial instruments embedded in an ecosystem where failure, experimentation, and opacity are routine.

For users considering stablecoins as long-term savings vehicles, caution is warranted. Unlike deposits in insured bank accounts, holdings in stablecoins do not benefit from government guarantees. If a stablecoin fails, the user has little legal recourse. Additionally, while stablecoins may resist local currency devaluation, they are still subject to inflation in their pegged currency. Holding USDC may insulate a user from Argentine peso depreciation, but it does not protect against broader erosion of purchasing power in the US dollar. *A stablecoin is only as strong as the economic and institutional scaffolding behind its peg.*

Another consideration is regulatory uncertainty. Authorities around the world are actively reassessing how stablecoins should be classified, regulated, and supervised. Depending on the jurisdiction, stablecoin usage may incur reporting obligations, tax implications, or even legal prohibitions. Central banks are increasingly wary of private digital currencies that could compete with sovereign money. As central bank digital currencies (CBDCs) evolve, the space that stablecoins currently occupy may shrink, become more regulated, or bifurcate into state-sanctioned and grey-market variants.

Ultimately, the decision to use stablecoins should follow a clear litmus test: *Does their functionality solve a problem the user actually has?* If the answer is yes—cross-border friction, banking exclusion, or DeFi liquidity—then stablecoins can be powerful tools. But if the appeal is based purely on assumption, convenience, or promotional hype, caution is essential. Financial literacy is the best defence. Non-technical users don't need to audit smart contracts or model reserve ratios, but they do need to ask pointed questions: Who issues this token? What backs it? What happens if redemptions spike? Has it broken its peg before? Can I get my funds back if something goes wrong?

Stablecoins are not inherently safe or unsafe. They are instruments, and like all instruments, their effectiveness depends on how—and why—they are used. They are at their best when serving clear, time-bound functions and at their worst when mistaken for guarantees. For the thoughtful user, they open new doors. For the careless, they hide old traps in modern wrappers. Understanding the trade-offs is not just prudent—it is the only way to make use of stablecoins without being misled by the illusion of safety.

Chapter 9
NFTs and the Tokenisation of Everything

Ownership has always been as much a social construct as a legal one, upheld by collective agreement about what belongs to whom and on what grounds. Land titles, patents, copyright claims, even physical money all depend on this shared trust. Blockchain, in contrast, offers the possibility of encoding ownership directly into a cryptographic ledger—transparent to all, tamper-resistant by design, and native to the digital realm. Non-fungible tokens (NFTs) are not merely whimsical artefacts for trading cartoon apes or exorbitantly priced JPEGs; they represent a new language for signalling individuality, scarcity, and provenance in cyberspace. What began as novelty now sits at the frontier of how we define possession, identity, and value in the digital age.

At their essence, NFTs are unique digital records—tokens representing assets that are non-interchangeable. Unlike cryptocurrencies such as Bitcoin or Ethereum, where each unit is identical and fungible, NFTs draw value from their singularity. They certify uniqueness: this asset, this edition, this chain of ownership. Crucially, the token rarely contains the content itself, a point often misunderstood; instead, it references the content, linking a blockchain entry to metadata describing the asset. The significance lies less in the digital file than in the token's status as a canonical receipt—publicly verifiable and resistant to forgery. This principle has sparked a surge in digital art markets, profile-picture projects, and speculative trading. Yet to stop there is to mistake the trappings for the substance. NFTs are not about art; they are about authentication.

It is easy to be distracted by the spectacle. The market is saturated with pixelated avatars selling for millions, generative art misrepresented as high culture, and influencers minting vanity projects to capitalise on hype. Beneath this froth, however, a more profound shift is occurring. The true innovation is not the assets being traded but the transactional infrastructure itself. Digitally native proofs of ownership enable interactions previously impossible. Imagine event ticketing: a concert promoter could issue NFT tickets that are traceable, programmable, and tamper-resistant. Access rights could be transferred, expirations coded into smart contracts, and royalties automatically distributed upon resale. This logic extends to real estate, intellectual property, and credentials—diplomas, driver's licences, or medical certifications could exist as NFTs: portable, verifiable, and forgery-resistant.

Yet such possibilities provoke deeper questions about ownership in a digital context. In conventional markets, ownership confers control and responsibility. A homeowner can live in, modify, or rent their property—but must maintain it, pay taxes, and comply with regulations. With NFTs, the picture is murkier. Purchasing a digital image NFT does not convey ownership of the image itself, nor the copyright unless explicitly transferred. What one owns is the token pointing to the image, and potentially a license to display or resell. For some, this suffices—the symbolic act of possession inscribed on-chain. For others, it underscores an ambiguity: can something be truly owned if the object remains infinitely reproducible, non-exclusive, and revocable by the host?

The challenge is conceptual rather than technological. We are reconsidering property in a realm where scarcity is artificial. Society has confronted similar tensions before: intellectual property law emerged to manage the industrial reproduction of ideas—books, music, inventions. The internet shattered many of those boundaries, making duplication trivial. Blockchain, paradoxically, reinstates controlled scarcity to impose order. NFTs are the latest attempt to reconcile digital replicability with economic differentiation, making uniqueness programmable once more.

Reality often diverges from promise. For every artist earning a living through NFT sales or brand leveraging fan engagement authentically, there are countless speculative ventures driven by hype. Markets fuelled by FOMO have led many to conflate fleeting price spikes with enduring value. Collections are minted en masse, liquidity fabricated through wash trading, and newcomers enticed into ecosystems they scarcely understand. The result is bifurcation: some prosper, others lose everything. NFT trading mechanics often mirror those of penny stocks or altcoins: thin order books, opaque valuations, and heavy reliance on community sentiment. Narrative frequently substitutes for fundamentals.

The tension between speculation and utility is pivotal. For NFTs to endure beyond early adoption cycles, they must offer more than financial upside. They require utility, context, and permanence: music NFTs unlocking backstage access; loyalty tokens granting DAO voting rights; digital twins of physical goods verifying authenticity and provenance. These are active experiments. Scaling them demands clarity around standards, interoperability, and user experience. Participation should not require mastery of token standards or gas fees. Just as the internet became invisible infrastructure, NFTs must integrate seamlessly—significant without being obtrusive.

Perhaps the most provocative implication lies in identity. Web2 platforms rent space from users: profiles, digital footprints, and personas monetised and controlled by companies, vulnerable to censorship. NFTs hint at an alternative: self-sovereign digital identities portable across platforms. A reputation system on-chain could embody transferable, programmable trust, skill, or participation. Yet this raises new concerns—privacy, surveillance, exclusion. The transparency that enables trustlessness may erode anonymity.

NFTs are more than a new asset class; they are a substrate for value expression. Their power derives from the systems built atop them. Much contemporary activity is experimental, skirting the edges of art, finance, and community. But these edges are converging, signalling a broader transformation: from centralised to decentralised ownership networks; from platform-controlled content to user-defined relationships; from passive consumption to active participation. The tokenisation of everything is not a forecast—it is a trajectory. NFTs constitute the grammar of this movement, the syntax through which it takes shape.

This chapter does not seek to celebrate or condemn NFTs, but to dissect them. We aim to move past noise, headlines, and hype cycles to understand what NFTs are, how they function, why speculation surrounds them, and where their most compelling applications lie. More crucially, we interrogate the assumptions beneath them: what does ownership mean in a digital age? How is value defined when scarcity is synthetically imposed? And how can systems be designed to reward creativity, preserve integrity, and broaden participation without descending into digital feudalism?

There is no single answer—but these are questions worth asking. As the lines between asset and experience, content and commerce, user and owner blur, NFTs represent not the conclusion of the story but one of its most urgent chapters.

What an NFT Actually Is

It is entirely possible to spend hours reading about NFTs and still not come away with a precise understanding of what they are. That is partly by design. The NFT ecosystem, at its loudest, thrives on confusion—elevating slogans, celebrity endorsements, and speculative fervour over technical clarity or functional literacy. Strip away the noise, however, and the underlying idea is surprisingly elegant: an NFT is a unique, traceable, programmable digital certificate of ownership. It is not, contrary to popular assumption, a digital artwork, a video clip, or a meme. Rather, it is the verifiable proof—anchored on a blockchain—that you own something specific, distinguishable, and not interchangeable with anything else. *This shift from what the token "is" to what it "represents" is fundamental.*

To appreciate why NFTs matter, one must first understand their contrast with *fungible* assets. A fungible asset is one whose individual units are interchangeable. A ten-pound note is fungible: any other ten-pound note will do. One Bitcoin is the same as any other Bitcoin. By design, such assets are optimised for equivalence, scale, and liquidity. NFTs, or non-fungible tokens, reject this paradigm. They represent *non-interchangeable* assets—things that are distinctive, like a signed first edition, a property deed, or a concert ticket for a specific date and seat. The key is *particularity*. NFTs are built to encode uniqueness and traceability into assets that would otherwise be indistinct when digitised.

Technically speaking, NFTs are smart contracts deployed on a blockchain—usually Ethereum, though other blockchains like Solana, Tezos, and Polygon are also used. Each NFT is associated with metadata—structured information about what it represents—and a token ID that makes it individually addressable. Most NFTs also include a link to off-chain data (usually an image or file hosted elsewhere), although newer protocols are exploring on-chain storage for permanence. This metadata is what defines the NFT's uniqueness: it may describe the properties of a digital artwork, a virtual land parcel in a metaverse game, or a certificate verifying access to a private event.

The most common misconception is that the NFT *is* the art. It is not. In most cases, the image or video lives off-chain, stored on centralised servers, IPFS (a decentralised file system), or cloud storage providers. What you buy when you purchase an NFT is not the file, but a token that *points to it*, along with whatever rights the issuer assigns to it. These rights can range from nothing at all (purely symbolic ownership) to limited usage rights, or, in rare cases, full commercial and copyright ownership. This variability is a source of both flexibility and confusion. Without legal standardisation, much of what NFT buyers believe they own is based on community norms rather than enforceable rights. *Owning an NFT does not automatically mean owning the thing it references.*

This is where NFTs diverge sharply from other digital assets. Cryptocurrencies are assets unto themselves; NFTs are proxies—digital wrappers for assets that may be tangible or intangible, static or dynamic, trivial or highly consequential. This gives NFTs remarkable versatility. They can represent artworks, but also academic credentials, medical records, patents, virtual clothing, or in-game weapons. They can be used to build loyalty systems, manage membership access, and even govern decentralised organisations. The unifying thread is *uniqueness plus provenance*, recorded on an immutable ledger.

What makes NFTs valuable is not the art style, the branding, or the hype (although all of these can influence price), but the *ownership record.* A digital artwork without an NFT is infinitely reproducible and difficult to monetise at scale. The same artwork attached to an

NFT becomes trackable, saleable, and capable of embedding royalty logic—ensuring that the original creator gets a percentage of future sales. This royalty function is a major innovation, giving artists and creators a new financial instrument: programmable resale rights. With each transaction, value can flow automatically back to the source—something nearly impossible to enforce in traditional markets.

However, NFTs are not only tools for creative industries. Their broader potential lies in administrative trust. Institutions that issue certifications, authorisations, or claims—such as universities, governments, or banks—can use NFTs to create digital artefacts that are secure, verifiable, and portable. A university degree issued as an NFT cannot be forged. A birth certificate on-chain can be retrieved without bureaucracy. A land title tokenised on a blockchain becomes resilient against loss, manipulation, or disputes. These applications are less sensational than NFT auctions but arguably more transformative.

To understand how NFTs differ from other crypto assets, consider the logic of scarcity. Bitcoin is scarce by protocol: there will only ever be 21 million coins. NFTs, in contrast, are scarce by design choice. Creators define the number of tokens, their attributes, and their issuance schedule. This introduces subjectivity and trust into systems that otherwise aspire to be trustless. While the blockchain records ownership transparently, the *meaning* of what is owned is often opaque. What rights do I have? What happens if the server hosting the artwork disappears? What if someone mints an identical copy on another chain? These are not yet resolved, and the answers vary by platform, project, and jurisdiction. *The infrastructure is decentralised; the implications are still deeply contextual.*

A useful analogy is the deed to a house. The paper itself has no intrinsic value. Its significance derives from the legal, social, and institutional systems that recognise and enforce what it represents. NFTs, similarly, are only as meaningful as the frameworks around them—technical, legal, cultural. Right now, those frameworks are patchy. But they are evolving. Standards like ERC-721 and ERC-1155 define how NFTs are structured; layer-two solutions aim to reduce transaction costs; marketplaces compete on usability, curation, and compliance. Over time, what feels experimental will become infrastructural.

This maturation also demands clearer distinctions between NFTs as collectibles, NFTs as utilities, and NFTs as credentials. A collectible NFT might derive its value from aesthetics, cultural relevance, or scarcity. A utility NFT might grant access to software, communities, or physical products. A credential NFT might attest to identity, skill, or authority. Each of these categories carries different expectations, risks, and rights. Understanding which type of NFT one is interacting with is essential—not just for investors, but for users, creators, and regulators. *NFTs are not a monolith. They are a format.*

There is also an important epistemic shift involved. For centuries, ownership has been tied to physicality: to have meant to hold. In digital environments, this breaks down. Control without possession, access without holding, visibility without sovereignty—these paradoxes define online life. NFTs attempt to restore a kind of integrity to digital ownership, but the results are still uneven. Can ownership be meaningful when the asset is ephemeral, hosted elsewhere, and accessible to all? Or is it the symbolism—the ability to say "this is mine, provably"—that carries value? This ambiguity is not a flaw; it is the terrain on which the next phase of digital culture is being built.

The most forward-thinking view of NFTs treats them not as an endpoint but as an *interface*—a bridge between identity, value, and verification in a world increasingly governed by data. Their real utility may not be in art sales or collectables, but in giving individuals portable, programmable representations of who they are, what they own, and what they're entitled to. That identity could span financial accounts, medical records, creative work, educational history, or digital reputation. The NFT, in this vision, is less about asset speculation and more about *sovereignty over digital footprint.*

Still, the current NFT ecosystem is fragile. It is dominated by speculation, often inaccessible to newcomers, and frequently misaligned with its own ideals. Scams are common. Standards are immature. Legal interpretations are inconsistent. Much of the infrastructure is still controlled by centralised platforms. For NFTs to fulfil their potential, the emphasis must shift from volume to clarity, from novelty to reliability, from profit-maximisation to value creation. *Understanding what an NFT actually is—and isn't—is the first step toward building that foundation.*

This clarity matters, because the stakes are rising. As more sectors explore tokenisation, and as more individuals experiment with owning and issuing NFTs, the demand for coherence will intensify. That means better user experiences, stronger legal protections, and richer cultural understanding. It means moving beyond the shorthand of "digital collectibles" toward a more nuanced literacy of digital property. And it means ensuring that the conversation is driven not by hype or cynicism, but by *thoughtful inquiry* into what ownership should look like in the digital century.

NFTs, then, are not just a curiosity. They are a prototype for a broader shift in how we encode, express, and exchange value. They will evolve—technically, legally, and culturally. But their essence is already clear: they give form to the intangible, and permanence to the ephemeral. That is both their power and their provocation.

NFTs Beyond Art and Hype

The idea that NFTs are limited to cartoon apes, pixelated punks, or digital trading cards is not only misleading—it actively obscures the far more transformative implications of non-fungible tokens. While popular culture has tethered the term "NFT" to speculative art markets and celebrity stunts, the underlying technology is quietly reshaping how we define ownership, access, and authenticity across industries. It is not about the medium; it is about the mechanism. And once we strip away the noise, the core concept—a verifiable, programmable record of uniqueness—proves adaptable to challenges well beyond the art world.

Consider ticketing. It is an industry plagued by counterfeit sales, scalping, and opaque secondary markets. NFTs offer a way to issue digital tickets that are not only verifiable and non-duplicable but also programmable. A concert promoter can cap resale prices, collect royalties on secondary trades, or restrict access to verified fan wallets. Every transaction becomes traceable, making fraud nearly impossible. More importantly, the experience can extend beyond the event itself. NFT tickets can unlock backstage content, permanent digital memorabilia, or early access to future shows. What was once a one-off QR code becomes a persistent digital asset with lifecycle value. *The simple act of attending an event becomes tokenised, authenticated, and potentially monetised.*

The real estate sector presents a more complex, but no less compelling, frontier. Property transactions are notoriously bureaucratic, paper-laden, and prone to friction. Tokenising real estate through NFTs—whether entire buildings or fractional ownership—could streamline transfers, reduce legal overhead, and improve liquidity in a traditionally illiquid market. Platforms experimenting with real estate NFTs already exist, especially in jurisdictions where digital land registries can be reconciled with blockchain-based titles. An NFT representing a property could carry with it not only the title deed, but also embedded rules for resale, lease terms, or community governance. While legal integration remains uneven, the directional logic is persuasive: *turn static records into programmable, transferable assets.*

Intellectual property is another domain ripe for transformation. Copyrights, trademarks, patents—these are often abstract, territorial, and difficult to enforce globally. NFTs offer a path toward standardising digital provenance and licensing. A musician might mint an NFT that includes not just their song but also a clear set of permissions: streamable rights, remix licenses, or commercial usage tiers. Ownership can be divided, royalties automated, and attribution permanently recorded. For creators, this marks a shift from trust to code—from relying on third parties to honour rights, to embedding those rights directly in the asset. The technology does not replace legal frameworks, but it *augments them with precision and transparency.*

Identity, often overlooked in NFT discussions, may ultimately prove the most consequential application of all. In a world where digital interactions increasingly shape opportunity, reputation, and access, a verifiable online identity is essential—and perilously lacking. Centralised platforms hold fragmented data on users, while individuals lack portable control over their credentials. NFTs could anchor a self-sovereign identity system in which diplomas, certifications, medical records, or employment histories are tokenised and tied to a single, user-controlled wallet. Each credential is unique, verifiable, and resistant to tampering. Unlike usernames and passwords, these tokens cannot be easily faked or forgotten. They establish a durable, composable form of identity—one that is less about login credentials and more about *provable history.*

Of course, none of these applications are free from complexity. Ticketing NFTs must grapple with privacy and anti-scalping regulations. Real estate NFTs raise questions of jurisdictional enforcement and digital custody. Intellectual property NFTs need clarity on legal interoperability. Identity NFTs touch on sensitive areas of surveillance, consent, and data sovereignty. The tools are neutral; the design choices are not. *Embedding trust, fairness, and usability into NFT systems is a design imperative, not a technical afterthought.*

To make sense of the proliferation of use cases, one must understand that NFTs operate more like infrastructure than products. They are not simply digital collectables, but primitives—modular components that can be assembled into new economic, social, and administrative structures. Think of them as building blocks for redesigning institutions that currently depend on centralised record-keeping: notaries, licensing agencies, event promoters, even governments. Their defining feature is not art but *verifiable digital uniqueness*. That changes how we track rights, ownership, and entitlements across both digital and physical contexts.

NFTs also carry philosophical implications that extend beyond utility. What does it mean to own something digitally—not just access it, but to possess a verifiable claim to its uniqueness? What kind of value can be conferred by a token that exists entirely on-chain, but grants privileges off-chain? When we own a token representing access to a community, a course, or a physical good, *what exactly is being owned*—the thing, the access, the status, or some combination thereof? These are not abstract questions. They shape how NFT-based systems are interpreted, regulated, and used in the real world.

As speculative fervour cools, these quieter, functional applications are gaining ground. Universities are piloting NFT diplomas. Airlines are exploring tokenised loyalty schemes. High-end retailers are using NFTs to guarantee product authenticity. Governments are experimenting with blockchain-based land registries and licences. What unites these efforts is not ideology but *instrumental value*: the desire for records that are tamper-proof, portable, and programmable. The blockchain becomes not a slogan, but a substrate for reliable systems.

Yet there remains a tension between innovation and incumbency. For NFTs to flourish beyond hype, they must coexist with existing institutions—banks, courts, regulators, professional bodies—many of which move slowly and resist structural change. This requires translation, not just advocacy. Legal scholars must help codify NFT-based rights. User-experience designers must make wallets comprehensible to non-technical users. Entrepreneurs must anchor NFT projects in genuine utility rather than gamified speculation. *The shift from speculative asset to trusted tool requires infrastructure, governance, and cultural literacy.*

Critics often dismiss NFTs as frivolous or faddish. And they are not entirely wrong—there is noise, grift, and hollow marketing. But the presence of poor implementations does not invalidate the underlying architecture. One can mock early email spam and still recognise the internet's transformation of communication. Similarly, NFTs as a class of innovation deserve to be decoupled from their loudest promoters and examined on the basis of *what they enable*. That lens reveals not a speculative mania, but a new grammar for digital ownership—one capable of encoding rights, access, and value in ways that traditional systems cannot easily replicate.

As the technology matures, the most compelling NFT applications will likely be the least visible. The art will recede; the function will remain. Tokenised credentials will sit quietly in wallets. NFT-based licenses will govern software access without ceremony. Identity NFTs will unlock resources, not headlines. Like most foundational technologies, their success will be measured not by visibility but by *invisibility*—when things simply work better because they are anchored in verifiable uniqueness.

In the end, the true promise of NFTs lies not in art auctions or profile pictures, but in their capacity to upgrade the most fundamental layer of civilisation: *trust in records*. A society that can issue, transfer, and verify claims—securely, transparently, and without intermediaries—is a society that can coordinate more efficiently, inclusively, and fairly. That is not a hype cycle; it is a civilisational step forward. NFTs, if guided wisely, will not just decorate our digital lives—they will scaffold them.

Speculation vs. Ownership

The allure of life-changing wealth has always had a gravitational pull on human decision-making, and nowhere has that magnetism been more vividly amplified in recent years than in the NFT market. In 2021, a collage by the digital artist Beeple sold for $69 million at Christie's—a sale that triggered a cascade of speculative frenzy. Around the same time, an unremarkable cartoon rock JPEG changed hands for over $1.3 million. Yet, for every meteoric rise, there were tens of thousands of NFTs that lost 90% or more of their value, leaving their buyers holding what amounted to glorified receipts for assets no one else wanted. The extreme asymmetry in outcomes begs an essential question: what is the difference between speculation and ownership in the NFT space, and why does it matter?

To understand this divide, we must first acknowledge that NFTs are not assets in the traditional sense. An NFT, or non-fungible token, is a unique digital certificate of ownership—recorded on a blockchain—that links to an asset, which may or may not have enduring value. Unlike Bitcoin, where each coin is interchangeable and therefore "fungible," NFTs are designed to be one-of-a-kind. This uniqueness can be applied to artwork, contracts, music, gaming items, virtual land, or nearly anything else that can be digitally represented. But owning an NFT does not necessarily mean owning the underlying intellectual property, nor does it guarantee economic return. In this ambiguity lies the crux of the problem.

Speculation, by nature, is the act of buying something primarily because one believes someone else will pay more for it later. Ownership, in contrast, is about intrinsic value—having something that delivers utility, meaning, or yield regardless of future price fluctuations. In traditional investing, this distinction is seen in the difference between buying a rental property for its income stream versus flipping it for a quick profit. In the NFT context, these boundaries are often blurred, partly because many assets have no tangible yield or inherent function beyond market perception.

Consider the speculative psychology that fuels many NFT purchases. Scarcity is often manufactured—collections like Bored Ape Yacht Club or CryptoPunks are limited in number, and their value is largely driven by social signalling, exclusivity, and hype. Buying one often carries the hope that it will become a status symbol, and that demand will remain high. But this is a fragile equilibrium. Unlike fine art or rare watches, NFTs exist within a hyper-accelerated digital landscape, where memes die fast, communities are fickle, and the emotional half-life of novelty is alarmingly short. What was "iconic" yesterday may be forgotten tomorrow.

At the peak of the NFT mania, many first-time buyers entered the market with minimal understanding of blockchain mechanics, provenance, or intellectual property rights. The simplicity of buying with a few clicks on platforms like OpenSea, combined with the viral success stories of overnight millionaires, created an environment where critical thinking was often replaced with FOMO—fear of missing out. This herd behaviour resulted in vast sums chasing questionable projects, often with unclear roadmaps, anonymous developers, and zero long-term vision. Some were outright scams. Others were genuine experiments in digital culture. Most fell somewhere in between.

Contrast this with ownership models that emphasise utility. Some NFTs function as access keys, unlocking membership in digital communities, early access to content, voting rights in decentralised organisations, or recurring benefits. These tokens carry value because they *do* something. They shift the NFT from a mere collectible to a functional tool. In gaming, for instance, NFTs can represent in-game assets that players actually use. In music and media, they can provide fractional royalties or fan engagement. In identity systems, they can act as decentralised credentials. These are early examples of ownership where the NFT is not just a placeholder for speculative dreams, but a digital artefact with embedded purpose.

However, even within utility-focused projects, speculation is hard to disentangle. The idea that a membership token could appreciate in value due to demand from newcomers introduces an economic loop that can mirror pyramid dynamics. If the value of an NFT is heavily reliant on future entrants rather than the ongoing utility it provides, we are back in speculative territory—just with better marketing.

There is also a philosophical tension at play. Ownership in the physical world is bounded by legal systems, tangible limits, and centuries of precedent. In the digital realm, it is less anchored. What does it mean to "own" a URL link that points to a file hosted on a decentralised server? What happens if the hosting provider disappears, or the file is altered? Does the NFT still represent anything? These aren't abstract questions—they touch the very heart of digital permanence and trust. True ownership should imply control, longevity, and clarity. Many NFTs offer none of these with certainty.

The volatility of NFT valuations further complicates the landscape. Traditional markets are also speculative to a degree, but they operate within regulatory frameworks, disclosure requirements, and investor protections. NFT markets remain largely unregulated, which invites extreme behaviour. Price manipulation through "wash trading"—where an owner buys and sells their own NFT at inflated prices to create an illusion of demand—is disturbingly common. Celebrities promote projects without disclosing financial ties. Influencers engage in pump-and-dump schemes. In this ecosystem, discerning genuine ownership from frothy speculation requires more than enthusiasm—it requires rigour.

That said, speculation is not inherently evil. It plays a role in price discovery and risk capital allocation. The problem is not that people speculate—it's that they do so without understanding the game they're playing. For a seasoned investor or digital native who recognises the volatility and treats NFT speculation like venture capital—placing bets across many high-risk projects—the activity may be rational. For a newcomer who believes that a cartoon monkey will pay their mortgage, the same activity is financially reckless. The emotional highs and lows can be profound: elation at a quick flip, despair at an illiquid bag, tribalism around "floors," and existential panic during bear markets. These are not just financial events—they are psychological dramas, unfolding in real time on public blockchains.

To bring clarity to the chaos, one must develop a personal framework for evaluating NFTs beyond aesthetics and hype. Ask: What does this token *do*? Who created it, and why? Is the value driven by speculation alone, or is there lasting functionality? Can this asset survive a market downturn? What rights, if any, does the owner possess? Without clear answers, you're not owning—you're gambling.

In the coming years, the NFT landscape will likely bifurcate. On one side will remain the cultural casino: speculative tokens tied to identity, meme-worthiness, and trend cycles. On the other will grow a more sober class of NFTs—those grounded in enterprise use cases, verifiable utility, and institutional-grade infrastructure. These won't generate headlines as flashy as million-dollar JPEGs, but they will reshape how digital rights, data, and property are represented and exchanged.

Ultimately, the true power of NFTs lies not in speculation, but in transformation—the ability to encode, verify, and transfer unique digital claims in ways previously impossible. Ownership, when rooted in function, transparency, and accountability, has a future. Speculation, by contrast, is a flame that burns brightly and unpredictably. Knowing which fire you're playing with is the first step toward not getting burned.

How to Think About Digital Ownership

A file saved on a computer is not a possession in the traditional sense—it's a sequence of zeros and ones, replicated effortlessly and infinitely, subject to deletion or duplication in seconds. And yet, digital artefacts increasingly carry real monetary value, social status, and legal implication. We "own" music, eBooks, software licences, domain names, and now NFTs—non-fungible tokens that claim to prove digital ownership. But what does ownership actually mean in an era where possession can be copied, where authenticity is harder to define than ever, and where permanence is one catastrophic server error or protocol failure away from erasure? Ownership, once rooted in physical possession and legal title, now requires new cognitive tools—ones capable of parsing code-based scarcity, decentralised custody, and emergent concepts of identity and provenance.

At its core, ownership implies exclusive control, enforceable rights, and some form of recognised legitimacy. These assumptions are strained in digital systems. A JPEG stored on your hard drive can be shared with millions, indistinguishable from the original. A file hosted on the cloud can be revoked by the service provider. Even NFTs, which promise blockchain-based proof of provenance, often point to metadata or files hosted off-chain, rendering their permanence illusory unless supported by decentralised storage. In this context, *authenticity* becomes not just a question of file integrity, but of consensus trust—does the broader network, the market, and the legal system agree that you have rightful claim to this object?

That agreement is not trivial. In traditional art, ownership is recognised through provenance, signature, and occasionally forensic evidence. In the digital economy, ownership increasingly relies on smart contracts and blockchains to declare a unique claim on an otherwise replicable object. But that uniqueness is only meaningful if the community around it—whether it be art collectors, gaming participants, or financial stakeholders—accepts the terms of the contract and the rules of the platform. In that sense, *digital ownership is never purely technical; it is always social.* A cryptographic signature might show that you "own" a token, but without communal acknowledgement of what that token represents, its value collapses into abstraction.

This fragility forces a distinction between *ownership* and *control.* You might own an NFT, but do you control the underlying asset? If the asset is a link to an image hosted on a private server, what happens if the server disappears? If your digital library exists on a platform's terms of service, what recourse do you have when access is revoked? These questions are not hypothetical. Amazon has remotely deleted books from users' Kindles. Spotify has removed songs from libraries due to expired licences. The user may have paid, subscribed, or saved—but they never truly owned. What they held was conditional access, revocable and centrally managed.

The appeal of blockchain-based ownership stems from its promise to invert this paradigm. Rather than rely on centralised intermediaries, blockchains allow users to prove and transfer ownership through decentralised ledgers that no single party controls. Yet even here, the surface-level security can mask deep structural dependencies. An NFT pointing to an artwork hosted on IPFS (a decentralised file system) is only as robust as the network of nodes maintaining that file. If the file is not "pinned" by enough participants, it can vanish. Blockchain immutability does not equate to digital permanence unless all layers of the stack—storage, metadata, token standards—are decentralised and resilient. The *illusion of permanence* is one of the most dangerous misunderstandings in digital ownership.

The psychological component cannot be ignored. Ownership has always been entangled with identity, status, and agency. A family home is not just a financial asset—it is a memory vessel, a locus of stability. A collector's rare watch or first-edition book offers both aesthetic pleasure and cultural capital. In digital spaces, similar desires persist. People pay for "skins" in video games not because they change gameplay, but because they signal identity within the tribe. Profile picture NFTs operate the same way—a punk avatar on Twitter conveys early adopter status, cultural alignment, and sometimes wealth. Here, *symbolic ownership trumps functional utility*. You do not "use" the NFT in a practical sense; you wear it like a badge, visible to others in the networked crowd.

This leads us to value. Why does a token that confers no rights over an artwork's copyright, no income stream, and no utility command a six-figure price? Because *value is not only rational—it is narrative*. The story around an asset—the artist, the platform, the cultural moment—creates perceived scarcity and desirability. Just as the art world elevates certain names through gallery shows and curatorial prestige, NFT markets elevate projects through viral momentum and social proof. In this dynamic, the digital economy becomes a theatre of belief. What you "own" is often the belief of others in your asset's significance. This is not inherently flawed—it mirrors aspects of traditional collecting—but it demands a clear-eyed awareness of how perception, consensus, and value intertwine.

Legal frameworks lag behind this shift. Owning an NFT does not grant copyright, trademark, or enforceable access rights unless explicitly codified. The token is a proof of claim, but not necessarily a proof of entitlement. This has led to confusion, particularly when NFTs are resold or repurposed without the creator's consent. New platforms attempt to address this by embedding licensing terms into smart contracts or using NFTs to represent fractional intellectual property rights. But these solutions remain nascent and fragmented. Until law catches up with code, *digital ownership operates in a grey zone—part possession, part performance, part promise.*

The future of digital ownership likely lies not in mimicking traditional models, but in transcending them. Consider dynamic NFTs that evolve based on user input, environmental data, or time. These are not static assets, but living contracts—programmable artefacts that blur the line between property and experience. Or consider NFTs as identity layers—credentials, reputations, histories—that users carry across platforms in a decentralised web. Here, ownership is less about having an object and more about *being recognised for who you are.* This shift from possession to presence marks a conceptual evolution in what it means to own.

But with this evolution comes responsibility. Owning a digital asset in a self-custodial wallet means managing private keys, securing backups, and navigating complex interfaces. There is no customer service in a permissionless blockchain. Lose your key, and the asset is gone. This is empowerment and burden in equal measure. Many users may prefer the convenience of centralised custody—trusted exchanges, managed wallets, insurance protections. The tension between control and convenience will shape the trajectory of digital ownership for years to come.

Finally, the permanence of digital ownership is increasingly tested by cultural and environmental volatility. Blockchains may be immutable, but platforms go offline, tokens get deprecated, standards evolve. A token minted on an obsolete chain may still exist, but functionally die. Ownership, in that sense, is contingent not just on technical persistence, but on *ecosystem continuity*. To own something digitally is to be tethered to a web of dependencies—protocols, storage systems, community consensus, regulatory clarity. This interdependence is not weakness; it is a new form of digital ecology. Understanding it is essential for anyone navigating this space.

To think clearly about digital ownership is to ask the uncomfortable questions: What am I buying? Who controls it? What happens if the platform dies? Does this asset give me rights, access, or mere appearance? Can I transfer it freely? Is the value I perceive shared by others, or is it a private fiction? These questions are not cynical; they are necessary. In the fog of innovation, clarity is rare and priceless. The tools of ownership are being rewritten—not with deeds and signatures, but with hashes and contracts, communities and consensus. Those who treat this shift with nuance, scepticism, and philosophical curiosity will be better equipped not only to participate—but to shape the meaning of ownership in the decades to come.

Chapter 10
Crypto and the Law—What Rules Apply?

When money sheds its physical form, the law is inevitably left scrambling to catch up. For centuries, financial systems relied on borders, paper ledgers, and central institutions. Cryptocurrencies, by contrast, operate untethered: a wallet created in London can receive funds from São Paulo, dispatch them to Tokyo, and store value across decentralised ledgers scattered over hundreds of nodes worldwide—all without passing through a single bank or customs checkpoint. The consequences for legal frameworks are profound. Crypto does not break the law by default; rather, it exposes the law's inadequacy, its design never intended for assets that behave in this manner. Regulatory lag is not merely slow—it is structurally misaligned. This friction introduces risk, confusion, and vulnerability for everyone from first-time investors to seasoned institutions. This chapter explores that dissonance and, crucially, equips you to navigate it with insight.

One striking feature of crypto regulation is its patchwork inconsistency. A token considered legal in Switzerland may be classified as a security in the United States, a currency in Japan, banned outright in China, and unregulated in El Salvador. These distinctions are far from trivial. They dictate whether trading is permissible, how taxes apply, what reporting is required, and whether mere possession might constitute a legal violation. A decentralised technology collides with a world of centralised jurisdictions, producing a regulatory landscape riddled with contradictions. For users, the key takeaway is blunt: where you live still matters. Ignoring that fact can expose you to legal, financial, and reputational peril, even when your actions feel inconsequential.

Taxation is an area where naivety is especially costly. Many newcomers assume crypto gains are exempt or that decentralised wallets evade oversight. Both assumptions are dangerously wrong. In the UK, HMRC treats crypto as property, making capital gains tax applicable when tokens are sold, swapped, or even used to purchase goods. In the US, the IRS has aggressively enforced compliance, compelling exchanges to report user data and embedding crypto-specific questions into tax filings. Across Europe and Asia, similar regimes have emerged. A gain—even converting one token to another—may constitute a taxable event. Ignorance is no defence. Decentralisation does not equate to invisibility. Public ledgers offer transparency; what is gained in openness is lost in plausible deniability.

Losses, too, pose unique complications. Misplace your private keys, and the assets vanish—irretrievably. Banks allow password recovery; crypto does not. This reality introduces grey legal areas. Can lost crypto be treated as a capital loss? Some jurisdictions allow it under narrow conditions; others do not. Inheritance becomes similarly fraught: without access to keys, a digital estate may disappear entirely. These issues are not technical footnotes—they are legal challenges with consequences for taxation, succession, and fraud prevention. Crypto demands both careful self-custody and proactive accountability. The system will not protect you unless you engineer your own safeguards.

Privacy, once celebrated as crypto's core promise, now faces legal scrutiny. Regulators worldwide enforce KYC (Know Your Customer) and AML (Anti-Money Laundering) mandates, obliging platforms to verify identities, monitor transactions, and report suspicious behaviour. Exchanges must comply or risk sanctions. Users face a trade-off: how much privacy are they willing to surrender for access? Decentralised exchanges often offer greater anonymity but minimal recourse; centralised platforms provide convenience and customer support, at the cost of surveillance. There is no universal answer, but every user must understand the tension between freedom and compliance. Anonymity may feel like a right, but in financial law it is increasingly treated as a potential risk.

The rationale behind these regulations is not imagined. Crypto has been used in ransomware payments, darknet transactions, and cross-border capital flight. But blanket restrictions risk penalising legitimate users, stifling innovation, and conflating experimentation with criminality. The US Treasury's 2022 sanctioning of Tornado Cash—a privacy protocol on Ethereum—illustrates this tension. Can open-source code be sanctioned? Can developers be liable for how their code is used? These questions are no longer theoretical;

they define the limits of legal and moral responsibility in crypto development. The law is beginning to treat protocols as actors, attributing intent, responsibility, and liability, with implications that are still unfolding.

So how does a prudent, law-abiding crypto user operate without a legal degree? Start with foundational principles. First, know your local laws: blockchain may be global, but obligations are local. Second, maintain meticulous records: every trade, wallet transfer, or staking reward should be logged. Automation tools exist, but discipline is indispensable. Third, assume traceability: treat the blockchain as a public ledger, not a black box. Finally, when uncertain, rely on regulated platforms; registration with a national financial authority increases the likelihood of compliance and protection. These practices may feel burdensome, but they safeguard both your assets and, in some cases, your liberty.

Crypto empowers individuals like no previous financial system—but with that empowerment comes unparalleled responsibility. There is no bank to call if funds vanish, no regulator to appeal to if a smart contract fails, no automatic compliance checks. Users are simultaneously custodian, accountant, compliance officer, and security engineer. This is not decentralised utopia; it is operational maturity. Engaging with crypto is not rebellion; it is self-regulation under extreme conditions.

As governments navigate the implications of digital assets, regulatory futures remain contested. Some jurisdictions will experiment with innovation-friendly frameworks; others will enforce restrictive policies. Cross-border agreements may arise slowly, with political compromise always lagging behind technological adoption. Meanwhile, users must act with prudence, clarity, and a commitment to learning. Legal certainty may evolve, but personal responsibility begins now. There is no waiting for perfect regulation. Participating in crypto means already operating under the law—you only need to know which one, where, and how it applies.

This chapter does not grant immunity. Instead, it offers conceptual clarity, practical guidance, and a mindset of informed diligence. In a world where ignorance is perilous and compliance increasingly mandatory, understanding the rules is not a restraint on innovation—it is a prerequisite for sustainable participation. Ultimately, the most powerful form of crypto ownership is not merely custody of keys; it is mastery of your rights.

Global Regulation Is a Mess

It is entirely possible for a cryptocurrency to be considered a security in one country, a commodity in another, and a banned asset in a third—all at the same time. That fact alone illustrates the fundamental regulatory chaos that surrounds digital assets globally. Unlike traditional financial instruments, which developed within nation-state structures and were regulated accordingly, cryptocurrencies emerged as *borderless by design.* They are protocols before they are products, and networks before they are securities. Yet they now find themselves subject to the legal frameworks of over 190 jurisdictions, many of which are still scrambling to understand what they are regulating. *The law is lagging behind the code—and the resulting mismatch is not merely bureaucratic; it is structural, strategic, and deeply consequential.*

This disjointed regulatory landscape is not simply inconvenient; it creates significant risk for everyone involved in crypto markets, especially small investors and non-institutional participants. For one, there is no consistent answer to the question: *what, legally, is a token?* In the United States, the Securities and Exchange Commission (SEC) relies on the 1946 Howey Test to determine whether a digital asset is a security—an approach that many critics argue is ill-fitted to 21st-century innovations. Meanwhile, in Switzerland, the Swiss Financial Market Supervisory Authority (FINMA) categorises tokens based on their utility, payment function, or underlying assets, applying different regulations to each. Japan treats certain cryptocurrencies as legal forms of payment; China bans them entirely; the EU recently passed MiCA (Markets in Crypto-Assets Regulation), an attempt to standardise oversight across member states. *The same digital asset can be legal, quasi-legal, or outright criminal depending on which jurisdiction you are standing in—and that's not a sustainable basis for global finance.*

The problem is compounded by the fact that regulation often trails sentiment. After major market crashes or fraud scandals—such as the collapse of FTX or the implosion of TerraUSD—governments tend to react with heightened scrutiny and politically charged regulatory proposals. This reactive approach results in policies that are designed more to appear decisive than to provide effective long-term governance. In some cases, the regulations are so vague or contradictory that even legal professionals struggle to provide clear guidance. Crypto projects find themselves caught between competing obligations: comply with local law and lose decentralisation, or maintain decentralisation and risk regulatory sanctions. *What emerges is not clarity, but a chilling effect—on innovation, on entrepreneurship, and on trust.*

This legal fragmentation also affects how infrastructure is built. Exchanges that operate globally must design geo-fencing tools to block users from specific countries, adjust trading pairs based on regional compliance, and continually update their terms of service to reflect an ever-shifting mosaic of obligations. Projects may choose to avoid jurisdictions with high regulatory uncertainty altogether, which limits user access and creates uneven opportunities across regions. Decentralised finance (DeFi) platforms, which often lack a central legal entity, face existential questions: can a protocol be sued? Can code be held accountable? These are not academic hypotheticals—they are questions that regulators and courts are now actively testing. *The legal system assumes a central actor. Crypto, by its nature, often has none.*

For small investors, the cost of this inconsistency is both practical and psychological. On a basic level, users may unwittingly break the law by using a platform or token that is legal elsewhere but restricted in their country. Airdrops might trigger tax obligations in one country but not in another; staking rewards may be treated as income, capital gains, or not taxed at all, depending on the jurisdiction. Even something as simple as transferring funds between wallets can carry different implications across borders. Investors must therefore operate with a degree of vigilance that is disproportionate to the size of their holdings. *Crypto demands not only financial literacy but jurisdictional awareness—something most casual investors are neither trained for nor expecting.*

Moreover, this regulatory incoherence creates uneven investor protections. A user defrauded on an unlicensed exchange in the UK may have no recourse, while a counterpart in the EU under MiCA might have access to compensation mechanisms. Consumer rights, fraud protections, dispute resolution processes—all are contingent on geography, despite the underlying technology being the same. This asymmetry breeds a false sense of universality. Many assume that because crypto operates globally, it is governed globally. But governance remains local, parochial, and fragmented. *The blockchain is global. The law is not.*

Philosophically, this poses a deeper challenge: how do you regulate a system that was designed, at least in part, to bypass traditional regulation? Satoshi Nakamoto's original vision for Bitcoin was explicitly distrustful of central authorities. Subsequent innovations—smart contracts, DAOs, DeFi, NFTs—have followed this ethos, emphasising autonomy and programmability over institutional compliance. But when crypto systems intersect with real-world economies—when tokens are traded for fiat, when projects raise capital, when users demand protection—the absence of legal frameworks becomes untenable. The paradox is this: *crypto needs law to scale, but law struggles to map itself onto crypto.*

Some argue that the only viable solution is global regulatory harmonisation—a set of shared principles that can be adapted to local contexts but provide overarching coherence. Efforts like the Financial Action Task Force (FATF)'s guidelines on virtual assets are a step in this direction, but implementation remains patchy and politically fraught. Others advocate for "regulatory sandboxes," where governments allow limited experimentation under supervised conditions. Still others suggest that decentralised governance models—token-based voting, on-chain compliance layers—can provide an alternative to traditional legal enforcement. Yet none of these approaches has achieved consensus or scale. *The regulatory future of crypto is being debated in real time, with no clear endpoint in sight.*

The implications are not merely technical. They affect the kinds of innovation that get funded, the users who feel safe participating, and the entrepreneurs who decide whether to launch in London, Lisbon, or Singapore. Regulatory messiness distorts markets, not just by creating friction but by privileging incumbents who can afford to navigate the legal minefield. It also opens the door to arbitrage, where bad actors exploit differences between jurisdictions to hide assets, launder funds, or defraud users. The result is not a free market but a skewed one—where access, trust, and accountability depend as much on where you are as on what you do.

To move forward, what is required is not only legal reform but regulatory imagination. Policymakers must think beyond existing categories—securities, currencies, commodities—and recognise that crypto represents a new asset class with unique properties. They must engage with developers, users, and legal scholars to craft frameworks that are both enforceable and innovation-friendly. This means moving from a mindset of prohibition to one of participation: not just *how do we control crypto?* but *how do we integrate it responsibly into our legal and economic systems?* It is a harder question, but a necessary one.

For now, users must navigate this mess with care, humility, and an awareness that the rules may change tomorrow. Compliance is not a one-time decision but an ongoing process. And the most valuable asset in crypto may not be a token at all—it may be regulatory foresight. Those who understand the legal terrain, who think critically about jurisdictional risk, who build or invest with clarity rather than hype, will be better positioned to thrive not just technically, but legally. *Because in a fragmented world, understanding the rules is not just about staying safe. It's about staying in the game.*

What You're Responsible For

It is often said that cryptocurrency liberates individuals from institutional dependence. What is said less often—but matters more—is that it also imposes a profound shift in personal responsibility. In traditional finance, lost access can be remedied with a phone call to a bank. Tax obligations are mediated by employers, brokers, or accountants. Identity is recoverable through legal processes. In crypto, by contrast, *you are the bank, the back-office, the compliance department, and the custodian—all in one.* This promise of sovereignty comes bundled with an obligation: to understand and manage the legal, technical, and fiscal dimensions of your holdings, even when those obligations are counterintuitive or invisible at first glance. The consequences of misunderstanding this are not theoretical. They are material, enforceable, and increasingly common.

Nowhere is this more pressing than in the realm of tax. While many retail investors mistakenly believe that cryptocurrency is "unregulated," tax authorities around the world are crystal clear: *crypto transactions are taxable events*. The ambiguity lies not in whether you owe taxes, but in the complexity of calculating them. Most jurisdictions treat cryptocurrencies as property, not currency. This means that capital gains rules apply—just as they would if you sold shares or real estate. Every time you convert crypto to fiat, swap one token for another, or spend crypto on goods and services, you may generate a gain or loss relative to your cost basis. If you're paid in crypto for freelance work, that income must be declared at the fair market value on the day received. If you stake tokens or earn yield through DeFi, those earnings are likely to be taxable—though the precise categorisation (as income, interest, or capital gain) varies widely between jurisdictions.

In the United Kingdom, HMRC requires individuals to keep detailed records of every crypto transaction, including the date, value in GBP at the time, nature of the transaction, and wallet addresses involved. Similar expectations exist in Australia, Canada, and the United States, where the IRS has increasingly prioritised crypto reporting. Failing to disclose crypto activity is not a minor oversight; it is treated as tax evasion. And ignorance—however genuine—is not a defence. What complicates matters further is that the infrastructure for crypto tax compliance is still immature. Many decentralised exchanges provide no transaction history, and even centralised platforms differ in how they report data. Users must often reconstruct their financial history across wallets, platforms, and chains, with no single source of truth. *You are responsible for assembling the puzzle, even when the pieces are scattered.*

Then there's the matter of reporting thresholds. In some countries, simply holding above a certain value of crypto may trigger mandatory disclosures. In others, transfers over a threshold (say, £5,000) may require enhanced due diligence or trigger suspicion of money laundering. AirDrops—tokens distributed for free—can also be taxable at the moment of receipt, even if their value plummets afterwards. NFTs, often considered novel and confusing, are still treated as taxable property. The lack of harmonised standards means that two people performing identical crypto actions may owe vastly different taxes depending on their country of residence. *The burden falls on the individual to know which rules apply, and when.*

Beyond tax, there's the stark question of loss and liability. If you lose access to your private keys—the cryptographic credentials that control access to your wallet—there is no password reset, no call centre, no recovery protocol. The crypto you hold becomes inaccessible, potentially forever. Estimates suggest that over 20% of all Bitcoin is lost in this way—locked away in wallets whose keys are forgotten, misplaced, or destroyed. This is not a glitch in the system. It is the system working exactly as designed. Ownership in crypto is secured by possession of private keys; without them, ownership cannot be enforced. This design principle, rooted in cryptographic trustlessness, places an extreme premium on *personal operational security*. That means securing your seed phrases offline, using hardware wallets when appropriate, and understanding the trade-offs of self-custody versus custodial platforms.

Even with custodial platforms—like centralised exchanges—the risk does not disappear. If the platform is hacked, mismanaged, or collapses (as FTX did), your assets may be frozen or lost entirely. Legal recourse may be limited, particularly if the company is based offshore or if you are an unsecured creditor in bankruptcy proceedings. Some platforms offer insurance or compensation schemes, but these vary in quality and enforceability. Others operate in legal grey zones, where user protections are minimal or non-existent. *When you delegate custody, you also delegate control—and potentially your legal rights.*

Another often-misunderstood area of responsibility lies in the obligations around Know Your Customer (KYC) and Anti-Money Laundering (AML) compliance. Increasingly, users are being asked to verify their identity, provide documentation, and justify the source of their funds—even on platforms that once prided themselves on anonymity. While this may feel intrusive, it reflects growing pressure from regulators to bring crypto into alignment with broader financial regulations. Failure to comply with KYC checks can result in frozen accounts, denied withdrawals, or permanent bans. More importantly, attempting to circumvent these systems—through mixers, proxy wallets, or false identities—can attract serious legal consequences. In some jurisdictions, such actions are classified as financial crimes, with penalties that include asset forfeiture or imprisonment. *The days of casual anonymity are ending—not through technical failure, but regulatory force.*

And yet, responsibility does not end with compliance. There is a broader ethical and operational responsibility to understand what you are participating in. When you approve a smart contract, do you understand the permissions you are granting? When you interact with a DeFi protocol, do you know the risks of impermanent loss or oracle manipulation? When you mint or buy an NFT, have you verified the authenticity and provenance of the token? These are not mere technicalities. They are the scaffolding of digital ownership. And they cannot be outsourced—not to developers, not to platforms, not to the community. *In crypto, ignorance is risk. Complacency is exposure. Delegation is liability.*

This is not to suggest that participation in crypto requires a law degree or a software engineering background. But it does require a mindset shift. The user is not just a consumer but a participant in a complex, evolving system. Rights are earned through knowledge, not granted by default. Protections are opt-in, not imposed. Mistakes are not always reversible. And while regulators are slowly catching up, the current architecture still assumes a level of self-sufficiency that few other financial systems demand.

The promise of crypto—accessibility, sovereignty, transparency—remains compelling. But its practice demands clarity, discipline, and an unromantic grasp of what responsibility truly means. It means filing taxes not only on realised gains but on unexpected income. It means securing your assets beyond convenience, planning for worst-case scenarios, and treating your digital footprint as both financial and legal data. It means resisting the temptation to dismiss regulation as irrelevant or obsolete, recognising instead that the intersection of technology and law is where legitimacy is forged.

Ultimately, to be "your own bank" is not simply a slogan—it is a legal and logistical reality. It entails rights, yes, but it also imposes duties. You must know what you hold, how it is categorised, where it is stored, and under which jurisdictions it falls. You must understand that compliance is not a one-time checkbox but a continuing act of engagement. And you must acknowledge that the consequences of neglect are borne not by the system, but by you. *Because in the world of decentralised finance, the margin between liberation and liability is measured not in ideology, but in understanding.*

KYC, AML, and Your Privacy

In the early mythos of cryptocurrency, anonymity was not just a feature—it was a principle. Bitcoin's pseudonymous structure promised a financial system untethered from identity, permission, or surveillance. But ideals collide with institutions, and as crypto moved from fringe to mainstream, so too did it move from ungoverned to scrutinised. Today, Know Your Customer (KYC) and Anti-Money Laundering (AML) requirements have become routine elements of any serious crypto exchange or financial service. They sit at the crux of a growing global push to fold decentralised finance into the existing legal order. But they also raise a profound question: *What should be the price of participating in the financial system—compliance or privacy?* And more urgently, who gets to decide?

At their core, KYC and AML are legal frameworks designed to prevent financial crime. The premise is simple: criminals rely on anonymity to launder money, fund terrorism, evade sanctions, and engage in illicit trade. If financial institutions are required to verify their users' identities (KYC) and monitor transactions for suspicious activity (AML), these actors can be excluded, flagged, or prosecuted. That, at least, is the theory. In practice, the scope of these regulations has expanded significantly over the past two decades. Following the 2001 Patriot Act in the United States and successive EU AML directives, financial service providers—including crypto exchanges, wallet custodians, and even some NFT platforms—are now compelled to collect substantial personal information from users. This includes names, addresses, identification documents, and sometimes even biometric data or proof of income. The goal is accountability. But the result, for many, is surveillance.

This raises an inherent tension. On the one hand, financial crime is real, and unchecked crypto anonymity provides fertile ground for bad actors. Chainalysis, a blockchain analytics firm, has documented how billions in illicit funds flow through cryptocurrency networks each year—often facilitated by obfuscation tools like mixers or privacy coins. On the other hand, the vast majority of crypto users are not laundering money. They are sending remittances, participating in decentralised finance, investing in digital assets, or securing savings in unstable economies. For these users, the imposition of KYC can feel not only intrusive but counterproductive. *Why should a Nigerian developer or a Venezuelan student be required to upload sensitive personal data to an offshore exchange just to access the global economy?* For many, privacy is not a cover for crime—it is a precondition for safety.

Moreover, the infrastructure of KYC is itself deeply flawed. Data breaches are common. Centralised exchanges are lucrative targets for hackers, and countless user databases have already been compromised—often without recourse. When users submit KYC documents, they are placing trust in platforms that may not be regulated in their own jurisdiction, may lack cybersecurity standards, or may have ambiguous accountability in case of misuse. And even when data is securely stored, it can be legally shared with third parties or governments under vague pretexts. The result is a growing global apparatus of financial data collection whose scope and safeguards are often opaque. *We have normalised surveillance in the name of security, without meaningfully debating its limits.*

Yet the crypto industry is not monolithic in its response. Some platforms, especially those seeking institutional adoption, embrace full KYC and AML compliance as a signal of legitimacy. They argue that regulatory alignment is necessary to scale, to earn public trust, and to access banking infrastructure. Coinbase, for example, has prioritised regulatory compliance in its expansion strategy, even if that means excluding users in jurisdictions where KYC infrastructure is underdeveloped. Others, like Binance, have historically taken a more permissive approach—offering limited KYC services until pressured by regulators. Still others, particularly decentralised protocols like Uniswap or Aave, resist KYC altogether, citing their status as code rather than institutions. These platforms claim that because they do not custody user funds or directly intermediate transactions, they should not be subject to traditional financial reporting obligations. Regulators, predictably, disagree.

This divergence highlights a deeper ambiguity: *What constitutes a "financial institution" in a decentralised system?* If anyone can deploy a smart contract, and users can interact with protocols through wallet addresses alone, who bears the responsibility for KYC and AML compliance? The developer? The DAO? The user? Legal clarity on these questions remains limited, and interpretations vary wildly by jurisdiction. In the EU's proposed Markets in Crypto-Assets (MiCA) regulation, there is language that would require certain DeFi projects to conduct KYC if they are deemed to provide services. In the US, the debate continues over whether software developers can be held liable for the uses of their code. And globally, the Financial Action Task Force (FATF) has published guidelines urging countries to impose the "Travel Rule" on crypto—requiring that sender and receiver information accompany transactions between exchanges. These shifts signal a clear direction: *the legal system is converging on identity as the price of participation.*

But is it the right price? That question remains unresolved. Privacy advocates argue that financial privacy is a civil right—not a privilege contingent on trustworthiness. Just as we would not tolerate email providers reading our messages or libraries logging our reading habits, we should not accept that every financial move must be traceable by default. Tools like zero-knowledge proofs, decentralised identifiers, and selective disclosure protocols offer potential middle grounds—enabling users to prove legitimacy (such as being over 18 or not on a sanctions list) without revealing all personal details. These technologies are nascent but promising. They suggest a future in which compliance and privacy are not mutually exclusive. But for now, that future is unevenly distributed.

The practical implication for most users is a choice. To use major exchanges, onboard into fiat, or access regulated DeFi platforms, one must provide identifying information. There is little room for negotiation. This is particularly true in countries with strict capital controls, where users may find themselves locked out of global markets unless they engage in peer-to-peer transfers or riskier decentralised alternatives. Conversely, those who value anonymity may seek refuge in non-KYC platforms, decentralised protocols, or privacy-preserving assets. But doing so often entails additional risk—of fraud, of legal exposure, or of irrecoverable loss.

The more critical insight, though, is that *privacy is not binary—it is contextual.* Submitting KYC to a reputable platform may be a rational trade-off for someone buying small amounts of crypto as an investment. But for an activist in an authoritarian state, even a traceable transaction could be life-threatening. For a journalist moving funds across borders, anonymity may be essential, not optional. The problem is that current regulations do not distinguish between these cases. They assume a world of trustful institutions, benign governments, and universal access to rights. That world does not exist for everyone.

And so we return to the tension: between the law's desire to know and the individual's desire to be left alone. Between security and freedom. Between systemic accountability and personal autonomy. These are not technical problems to be engineered away. They are political questions, ethical dilemmas, and societal decisions. As crypto continues to globalise, the pressure to resolve them will intensify—not just in legislation, but in code, in corporate policy, and in cultural norms.

The task, then, is not to pretend that anonymity and compliance can always be harmonised. Nor is it to glorify privacy at the cost of justice. Rather, it is to insist that *the architecture of financial identity be designed with deliberation, consent, and transparency.* That users understand what they are surrendering, to whom, and why. That compliance be proportional, not indiscriminate. And that privacy be protected not as a niche concern, but as a foundational value of any free and equitable digital economy.

In the end, privacy is not the absence of visibility—it is the presence of control. In a world where data is capital and identity is currency, that distinction may well define the next phase of financial modernity.

How to Stay on the Right Side of the Line

For most people dipping their toes into the waters of cryptocurrency, the largest risk isn't some esoteric bug in a smart contract or the volatility of meme coins—it's unintentionally breaking a law they didn't know existed. Unlike traditional financial systems, where banks and institutions bear much of the legal responsibility on behalf of their customers, crypto transfers the burden almost entirely to the individual. You don't need to know every nuance of securities regulation, tax code, or anti-money laundering statute to use crypto, but you do need a framework for behaving responsibly within an evolving and often contradictory legal environment.

The key challenge lies in the fact that *the rules you're expected to follow vary wildly depending on where you live, what type of assets you hold, and how you use them.* Yet ignorance offers no protection. Authorities in most jurisdictions expect crypto users to make reasonable efforts to comply with applicable laws—even if those laws are still catching up with the technology.

The first and most foundational concept to internalise is this: *if you control your crypto assets directly, you also control the legal liability that comes with them.* Custodial platforms like exchanges and wallets sometimes help intermediate regulatory responsibilities—especially when they're registered in jurisdictions with strict compliance regimes. However, as soon as you move funds to a private wallet or engage in peer-to-peer transactions, you are effectively your own bank, accountant, and legal counsel.

So how does a well-meaning user avoid trouble without needing to hire a barrister or become a blockchain forensic analyst? It starts by learning to spot where the legal landmines typically lie, then building simple, durable habits that reduce your exposure over time.

Keep records—religiously. Most governments now treat cryptocurrency as taxable property. This means every disposal—whether you sell coins for cash, trade them for another token, or use them to buy a coffee—can trigger a capital gains event. Many users are surprised to learn that even converting Bitcoin to Ethereum might create a reportable tax liability. Without accurate records of acquisition dates, purchase prices, and transaction histories, you'll find yourself scrambling when it's time to file. Worse still, failure to report crypto income accurately can be interpreted as tax evasion—a crime in most jurisdictions. The habit to develop here is simple but non-negotiable: *document everything.* Use tax software that integrates with your wallets and exchanges. Export transaction logs regularly. Store backups securely and redundantly. Your future self will thank you, especially if you're ever audited.

Next, understand the difference between *platform compliance* and *personal responsibility.* Just because a platform allows you to make a transaction doesn't mean it's legal to do so. For instance, certain decentralised exchanges do not restrict access based on jurisdiction, meaning users from countries where those services are prohibited can still technically use them. Doing so may breach local laws—especially those related to securities or sanctioned assets. Platforms may claim decentralisation as a defence, but *regulators increasingly expect individual users to perform their own due diligence.*

The same principle applies to the rapidly expanding universe of tokenised assets. Buying a token that represents a share of a real estate investment, for example, could be considered an unlicensed securities purchase depending on where you live. Don't assume that the mere existence of a token on the blockchain legitimises it. Ask critical questions: Who issued it? What rights does it confer? Is it backed by real assets? Is it registered or exempt from registration under your local securities laws? In practice, if a token promises profit from the efforts of others—particularly if you're a passive holder—there's a chance regulators may classify it as a security. *When in doubt, be conservative.*

Another emerging legal frontier concerns *cross-border transfers.* Many countries impose restrictions on moving large sums of money across borders, especially without disclosure. Sending a few thousand pounds' worth of crypto to a friend in another country may not raise any red flags, but larger or repeated transfers can attract regulatory scrutiny. Even if you're not laundering money, your transactions might resemble someone who is. This is especially true if you use privacy tools like mixers or shielded addresses—technologies that, while legal in some jurisdictions, can attract suspicion in others. If your goal is privacy rather than opacity, look for regulated platforms that offer strong data protections without triggering red flags.

KYC and AML compliance is not just about onboarding—it affects how your data is stored, how suspicious activity is flagged, and whether your transactions are subject to ongoing monitoring. Many users forget this and are shocked when exchanges freeze their accounts or request updated documentation years after opening an account. The best practice here is to use reputable platforms with clear compliance policies—and to keep your own records of KYC submissions, including the dates and documents provided. This helps demonstrate good faith if you ever need to prove your identity or intent to regulators.

What about decentralised platforms that don't require KYC? While these can offer flexibility and anonymity, they also come with greater legal ambiguity. Using non-KYC platforms to bypass national restrictions is risky. Regulators may retroactively target participants in decentralised ecosystems, particularly if the projects are deemed to facilitate illicit finance. If you prefer the autonomy of decentralised finance (DeFi), approach it with caution: favour protocols with transparent governance, public audits, and strong community reputations. Avoid anything that smells of evasion, secrecy, or regulatory arbitrage. *The absence of regulation is not the same as legal immunity.*

Lastly, adopt a simple rule of thumb: *if something feels too clever, it probably is.* Tax-loss harvesting strategies that involve selling assets and immediately buying them back, wash trading between wallets you control, or routing funds through multiple exchanges to "lose the trail"—these may technically work in the short term, but they are rarely worth the long-term risks. Regulators are increasingly investing in blockchain analytics tools that can detect patterns of behaviour, even when identities are obscured. Being clever is not the same as being compliant—and the latter always wins in the long run.

In truth, the most effective compliance strategy for ordinary users is not technical sophistication, but behavioural consistency. Stay informed. Use regulated platforms where possible. Report your transactions honestly. Don't try to outsmart the law. And remember: the purpose of regulation is not to punish, but to provide clarity and protection—*when it's functional, it exists to serve people like you.*

The crypto world rewards initiative, but it also punishes negligence. You don't need to be a legal expert to operate safely, but you do need to respect the rules—even the ones that haven't been written yet. And in a space where innovation moves faster than legislation, *prudent habits will protect you better than clever schemes ever could.*

Chapter 11
Beyond Bitcoin—What's Next for Crypto?

The popular imagination still pictures cryptocurrency as a gleaming digital coin embossed with a capital B. Bitcoin remains the emblem, the cultural anchor, the first to defy the orthodoxy of traditional finance, and the default reference point in debates about value, decentralisation, and monetary freedom. Yet if Bitcoin sparked the revolution, it is no longer its gravitational centre. The action has shifted inward—into architecture, protocols, and systems that rarely make the headlines. The pressing question today is not whether crypto will endure, but in what form it will ultimately stabilise.

To grasp that, one must look past the coin itself and examine the deeper, quieter strata: Ethereum's programmable ledger, the rise of decentralised finance (DeFi), the experimental contours of decentralised autonomous organisations (DAOs), and the elegant problem-solving offered by Layer 2 solutions. These developments seldom generate viral headlines, yet they carry far more weight in shaping the real-world trajectory of crypto. If Bitcoin is the symbol, these layers constitute the substance.

Ethereum, for example, is more than a cryptocurrency—it is a platform. While Bitcoin was conceived as a narrowly focused tool for secure, decentralised value transfer, Ethereum was built as a general-purpose infrastructure for decentralised applications. Its smart contracts—self-executing code running on the blockchain—enable everything from tokenised assets and lending protocols to digital art and automated governance. Ethereum transformed the blockchain from a ledger into a canvas. Other platforms have emerged, but Ethereum's maturity and influence continue to define development norms and architectural standards across the ecosystem.

Arguably, Ethereum's most enduring contribution is conceptual. It demonstrated that programmability—not scarcity—is crypto's second act. Bitcoin proved that money could exist outside central banks; Ethereum showed that entire financial systems could be removed from institutional control and reconstructed with code rather than bylaws. This insight underpins DeFi, which displaces traditional intermediaries—banks, brokers, custodians—with transparent, auditable algorithms. Borrowing, lending, trading, and asset management can all occur without human intermediation, replacing trust with mathematics and oversight with transparency.

DeFi is not mere idealism. It provides tangible advantages: lower fees, round-the-clock availability, global accessibility, and programmable incentives. But there is a cost. Without intermediaries come no safety nets. Smart contract vulnerabilities, token volatility, and governance risks can compound quickly. Regulatory uncertainty further complicates matters, creating a realm where opportunity and fragility coexist. The systems are robust in some respects, brittle in others. DeFi, therefore, functions both as proof of concept and cautionary tale: radical efficiency can masquerade as systemic risk if not properly engineered.

DAOs, meanwhile, challenge the very notion of organisation. Without CEOs, boards, or conventional hierarchies, DAOs operate through smart contracts and token-weighted voting. The promise is transparency, efficiency, and global accessibility. Reality, however, is messier. Accountability becomes opaque, voter apathy threatens decision-making, and plutocracy can emerge from the very mechanisms intended to democratise governance. Some DAOs manage venture capital pools, others fund decentralised protocols, distribute grants, or even acquire tangible assets. They reveal the potential of collective governance—and its vulnerabilities when incentives diverge or participation wanes.

Underlying both DeFi and DAOs is a shared bottleneck: scalability. Ethereum's base layer, while secure and decentralised, is slow and costly under heavy load. Gas fees spike unpredictably, pricing out ordinary users. Layer 2 protocols—rollups, sidechains, and hybrid architectures—aim to alleviate this pressure, processing transactions off-chain and settling them on-chain in batches. These solutions are not merely technical niceties; they are essential for mainstream usability. Without them, open finance risks becoming an exclusive playground for the technically adept and the affluent.

As the tools evolve, scrutiny follows. Regulators now examine everything from stablecoins to decentralised exchanges. They face unprecedented questions: who is liable when a smart contract fails? Can financial supervision function when protocols have no CEO? For users, this means uncertainty. Rules are patchwork, unsettled, and sometimes contradictory. Crypto is becoming as much a legal system as a technical one, demanding literacy in both spheres.

And so comes the philosophical inquiry: is the revolution still arriving? Early advocates imagined a world where decentralised systems would dismantle central banks, displace conventional finance, and reshape the internet around peer-to-peer sovereignty. Some of that vision has materialised. Much has not. Instead, we see bifurcation: crypto as an alternative financial layer for the unbanked, curious, or speculative; and crypto as a technological substrate increasingly integrated into legacy institutions. Banks now custody Bitcoin; governments explore central bank digital currencies; venture capital pours billions into Web3 ventures.

The central tension is not victory or defeat—it is control. Who writes the rules? Who enforces them? Who can participate? These questions will determine whether crypto realises its transformative potential or becomes another feature of entrenched systems.

For the discerning reader, this chapter offers more than a survey of tools. It is an invitation to perceive crypto as an ecosystem with competing logics. Platforms and protocols—Ethereum, DeFi, DAOs, Layer 2s—are not endpoints but building blocks. Their design choices are far from neutral. Each embodies a vision of how digital value flows, who should govern it, and why it matters. As adoption widens, debates that once seemed niche become central to banking, governance, identity, and infrastructure.

Bitcoin broke the mould. What follows is still being written.

The Ethereum Ecosystem

Ethereum was not the first blockchain, but it was the first to treat a blockchain as more than a ledger. To understand Ethereum is to grasp a shift in what a decentralised network can be—not simply a tool for recording transactions, but a general-purpose infrastructure for running programmable applications. This conceptual leap, though technically subtle, has transformed the scope of what crypto can enable. Bitcoin aimed to disintermediate money. Ethereum aims to disintermediate everything.

At the core of Ethereum lies a simple but powerful idea: *programmable trust*. Unlike Bitcoin, whose protocol is intentionally rigid to preserve its singular use case as digital gold, Ethereum is designed to be flexible. It introduces the Ethereum Virtual Machine (EVM), a decentralised computing environment that executes code across thousands of nodes worldwide. This makes it possible to write smart contracts—automated scripts that run exactly as programmed, without the possibility of downtime, censorship, or third-party interference.

Smart contracts are the building blocks of Ethereum's ecosystem. A smart contract can be as basic as a token that represents a digital asset or as complex as a decentralised insurance protocol, a lending platform, or a voting system. Once deployed, a smart contract is immutable in logic and transparent in execution. It replaces institutional trust with software enforcement. This has wide-reaching implications, not only for finance but for governance, commerce, identity, and beyond.

The range of applications built on Ethereum today is vast and growing. At one end are decentralised finance protocols like Aave, Uniswap, and MakerDAO, which offer borrowing, lending, and asset trading without intermediaries. At the other are decentralised social networks, non-fungible token marketplaces, and even experimental games where users truly own their digital assets. These are not speculative add-ons; they represent a new design pattern for how software can function: autonomous, interoperable, and user-controlled.

This model of decentralised applications (dApps) relies on Ethereum not as a currency but as a coordination layer. Ether (ETH), its native token, is used primarily to pay for the computational work of executing smart contracts—what the network calls "gas." This distinction is crucial. Ether is not simply held as a store of value; it is used. Every transaction, every application interaction, every contract execution consumes ETH to compensate the global network of miners or, post-Merge, validators. *Ethereum's value is thus not just financial but infrastructural.*

This infrastructure underpins what many refer to as Web3—a conceptual evolution of the internet from centralised platforms to decentralised protocols. Web1 was static pages; Web2 was interactive but platform-owned; Web3 aspires to be user-owned and protocol-governed. In this vision, Ethereum serves as the base layer: a substrate where ownership, identity, data, and computation are not intermediated by corporations but embedded in transparent code. It's a future where Facebook does not own your social graph, Google does not own your search history, and Apple does not own your wallet.

However, Ethereum's strengths are not without trade-offs. Its security and decentralisation come at the cost of scalability. Transactions on Ethereum are processed sequentially, and its block size is deliberately limited to maintain network decentralisation. This has led to congestion and high gas fees during periods of demand, pricing out smaller users and limiting application throughput. The result is a paradox: a democratising platform whose access can become exclusive.

To mitigate this, Ethereum is evolving. The transition from proof-of-work to proof-of-stake—a historic shift finalised in 2022 and known as "The Merge"—has drastically reduced energy consumption and opened the door to future performance upgrades. Yet the most significant scalability improvements are coming from Layer 2 solutions: separate protocols that run atop Ethereum to batch and compress transactions before submitting them to the base layer for security. These include optimistic rollups like Arbitrum and zk-rollups like zkSync, each with different trade-offs in speed, cost, and trust assumptions.

Layer 2s are not afterthoughts; they are essential to Ethereum's future. If Ethereum is to become the backbone of a decentralised internet, it must be both secure and performant. The Ethereum roadmap reflects this ambition: modularity, rollup-centric design, sharding, and eventually stateless clients. Each step is a move toward making Ethereum a public utility for programmable logic—accessible, scalable, and neutral.

Yet Ethereum's significance is not purely technical. It is *philosophical.* It challenges foundational assumptions about trust, coordination, and value. Institutions enforce agreements through contracts, courts, and enforcement. Ethereum enforces agreements through code and consensus. This does not eliminate human judgment, but it does relocate the point of trust. Instead of asking "Do I trust this counterparty?" we begin to ask "Do I trust this protocol?" This reframing has implications far beyond DeFi. It touches governance (can a community run itself via a DAO?), art (can provenance be verified without galleries?), and law (what happens when code becomes the final arbiter?).

Critics rightly point out that Ethereum-based systems are not immune to failure. Bugs in smart contracts have led to multi-million-dollar losses. Governance token systems can be captured by whales. Speculation can overwhelm utility. And the user experience—wallets, seed phrases, bridging between chains—remains unintuitive and fragile. These are not minor issues. But they are also not unsolvable. Many of Ethereum's greatest vulnerabilities stem not from its core architecture but from the immature tools, education gaps, and experimental edge of its ecosystem.

Still, it is worth noting what Ethereum has already achieved. It has hosted more than a million smart contracts, secured billions in user assets, and spawned an ecosystem of protocols, projects, and standards that function without central control. It has catalysed innovations in cryptography, identity, governance, and finance. It has been copied, criticised, forked, upgraded, and relentlessly stress-tested. And it has continued to evolve—decentralised in its development, global in its reach, and stubbornly difficult to categorise.

Perhaps Ethereum's most radical offering is not a particular product or protocol, but a new template for institutional logic. In the Ethereum worldview, systems can be open by default, coordination can be permissionless, and economic relationships can be restructured from the ground up. It is neither a utopia nor a foregone conclusion. But it is no longer an abstract promise. It exists, and it is being built in public, line by line, block by block.

To view Ethereum as merely "another cryptocurrency" is to miss the point. It is a computing substrate, a financial laboratory, a governance experiment, and a developer platform all at once. Its value lies not in its price chart but in its architecture—an architecture that invites anyone, anywhere, to write code that becomes law, to define ownership without intermediaries, and to reimagine systems that were previously taken as given.

Ethereum is not the destination. It is the scaffolding for what comes next.

DeFi, DAOs, and the Future of Finance

What if a bank could operate without bankers, a stock market without brokers, or an insurance provider without underwriters? This is not a hypothetical posed by futurists or science fiction authors, but a live question being answered—in real time—by the decentralised finance movement, better known as DeFi. It is not a single platform or company but a growing constellation of protocols built on public blockchains, most notably Ethereum. What makes DeFi radical is not its technology alone, but what that technology permits: *financial infrastructure without institutional intermediaries*. It is not that the old rules are being rewritten—it's that the tools themselves are replacing the need for the rule-writers.

At the heart of DeFi lies the principle of *composability*. In traditional finance, institutions build proprietary products—siloed systems bound by legal contracts and trust in central authorities. In DeFi, protocols are designed to interoperate like modular software. One protocol might provide stablecoins (digital assets pegged to fiat currencies), another might enable lending against those coins, and a third might offer insurance against smart contract failures. Each piece is autonomous yet compatible, and none requires permission to integrate. The outcome is not a closed financial institution but an open financial ecosystem—more like an operating system than a bank.

What makes this possible is the transparent, programmable logic of smart contracts. In DeFi, there are no bank managers, no compliance departments, no human gatekeepers. Everything is enforced by code. When you deposit funds into a DeFi lending protocol like Compound or Aave, your capital is matched algorithmically with borrowers. Interest rates are set dynamically by supply and demand. Collateralisation is enforced programmatically. Defaults are not handled by court order but by instant liquidation via on-chain mechanisms. *Trust is not transferred; it is rendered unnecessary.*

For many, this sounds absurd. And yet by mid-2021, the total value locked (TVL) in DeFi protocols exceeded $100 billion. Billions of dollars in assets were being lent, borrowed, traded, and insured—all without banks. There was no central board, no licensing authority, and in many cases, no corporate entity at all. What emerged was not a shadow financial system, but a parallel one—open-source, globally accessible, and profoundly experimental. It has since fluctuated with markets, yet the architecture remains, evolving with increasing technical rigour and conceptual clarity.

But the promise of DeFi is not merely efficiency. It is *re-architecting financial participation.* Traditional finance is constrained by geography, legal jurisdiction, and institutional bias. Opening a bank account, getting a loan, or trading equities depends on where you live, your credit history, and often the implicit gatekeeping of bureaucratic layers. DeFi, by contrast, runs on a borderless internet. If you have a smartphone and a crypto wallet, you can access complex financial instruments once reserved for institutions. The entry barriers fall away—not only for users but for builders. A single developer can launch a decentralised exchange, a synthetic asset platform, or a risk market, and within weeks it could be handling tens of millions in volume. That degree of leverage—intellectual and financial—has never existed in traditional finance.

Of course, with permissionless innovation comes profound risk. DeFi has been fertile ground for exploits, rug pulls, flash loan attacks, and governance manipulation. The same openness that allows global access also allows adversarial exploitation. A single coding error can be catastrophic. And because many protocols are unaudited, their complexity masks vulnerabilities even from their own creators. These risks are not theoretical; they have cost users hundreds of millions of dollars. But even amid setbacks, the DeFi community has shown an unusual resilience. Code is forked, protocols are patched, new primitives emerge from the ashes of failed ones. It is software as finance, iterated at open-source speed.

Where DeFi rewrites financial infrastructure, decentralised autonomous organisations (DAOs) seek to rewrite governance. A DAO is, at its core, an internet-native organisation run by code rather than corporate charters. Token holders vote on decisions—budget allocations, protocol upgrades, partnerships, and even compensation—via on-chain mechanisms. Unlike corporations, which are beholden to legal jurisdictions, DAOs exist only on-chain. They are not necessarily stateless, but they are *natively global.* Some DAOs manage investment funds (e.g., The LAO, MetaCartel Ventures), others operate grant programs (e.g., Gitcoin), and many serve as the governance layer for DeFi protocols themselves.

The allure of DAOs is not just their efficiency but their transparency. Every vote is recorded, every treasury movement tracked. This allows for a new type of institutional accountability—one enforced not by regulators or auditors but by code and community. However, DAOs are far from utopian. They face deep questions of voter participation, plutocracy (where the wealthy dominate governance), and the tension between decentralisation and operational competence. Many DAOs struggle to achieve quorum. Others devolve into internal politics or succumb to whale manipulation. And still others face existential questions when things go wrong: if no one is in charge, who is responsible?

Despite these issues, DAOs represent a fundamental shift in organisational theory. They challenge the idea that institutions must be anchored in geography, chartered by law, or operated by hierarchical leadership. Like DeFi, they move the locus of trust from people to protocol. They are not necessarily better, but they are categorically different. And like DeFi, they are less about replacing existing systems than about offering *alternatives*. Alternatives that are opt-in, modifiable, and continuously reimagined.

What connects DeFi and DAOs is more than their reliance on Ethereum. It is their *philosophy of minimised trust*. Both are attempts to rewire the architecture of finance and governance to reduce dependency on fallible institutions. This is not to suggest that trust disappears—only that it is reconfigured. Users must trust code, yes, but they can read it. They must trust markets, but those markets are open. They must trust community decisions, but the mechanisms of those decisions are visible and verifiable. That trade-off—between opacity and transparency, between centralisation and autonomy—is at the core of this new financial paradigm.

Still, it would be naïve to frame DeFi and DAOs as ready-made replacements for traditional institutions. They are not. They are emergent technologies in their adolescence—brilliant, flawed, unpredictable. They suffer from usability issues, legal grey areas, economic naivety, and social fragility. They demand a new kind of literacy from participants: not just technical, but economic and political. Engaging with DeFi means understanding risks that don't exist in regulated markets. Participating in a DAO means navigating governance mechanisms with no historical precedent. These systems are not turnkey. They require *thoughtful participation*.

Yet the direction of travel is unmistakable. From banks exploring tokenised assets to corporations experimenting with on-chain governance, the gravitational pull of these ideas is being felt even in the institutions they aim to disrupt. Central banks are studying programmable currencies. Asset managers are integrating DeFi yield strategies. Regulators are asking not how to ban these systems, but how to interpret them within existing frameworks. This is not endorsement, but it is acknowledgement. The genie is not going back in the bottle.

The future of finance will not be monolithic. It will likely be hybrid. Traditional institutions will adopt cryptographic infrastructure where it offers real gains—settlement speed, transparency, capital efficiency. Meanwhile, decentralised protocols will mature, professionalise, and interface more gracefully with the broader economy. There will be cross-pollination, and there will be friction. But the central question is no longer whether DeFi and DAOs matter. It is how much, how soon, and to whom.

To dismiss this movement as a passing trend is to misunderstand its trajectory. DeFi and DAOs are not endpoints. They are experiments—sometimes reckless, often imperfect, but fundamentally generative. They invite us to reimagine finance not as a product sold by institutions, but as a protocol embedded in networks. They force us to reconsider who controls capital, how decisions are made, and what mechanisms we use to enforce cooperation at scale.

What's at stake is not the price of a token, but the architecture of power.

What's a Layer 2, and Why Should I Care?

In April 2021, a single transaction on the Ethereum blockchain cost over $300 in network fees—just to approve the movement of a token. It was neither complex nor unusual. Yet it revealed a structural problem with early blockchain architecture: *public blockchains do not scale well.* For all their virtues—security, transparency, decentralisation—they face a hard limit on throughput. Ethereum, at the base layer, can handle roughly 15 to 30 transactions per second. That number is embarrassingly low when compared to global payment networks like Visa, which can process thousands per second. As adoption grows, the bottleneck tightens, and prices soar. The question becomes existential: *how can a global financial system run on infrastructure that breaks under its own popularity?*

Enter Layer 2 solutions—engineering responses to a problem that is neither temporary nor trivial. A Layer 2 (L2) is not a competitor to the main blockchain but a complement. It is built *on top of* the base layer (Layer 1), offloading transaction activity while preserving the security guarantees of the main chain. The idea is simple in concept but profound in implication: move most of the work elsewhere, and settle the results back on the blockchain only when necessary. If Layer 1 is the settlement layer, Layer 2 is the execution environment.

It's the difference between logging every conversation in a crowded room versus only recording the final agreement.

But what does this actually look like in practice? And why should the average crypto user—even a casual one—care?

Let's start with the two dominant categories of Layer 2 scaling: **rollups** and **state channels**. Rollups, particularly optimistic rollups (like Optimism or Arbitrum) and zero-knowledge rollups (zkSync, StarkNet), work by bundling hundreds or thousands of transactions into a single proof, which is then posted to the Ethereum mainnet. This batching mechanism allows the network to scale by orders of magnitude without sacrificing trustlessness. Transactions are still executed off-chain, but their integrity is verified on-chain. *It's a clever balancing act: decentralisation without congestion.*

State channels take a different approach. They allow participants to transact privately and rapidly off-chain, only settling the final state on-chain once the interaction is complete. Think of it like running a tab at a bar: you only pay once, but behind the scenes, dozens of individual actions have taken place. This model works well for scenarios involving repeated interactions between the same parties—say, gaming, micropayments, or subscriptions.

But the technical jargon, while important, is not the crux of the matter. The key insight is this: *Layer 2 exists to make crypto usable at scale.* Most users don't care about consensus algorithms or data availability proofs. They care about sending money quickly, trading tokens affordably, minting NFTs without paying more in gas than in art. Without Layer 2s, these use cases remain niche, or worse, elitist—accessible only to those who can afford triple-digit transaction fees.

What Layer 2s offer is *economic accessibility*. They change the unit economics of participation. A transaction that would cost $40 on Ethereum Layer 1 might cost $0.02 on Arbitrum. That difference is not cosmetic; it is transformative. It means a DeFi yield farmer in rural Indonesia can move capital without going bankrupt. It means a student can mint a certificate on-chain without it being financially irrational. It means the promise of Web3—open, programmable, decentralised interaction—is not gated by network congestion and speculative fees.

Still, there are trade-offs. Not all Layer 2s are equal in security, decentralisation, or user experience. Optimistic rollups, for example, assume transactions are valid by default but allow a challenge period (typically seven days) during which fraudulent activity can be contested. This delays withdrawal times, which is inconvenient for users needing fast access to funds. Zero-knowledge rollups, in contrast, offer near-instant finality and superior cryptographic guarantees but are more complex to build and currently limited in smart contract compatibility.

This introduces a subtle but essential point: *Layer 2s are not mere scaling hacks—they are governance choices.* Different models imply different assumptions about who validates, who controls the infrastructure, and what trade-offs are acceptable. Some L2s use centralised sequencers for speed, raising concerns about censorship resistance. Others push for full decentralisation, sacrificing throughput in the process. These architectural choices are not just technical—they are *political.* They determine who benefits, who is exposed to risk, and how trust is allocated in a supposedly trustless system.

Moreover, the proliferation of Layer 2s creates a new kind of complexity for users and developers alike. Where should a new application launch—on Optimism, Arbitrum, Base, Scroll, or StarkNet? Each L2 has its own technical stack, developer incentives, bridge risks, and user bases. Fragmentation becomes a real concern. Liquidity is scattered. Users must learn new wallets, manage bridging assets, and track balances across environments. For developers, this multiplies the burden of interoperability and support. For users, it adds friction at the very moment crypto seeks mass adoption.

That's where the emerging notion of *Layer 3* and interoperability protocols like Polygon AggLayer or zkSync Hyperchains come into play. These projects aim to unify fragmented ecosystems and create seamless experiences across Layer 2s—akin to how the web unified disparate networks into a single user-facing platform. If successful, this could abstract away the complexity for users entirely. Just as no one thinks about TCP/IP when browsing the web, crypto users might someday interact with a dApp without knowing—or needing to know—what Layer 2 they're on.

So why should you care about Layer 2?

Because without it, everything promising about crypto—from borderless finance to digital identity to on-chain coordination—remains a bottlenecked vision. Layer 1 chains like Ethereum provide robust security and decentralisation, but they were never designed to be high-throughput transactional highways. Layer 2s are the asphalt on that highway. They don't replace Layer 1—they *enable it to scale meaningfully*.

More importantly, understanding Layer 2 is not just about saving money on gas fees. It's about understanding where crypto is going. It's about recognising that *infrastructure design shapes user experience*. And that decisions made today about architecture, sequencing, and data availability will determine who gets to build, who gets to use, and who gets excluded.

For developers, Layer 2 opens a new design space—one where applications no longer need to compromise functionality to stay within gas limits. For institutional actors, it offers a low-cost, high-throughput environment that aligns better with regulatory demands and compliance workflows. For everyday users, it promises a Web3 that *feels fast*, *costs little*, and *just works*. And for the ecosystem as a whole, it represents the maturation of crypto from ideological prototype to usable infrastructure.

But the maturity of the space also invites a higher standard of scrutiny. Who governs these Layer 2s? Are they decentralised in name only? Can users exit safely if things go wrong? Can developers fork if platforms become extractive? These are not rhetorical questions. They are the design constraints of the next era of crypto infrastructure.

Layer 2 is not a buzzword. It is a battleground—one that determines whether blockchain stays a playground for the wealthy or becomes a substrate for global coordination. To care about Layer 2 is to care about inclusion, scalability, and the very viability of crypto's grand experiment. It is not just a layer of technology; it is a layer of consequence.

Is the Revolution Still Coming?

In 2009, Bitcoin appeared as a quiet provocation, a 9-page whitepaper from a pseudonymous cryptographer proposing an alternative to central banking and trust-based finance. By 2017, it had become a global spectacle, a volatile cocktail of idealism and speculation. In the years that followed, the ecosystem exploded: Ethereum redefined programmability, stablecoins promised monetary stability, and decentralised finance (DeFi) dared to reimagine banking without bankers. Yet today, after cycles of euphoric peaks and brutal contractions, the question hangs uncomfortably in the air: *is crypto still a revolution in motion—or merely a failed rebellion wrapped in clever code and capital flows?*

The answer depends on where one looks, and how one defines revolution. If by "revolution" we mean the abrupt dismantling of legacy financial institutions, the widespread adoption of decentralised networks, or the overthrow of fiat money, the movement looks stalled—if not discredited. But if we understand revolution as *a gradual but irreversible reconfiguration of infrastructure, norms, and power structures*, then crypto may be advancing not in noise, but in silence.

Let's start with the hype that's visibly receded. The NFT boom of 2021, which saw pixelated apes and algorithmically generated avatars sell for millions, now feels like a fever dream. Projects once hailed as the future of digital art lie abandoned. Similarly, the DeFi summer of 2020 brought unsustainable yields, dubious tokenomics, and unaudited smart contracts that emptied faster than they filled. Each boom ended in bust—speculators vanished, regulators sharpened their knives, and casual users recoiled. But it would be intellectually lazy to conflate these bubbles with the underlying innovations they distorted.

Hype collapses quickly. Infrastructure, when it survives the hype, endures. Consider stablecoins, often maligned as dull compared to memecoins or metaverses. Yet in many emerging markets, dollar-denominated stablecoins are now functioning as *de facto savings instruments and payment rails*, offering inflation resistance and cross-border liquidity to populations with failing currencies and predatory banking regimes. Circle's USDC and Tether's USDT are used daily not as investments, but as tools. That alone is a quiet revolution—one not announced on billboards or Twitter threads, but played out in remittance corridors and informal economies.

The same applies to blockchain as a settlement layer. Today, global banks and financial institutions—once publicly dismissive—are exploring tokenised assets, on-chain bonds, and distributed ledgers for clearing and custody. JPMorgan's Onyx platform, the Monetary Authority of Singapore's Project Guardian, and the European Investment Bank's digital bond issuance are not start-up experiments. They are sober, compliant, institutional commitments to the architecture of programmable finance. These developments lack the ideological purity that early crypto evangelists demanded, but they suggest something far more enduring: *integration without disruption*. The revolution, paradoxically, may arrive through co-option.

This raises a broader philosophical tension—*must revolutions always overthrow, or can they also rewire?* Many early adopters envisioned crypto as an insurrectionary force: unstoppable, decentralised, uncensorable. In some cases, it still functions that way. Dissidents in authoritarian states continue to use Bitcoin and Monero to escape financial surveillance. Whistleblowers use decentralised storage to publish sensitive data beyond the reach of deletion. Privacy coins remain legal grey zones in many jurisdictions precisely because they are effective. But the broader trajectory of the ecosystem is not towards radical detachment from existing power structures. It is towards entanglement, interoperability, and regulation. That is not failure—it is evolution.

However, to pretend that all is progress would be dishonest. Much of the crypto ecosystem remains structurally flawed. Most protocols are still dominated by a handful of whales, venture capital funds, and centralised exchanges. Governance, though touted as decentralised, is often opaque or easily manipulated. DAOs promised radically democratic coordination; most have become stagnant, performative, or captured by insiders. Technical debt accumulates. Security exploits persist. User experience remains unintuitive. For crypto to fulfil its promises, these foundational issues cannot be romanticised or ignored.

Scalability, too, remains a defining constraint. Ethereum's transition to proof-of-stake and the rise of Layer 2s like Arbitrum, Optimism, and zkSync mark real progress. But the dream of instantaneous, frictionless interaction—without gas fees, bridge risks, or wallet confusion—has not yet materialised. Until it does, mainstream adoption will be cautious at best. And even then, adoption alone is not the metric. *Adoption must be meaningful*, not just the migration of existing systems onto new rails.

That's where Web3 enters the debate, often cited as the next evolutionary stage: a decentralised internet where users own their data, identity, and assets. Yet Web3 remains in conceptual adolescence. Many applications are decentralised in name only, relying heavily on centralised infrastructure (Infura, Alchemy, Firebase) and gatekeeping platforms (OpenSea, MetaMask). True decentralisation is not a checkbox—it is a spectrum of trade-offs between usability, sovereignty, and security. The technology may be ready, but the incentives, culture, and education required to operationalise it at scale are still maturing.

So is the revolution still coming? Perhaps it depends on where one stands. From a regulatory perspective, the revolution is increasingly visible—and threatening. Governments around the world are no longer asking whether to regulate, but how, and how forcefully. The U.S. SEC has brought numerous enforcement actions against tokens, platforms, and projects. The EU has passed MiCA. China has banned much of the space outright. Yet regulation also brings clarity. It creates thresholds for legitimacy. It disambiguates innovation from fraud. The maturation of the legal framework may slow some speculative activity, but it may also clear a path for the builders who remain.

From a cultural standpoint, the revolution is fragmenting. There is no single "crypto community" anymore—there are multiple subcultures with divergent goals. Bitcoin maximalists focus on monetary sovereignty. Ethereum developers dream of composable applications. Solana builders chase speed. Privacy advocates demand zero-knowledge proofs. Memecoin traders hunt virality. This decentralised ethos is both strength and weakness—resilient to capture, but difficult to coordinate.

Yet perhaps that is the point. Revolutions rarely unfold in linear narratives. They are messy, recursive, and often only visible in retrospect. The printing press did not dismantle the Catholic Church overnight. The internet did not upend the media in a single decade. And cryptography—long considered an obscure subfield of mathematics—is now shaping geopolitics, finance, and governance.

What remains critical is the ongoing intellectual investment. That people are still asking hard questions—about the ethics of digital identity, the economics of tokenised labour, the philosophy of programmable law—suggests that the space has not stagnated. It has matured. The tone has shifted from evangelism to inquiry. That's a good thing. It means the conversation is no longer about speculative gains, but systemic design. About *what should be built*, not just what can.

So yes, the revolution may be less visible, less dramatic, and less certain than it once seemed. But it is still happening—in GitHub commits, protocol upgrades, jurisdictional debates, and cultural critiques. It is not the revolution the headlines promised. It is the one being forged by those still building, still questioning, and still refusing to settle for the status quo. That is the revolution worth watching. And perhaps, worth joining.

Chapter 12
Your Crypto Philosophy

The deeper one delves into cryptocurrency, the more it resembles a psychological landscape rather than a mere financial arena. Beyond the oscillating charts, protocol updates, and frenetic market cycles lies a question that few confront but none can escape: what does this technology demand of me? In a space dominated by volatility and novelty, technical skill or timing alone is insufficient; what is essential is philosophical clarity. Crypto is not only about ownership—it is about how one positions oneself in a domain that constantly probes attention, judgement, and conviction.

It is no coincidence that the loudest voices in crypto are often the least instructive. Speculators chase short-term gains, maximalists proselytise ideological purity, influencers amplify every trend, and fraudsters exploit uncertainty. The information landscape is dense, yet fragmented. You could follow hundreds of newsletters and still feel adrift. Hours on Discord may yield insight that evaporates almost instantly. And yet, for those willing to pause, reflect, and ask better questions—about risk, purpose, credibility, and learning—this same chaos becomes fertile ground for intellectual growth and strategic reasoning.

Clarity begins with recognising that there is no universal approach to "doing crypto." One participant treats it as a high-risk investment. Another experiments with on-chain governance. A third builds infrastructure for underserved communities. A fourth observes critically, cultivating insight without ever touching a token. All are legitimate, but each carries different responsibilities, stakes, and exposures. Without a conscious choice of posture, one is defined by the environment rather than one's own intent.

So, what role do you wish to inhabit? Investor, user, builder, observer—these categories are not mutually exclusive, but they frame distinct perspectives. Investors focus on allocation, security, and tax efficiency. Builders navigate protocol design, code audits, and community coordination. Users weigh privacy, usability, and product-market fit. Observers prioritise intellectual coherence, policy analysis, or cultural critique. Your personal crypto philosophy begins with naming what you aim to do and, crucially, why. This is not a fixed identity; it is a deliberate starting point.

With self-definition in hand, the next step is establishing a personal risk framework. Crypto is structurally different from traditional investments. Tokens may be illiquid. Projects can collapse overnight. Keys can be lost. Communities may fracture. Code can be exploited. Regulations may shift unexpectedly. These are not peripheral hazards—they are intrinsic to the system. Rational engagement begins with defining boundaries: what are you willing to risk, what conditions would trigger an exit, how frequently will you review assumptions, and how will you identify their failure?

Some adopt a "core-satellite" strategy: a modest, long-term stake in Bitcoin or Ethereum, surrounded by experimental positions in protocols, NFTs, or governance tokens. Others abstain financially but commit to deep study of sociotechnical dynamics. There is no universal prescription, only the perils of unreflective participation. Clarity does not guarantee success, but it fosters coherence and reduces anxiety.

Yet philosophical clarity is never static. Crypto evolves swiftly, and thinking must evolve with it. The challenge is distinguishing signal from noise in an ecosystem awash with Telegram threads, Medium posts, YouTube explainers, Substack essays, Twitter debates, and governance forums. Much of this content is urgent but trivial, loud but shallow. Success lies not in consuming more, but in filtering wisely.

Signal accumulates in sources that are patient, consistent, and reflective: technically literate researchers publishing open-source audits, legal scholars tracing regulatory shifts, contrarian investors elucidating thesis-driven portfolios, founders reflecting on failed DAOs. The most reliable insights do not shout—they accrue trust over time. The task is not to idolise, but to curate a small, diverse set of inputs and review them methodically.

Even the best-curated feed, however, can become a trap. The constant novelty of crypto is addictive: new tokens, exploits, governance battles. The risk is cognitive hijack. Many intelligent participants burn out, not from poor trades but from unstructured immersion. They mistake activity for learning, reaction for reflection. A sound crypto philosophy includes strategies for self-regulation: limiting social media, scheduling "offline audits" of holdings and assumptions, adopting a slow-learning model that prizes depth over recency.

A useful frame treats engagement as research. Formulate a thesis. Gather evidence. Write memos. Revisit assumptions periodically. Track only developments that intersect with your thesis. This curbs both FOMO and fatigue. It reminds you that the aim is not to absorb hype, but to construct a coherent worldview—a worldview that evolves yet remains anchored to deliberate inquiry.

Ultimately, a crypto philosophy is filter, scaffold, and mirror. It filters distractions from essentials, scaffolds learning, building, or investing, and reflects how values and vulnerabilities manifest within a volatile, experimental, human-driven system. While decentralised code powers crypto, the trajectory will be shaped by individuals who engage with intention rather than inertia.

This chapter offers no prescriptive roadmap. Instead, it invites reflection, deliberate design, and ownership of participation. Whether allocating capital, developing tools, contributing to discourse, or observing from the sidelines, engagement demands rigour. It demands philosophy. For crypto is not merely a market—it is a test of the kind of thinker and actor one chooses to be.

What Kind of Participant Do You Want to Be?

Crypto forces a decision that few other technologies demand: not simply whether you will engage, but *how*. It is not a passive medium like a film or a mobile app. It is a socio-technical ecosystem that implicates your judgement, your resources, your politics, your attention, and your identity. You cannot casually "use" crypto in the same way you might tap to pay with Apple Pay. To engage meaningfully is to take a position—whether you admit it or not. *That position deserves to be chosen consciously.*

The question—what kind of participant do you want to be?—is not rhetorical. It is foundational. It determines how you allocate time, interpret risk, process information, and filter signal from noise. It defines your relationship to volatility, novelty, and complexity. It determines whether crypto becomes a useful tool or an emotional liability. And most importantly, it aligns your actions with your values, rather than defaulting to the incentives of others.

Too many people stumble into crypto as speculators and never examine the frame. They follow prices, memes, personalities, and sentiment, believing they are "informed" because they check charts and Twitter. But watching a system is not the same as understanding it. Participating is not the same as investing. Buying tokens is not the same as believing in protocols. These distinctions matter because *your posture shapes your outcomes.*

There are at least four primary orientations: the investor, the builder, the user, and the observer. Each carries distinct motivations, responsibilities, and forms of value creation. None is inherently superior—but failing to choose, or blindly switching between them, is the fastest path to confusion.

The investor engages with capital. Their tools are asset allocation, custody, risk management, and tax optimisation. Their questions are: what is the thesis behind this token? What structural edge do I have? How does this protocol accrue value over time? What are the risks if the network fails, forks, or is regulated? A thoughtful investor treats crypto as a thesis-driven allocation, not a roulette table. They understand that most tokens trend toward zero, that market psychology is cyclical, and that long-term conviction must be paired with operational discipline. *They do not delegate due diligence to influencers.*

The builder engages with creation. Their tools are code, design, governance, and community development. Their questions are: what problem does this solve? Who are the users, and what do they need? Is the protocol secure? Is the incentive structure coherent? Will this be resilient in the face of attack, change, or apathy? Builders are often the least visible yet most consequential actors in the ecosystem. They operate in Github commits, not price feeds. *Their impact compounds slowly, but it lasts.*

The user engages with utility. Their tools are wallets, dapps, bridges, and services. Their questions are: does this work? Is it cheaper, faster, or more private than the alternative? What trade-offs am I making in terms of custody, compliance, or convenience? Users are the stress test of every protocol. They determine what scales and what breaks. In a decentralised world, users are not passive consumers; they are often co-governors, liquidity providers, and bug reporters. *Their experience shapes adoption more than any roadmap.*

The observer engages with perspective. Their tools are research, writing, teaching, and dialogue. Their questions are: what are the implications of this system? How does it reshape trust, identity, and coordination? What narratives are forming, and who benefits from them? Observers connect crypto to history, philosophy, policy, and culture. They are the bridge between technical change and social meaning. *They don't just explain what's happening—they ask why it matters.*

These roles are not rigid. One can move between them, or hold multiple perspectives at once. A builder can also be an investor. A user may become an observer. But clarity requires *prioritising one lens at a time.* Confusion sets in when someone trades like an investor but expects utility like a user. Or when someone builds infrastructure while reacting emotionally to token prices. Or when someone critiques policy without understanding protocol mechanics. The goal is not to pick a label but to *cultivate internal coherence.*

Part of this coherence involves clarifying your motivations. Are you here for financial gain, intellectual curiosity, ideological alignment, or technological empowerment? Do you care about privacy, permissionlessness, financial sovereignty, or simply not missing the next big thing? Are you looking to solve problems, make money, build reputation, or learn skills? *Your answer will shape your risk tolerance, time horizon, and ethical stance.* If you can't articulate your motivation, you are likely absorbing someone else's—and that rarely ends well.

It also means acknowledging your limitations. If you're not technical, don't pretend to audit smart contracts. If you're not legal-minded, don't assume regulatory immunity. If you're not emotionally stable during market swings, don't overexpose yourself to volatility. If you're time-poor, don't try to track everything. *Crypto is not a test of perfection—it is a test of self-awareness.*

Another crucial element of participation is information hygiene. Each role requires different filters. Investors need clarity on tokenomics, funding, governance, and runway. Builders need technical audits, developer documentation, and API reliability. Users need support channels, UX consistency, and fee transparency. Observers need longitudinal data, comparative frameworks, and cultural context. *Your filters must match your function.* Blindly consuming generalised noise will only blur your thinking.

What unites all roles, however, is the importance of *intentionality*. Passive engagement is a myth in crypto. Whether you're delegating votes, clicking airdrop links, or following influencers, you are participating in systems of value and trust. Even silence can be a form of consent. To opt in is to accept responsibility for outcomes—whether or not you understood them at the time. This does not mean paralysis. It means mindfulness.

Crypto, at its best, invites agency. You are not just a user of platforms; you are a co-creator of systems. You don't just react to changes—you can propose them. You don't just adopt technologies—you can fork them, govern them, improve them. But with agency comes responsibility. And with responsibility comes the need for reflection. The question—what kind of participant do you want to be?—is not asked once. It must be revisited regularly, as the space evolves and as your own interests shift.

In this light, participation becomes not merely economic or technical, but *philosophical*. It is a practice of aligning intention with action, belief with behaviour, knowledge with humility. It means resisting hype, cultivating discipline, and engaging with a posture of curiosity rather than urgency. It means recognising that your presence shapes the systems you touch—even if only slightly.

So pause, and ask: *Why are you here?* What do you hope to learn, build, earn, or contribute? What do you want to understand more deeply, and what do you prefer to leave untouched? How will you measure whether your engagement is meaningful—or merely habitual? The answers may change, but the inquiry must remain.

Because in crypto, as in life, *how you show up matters*. And showing up with clarity, humility, and purpose is still the most undervalued skill of all.

Designing Your Own Risk Rulebook

Risk in crypto is not merely a variable to manage—it is a lens that shapes perception, behaviour, and ultimately, outcomes. Unlike traditional finance, where risk is often measured and contained by institutions, regulation, and mature infrastructure, crypto demands personal responsibility at every turn. You are not just choosing what to buy; you are choosing what to believe, whom to trust, what to prioritise, and how to protect yourself. And unlike the static categories in a brokerage risk tolerance quiz, crypto's risks are *multi-dimensional, dynamic, and deeply psychological*. To navigate them, you don't need a law degree, a quant background, or a trading desk—you need a framework. A personal rulebook. Not to eliminate risk, but to *calibrate* it—deliberately, consistently, and in line with your own purpose.

Most people treat risk as something external, something that "happens" to them: prices crash, wallets get hacked, protocols fail. But the real danger often lies in the *absence of internal structure*. Without a rulebook, decisions are outsourced to market sentiment, Twitter threads, or a vague sense of FOMO. Exposure creeps up. Conviction is mistaken for hype. Cash management turns into emotional roulette. And what starts as curiosity turns into reactive compulsion. The role of a risk rulebook is to interrupt this drift—not with rigidity, but with reflection.

At its core, a crypto risk rulebook is a self-authored framework for engaging with volatility, uncertainty, and decision-making. It is not a trading strategy. It is not about optimising returns or timing tops. It is a practical system for aligning your actions with your *actual* appetite for uncertainty—not your aspirational one. It is a living tool, meant to be revisited, refined, and adapted over time. And crucially, it is yours. Not copied from a newsletter, not borrowed from a Twitter account, not dictated by an exchange dashboard. *Crafted, instead, by clarity.*

To begin designing such a rulebook, start with your capacity. This includes financial, emotional, and temporal capacity—not just how much money you're willing to risk, but how much *bandwidth* you can sustainably allocate to crypto without it compromising your other priorities. For example, someone with deep technical knowledge, flexible capital, and a full-time focus on blockchain can afford to engage with risk very differently from a part-time participant with limited liquidity and no programming experience. *If your capacity is low but your exposure is high, you are playing someone else's game with borrowed time.*

Next, articulate your thresholds. At what percentage of portfolio drawdown will you pause and re-evaluate? What level of protocol complexity are you willing to accept before stepping away? How many hours per week can you commit to monitoring, learning, or participating? These thresholds are not walls—they are early warning systems. Their function is not to force action, but to prompt attention. Without them, it becomes far too easy to rationalise every downturn as "normal" and every new feature as "essential." Your thresholds provide a check against narrative overfitting.

Equally important is defining your *principles*—the values that underlie your risk decisions. These could include beliefs about decentralisation, privacy, ownership, financial sovereignty, or open-source development. For example, if you believe that decentralisation is non-negotiable, you may avoid protocols with opaque governance—even if the yield is attractive. If you value custody, you may forgo exchange-based services despite their convenience. *Risk tolerance without values is merely opportunism.* And opportunism in crypto often ends in regret.

A functional rulebook must also specify *processes*—the concrete ways you evaluate, decide, and reflect. This might mean creating a checklist before making any new investment: What problem does this solve? Who are the founders? Is the code open source? What is the governance structure? Is there a clear business model? How are tokens allocated and vested? Similarly, you might build in post-action reviews: every quarter, re-examine your positions, your thesis, and your behaviour. Did you follow your process, or did you get swept up? Did your strategy perform within expectations, or did luck mask a bad decision? *Without review, learning stagnates.*

The rulebook should also include boundaries. These are not about austerity—they are about sustainability. Boundaries could include hard limits on trading frequency, on social media consumption, on speculative allocations, or on the use of leverage. For example, one might set a rule never to invest in projects where the tokenomics are not transparent, or never to keep more than a certain percentage of funds on centralised exchanges. Boundaries function as pre-commitments that *reduce cognitive friction* in moments of hype, fear, or doubt.

One often overlooked aspect is *emotional risk*. Crypto can be exhilarating—but it can also be destabilising. Sudden price swings, community infighting, rug pulls, and relentless novelty can create a low-grade psychological churn that leads to fatigue, compulsive behaviour, or decision paralysis. A robust rulebook accounts for this. It may involve structured breaks, a journal to track mood and reaction patterns, or a "cooling off" rule—no major decisions within 24 hours of significant gains or losses. The goal is not to suppress emotion but to *insulate decision-making from volatility-induced irrationality*.

Importantly, your risk rulebook is not static. It should evolve with your knowledge, context, and experience. As you learn more about custody, you may change how you store assets. As your income changes, your allocation limits may shift. As regulation evolves, your approach to compliance may need revision. The point is not to set rules in stone, but to create *a system of conscious revision*. Ideally, you revisit your rulebook quarterly—not reactively in a panic, but proactively in reflection.

It also helps to distinguish between different categories of exposure. There is *financial* risk—what happens if this asset loses value? There is *technical* risk—what happens if this protocol is exploited? There is *governance* risk—what happens if voting control consolidates? There is *legal* risk—what happens if regulators intervene? And there is *social* risk—what happens if this project loses legitimacy in the community? Each requires different safeguards. *A rulebook that treats all risks as financial will overlook the slow, compounding damage of structural fragility.*

Beyond individual safeguards, there is also the risk of *misaligned incentives*. Many of the loudest voices in crypto—whether influencers, venture funds, or protocol leaders—are talking their own book. They are not inherently malicious, but their incentives are rarely neutral. Recognising this, a risk rulebook must include *epistemic hygiene*: How do you evaluate sources? What criteria do you use to assess credibility? Are you exposed to contrarian views? Are you mistaking conviction for consensus? Intellectual integrity is a form of risk management.

Some may argue that such a framework is unnecessary—that crypto is too volatile, too fast-moving, or too unpredictable for rule-based thinking. But the opposite is true. The more chaotic the environment, the more essential the structure. A pilot flying into turbulence does not abandon instruments. They rely on them. *Crypto is full of turbulence. You need instruments you trust.*

This doesn't mean becoming inflexible or dogmatic. It means building a system that lets you *respond without reacting*. That filters out noise while remaining open to insight. That protects your downside while leaving room for upside. And most importantly, that turns your crypto experience from an emotional rollercoaster into a deliberate exploration.

Designing your own risk rulebook is not about playing it safe. It's about playing it smart. Not avoiding danger, but choosing your exposure with clarity. Not outsourcing responsibility, but owning your framework. In a space where everyone is selling certainty, it is an act of maturity to admit uncertainty—and to prepare for it.

Ultimately, your risk rulebook is a statement of self-respect. It says: I take my decisions seriously. I value my time, my capital, and my peace of mind. I am willing to engage—but on terms that are mine, not dictated by headlines, algorithms, or strangers online. That may not be the fastest way to profit. But it is the surest way to endure. And in crypto, *endurance is the edge that compounds.*

From Noise to Signal

Information overload is not a side effect of the crypto space—it's its native environment. The torrent of Discord threads, Telegram channels, Twitter feeds, Medium essays, GitHub updates, whitepapers, podcast episodes, Substack posts, YouTube explainers, and ever-shifting meme slang isn't accidental—it's structural. Crypto evolved not as a single industry but as a decentralised movement of builders, traders, philosophers, and opportunists, each broadcasting from their own frequency. And for someone seeking to genuinely understand rather than simply react, the challenge isn't just to *find information*, but to *filter signal from noise.* In other words, knowing *whom to listen to* becomes as critical as knowing *what is being said.*

The mistake many make at the outset is equating volume with authority. The loudest voices—the ones with the most viral tweets, the biggest Discord followings, or the slickest newsletter branding—are not necessarily the most trustworthy. Many are intelligent and well-meaning, but their incentives are often misaligned with the reader's learning goals. Traders may be optimising for engagement, protocol marketers for adoption, influencers for clout, and token holders for price appreciation. In such an environment, *cynical scepticism is insufficient; you need epistemic rigour.* Your objective isn't to "follow the right people" but to build *a system* that consistently exposes you to credible insight and reduces exposure to distraction, hype, or misinformation.

One of the most enduringly reliable sources of structured, high-quality thought in the space is research-driven content from reputable institutions. Reports and deep dives from firms like Messari, Delphi Digital, and Coin Metrics offer granular, well-sourced analysis that goes beyond speculation. They break down tokenomics, protocol mechanics, governance risks, user growth, and ecosystem dynamics with the kind of discipline one would expect in traditional equity research. While not all of their work is accessible without a subscription, even the free-tier material is a significant upgrade over social media discourse. *Their value lies not just in their data, but in the frameworks they model—how to ask the right questions, not just how to read the charts.*

Equally instructive, but in a very different register, are independent educators and commentators who maintain intellectual independence and long-term presence in the ecosystem. Bankless, for instance, despite its occasionally evangelical tone, has earned credibility by building a consistent body of content around Ethereum, DeFi, and digital identity. Their podcasts and newsletters—when taken with critical distance—can offer clarity on the motivations, trade-offs, and long-term aspirations of decentralised systems. Similarly, Chris Burniske, Linda Xie, and Haseeb Qureshi have established reputations for thoughtful analysis that blends technical literacy, economic reasoning, and philosophical curiosity. *The most valuable thinkers are rarely maximalists—they are bridge-builders, capable of seeing multiple sides of a debate without collapsing into relativism or dogma.*

For those who want to see what's happening at the protocol level, GitHub remains an indispensable tool. It isn't necessary to read code to use GitHub effectively. Watching commit frequency, issue discussions, and contributor engagement offers a window into the vitality and responsiveness of a project. A protocol with thousands of users but a stagnant repo may be a warning sign; one with modest usage but active developer dialogue may be a sleeper worth deeper examination. Complementing this are data aggregators like Dune Analytics, DefiLlama, and Token Terminal, which provide on-chain metrics, financial data, and visual dashboards. Used properly, these tools shift your information diet from opinion-based to *evidence-based.*

But tools and reports alone aren't enough. Crypto is not a closed system of technical documents—it's a live, participatory culture. And understanding it requires context, tone, and proximity to the debates shaping its evolution. That's where community-based forums—when carefully selected—become irreplaceable. Unlike noisy Twitter threads or shill-heavy Telegram groups, certain Reddit communities (such as r/ethereum or r/CryptoCurrencyMeta) host nuanced, long-form discussions where users hold each other accountable with citations and historical knowledge. More technically inclined readers may find value in ETHResearch or governance forums like those of MakerDAO, Optimism, and Arbitrum, where protocol direction is debated openly and transparently. *Signal is more likely to appear where incentives reward long-term thinking, not quick reactions.*

One paradox of seeking reliable crypto information is that *early access often correlates with higher risk of manipulation.* Many Discord servers and early-stage alpha groups cultivate an illusion of insider status while operating more like echo chambers or pump-and-dump incubators. Being "early" is not inherently valuable if the epistemic environment lacks rigour. Conversely, arriving "late" to a mature, well-moderated discussion often provides better signal than catching a trend during its speculative spike. *Quality information does not demand urgency—it rewards patience.*

A recurring theme across all high-signal sources is *transparency of motivation.* Are authors disclosing their holdings or affiliations? Are analysts explaining their assumptions and data limitations? Are educators willing to say, "I don't know," or revise earlier views? These subtle cues are more important than branding or popularity. In a landscape where hype often masquerades as conviction, humility becomes a proxy for credibility.

Of course, building a personal signal network also requires *active pruning.* This means unfollowing high-volume, low-insight accounts—even if they are entertaining. It means resisting the dopamine lure of outrage-based content. It means unsubscribing from newsletters that don't enrich your thinking. And it means periodically stepping back to ask: Is my current information diet helping me *learn*, or merely making me *feel informed*? The latter is an illusion that breeds overconfidence; the former cultivates intellectual resilience.

Some readers may gravitate toward tools that synthesise information. Aggregators like CryptoPanic or Feedly can help centralise updates from multiple trusted sources. Browser plugins like DeFiLlama's dashboards can surface protocol-specific insights without jumping between tabs. But curation, while convenient, is not a substitute for discernment. *Tools are only as useful as the intentionality of the person using them.*

Interestingly, some of the most profound insights about crypto do not come from crypto sources at all. Books on systems thinking, network theory, behavioural economics, or institutional design often offer deeper explanatory frameworks than the latest token pitch. Thinkers like Elinor Ostrom, James C. Scott, and Nassim Nicholas Taleb have all written in ways that illuminate decentralisation, incentives, and risk far more effectively than most Web3 whitepapers. *Signal doesn't always look like crypto—but it helps you see crypto more clearly.*

Finally, one must not confuse *learning* with *tracking*. Many newcomers believe that staying current is synonymous with staying informed. This leads to compulsive monitoring—of price feeds, Discord alerts, or crypto Twitter dramas—which paradoxically degrades clarity. Signal is not about being the first to know; it's about knowing what *matters*. This requires structured reflection, not constant reaction. A better approach is to define periodic review cycles—weekly synthesis sessions, monthly portfolio reviews, quarterly thesis revisions. Let information accumulate, then engage it with purpose. *Signal is what remains after noise has passed through a filter of attention.*

In a field as fast-moving as crypto, clarity is not a given—it is cultivated. It is the product of conscious choices: whom to follow, what to read, when to step back, how to think. There is no perfect list of sources, no ultimate feed. But there is a pattern: signal tends to emerge where people combine intellectual integrity, practical curiosity, and skin in the game. Follow that pattern, not the noise.

How to Stay Curious Without Getting Hooked

Curiosity is the intellectual engine of discovery, but in the crypto world, it often becomes bait. What begins as an innocent search for understanding quickly morphs into compulsive scrolling, price-checking, Discord lurking, and dopamine-driven headline hunting. This is not incidental. The crypto ecosystem is designed—intentionally or otherwise—to reward hyper-engagement. Tokens trade 24/7. News cycles shift hourly. Influencers, protocols, and projects compete not just for capital, but for your attention. *And once attention becomes the currency, curiosity turns addictive.* The problem isn't just the volume of information—it's the emotional architecture beneath it.

The modern crypto interface is indistinguishable from the gamified surfaces of social media. Apps like Twitter (X), Telegram, and Discord are not neutral venues of learning; they're behavioural feedback loops. Notifications trigger spikes of interest. Likes and retweets incentivise performative certainty. Hot takes outperform slow thinking. Amid this stream, genuine insight is possible—but only if you develop filters strong enough to resist the pull of continuous partial attention. *Staying curious without getting hooked requires more than discipline. It demands structure.*

Begin with *intentionality*. Ask yourself what you're trying to understand—and why. Are you learning about Ethereum's roadmap to grasp the future of decentralised computing? Or are you subconsciously seeking confirmation that your recent token purchase is wise? Are you listening to a podcast because it explains governance trade-offs in DeFi, or because the hosts are entertaining and fill a cognitive void during your commute? One is education; the other is sedation. *Awareness of motive transforms consumption into inquiry.* This doesn't mean you must become stoic or joyless, but it does mean developing an internal metric: did that hour of reading leave you clearer, or merely more anxious?

A second, often overlooked principle is *temporal separation*. Crypto moves fast—but that doesn't mean you have to. The myth of "you'll miss it if you're not plugged in" is precisely that: a myth. The core developments that shape the industry—protocol upgrades, governance votes, ecosystem migrations—unfold over weeks or months, not hours. Markets may move quickly, but *meaning moves slowly*. Instead of checking daily for micro-updates, develop a cadence. Perhaps one weekly reading session and one monthly synthesis review. This shift from "reactive monitoring" to "periodic reflection" not only reduces fatigue but sharpens insight. *Time is not the enemy of relevance—it is its filter.*

This ties directly into the value of *asynchronous media*. Podcasts, long-form essays, in-depth interviews, and whitepapers provide depth without urgency. Unlike Twitter, they don't push you toward real-time commentary or emotional response. They offer conceptual frameworks, not dopamine hits. Curating a small, reliable list of these resources—and revisiting them slowly—can rewire your informational instincts. When you learn to seek ideas rather than updates, *you create space for actual learning, not just informed anxiety.*

Of course, you'll still encounter the real-time firehose. News alerts. Token surges. Security exploits. Meme coins that 10x overnight. The trick isn't to avoid these entirely, but to *contain their influence.* One strategy is to compartmentalise: use a different browser, device, or time block for speculative news than for structured study. Another is to limit surface-level exposure—disable notifications, unfollow volatility chasers, and silence uncurated Telegram groups. *The goal is not abstinence but sovereignty over your attention.* You should be able to dip into the chaos and leave without being mentally hijacked.

Maintaining curiosity also depends on *trustworthy interlocutors.* Learning in isolation is harder than learning in dialogue. If you can find a small group of peers—online or offline—who share your values of clarity over hype, nuance over narrative, and patience over panic, then you create a shared scaffolding for meaning-making. These people don't need to be experts. In fact, the best learning communities are often composed of curious generalists who challenge each other respectfully, recommend resources, and resist the temptation to chase every new trend. *Conversation slows thought, and in slowness, wisdom has a chance to emerge.*

Equally important is the *ability to stop.* Curiosity becomes addiction not when it starts, but when it no longer knows how to end. The constant "next article," "next video," or "next alert" pattern leaves the brain in a perpetual state of anticipation. To counter this, create hard edges around your inquiry. Set a timer. Decide on a reading limit. Build mental rituals—such as summarising what you've learned in your own words or noting three new questions—to mark the close of an exploration. These boundaries signal to your brain that curiosity has done its job. *Closure is not the death of learning; it is what allows learning to integrate.*

One conceptual tool that helps here is distinguishing between *relevance and recency.* The crypto ecosystem thrives on the illusion that what just happened matters most. But if you orient your curiosity around relevance—how much something clarifies, informs, or transforms your understanding—you start to escape the tyranny of the timeline. A whitepaper from 2020 or a lecture from 2018 might deepen your thinking more than any current news post. This doesn't make you "out of touch." It makes you a *strategic learner* rather than a tactical consumer.

A practical framework for maintaining this balance is the "Three Lenses" approach: scan, study, and synthesise. *Scanning* is your light, time-boxed exposure to current headlines or updates. It satisfies curiosity without consuming you. *Studying* is where you slow down—reading technical posts, essays, or listening to detailed interviews. It's where deep understanding takes root. *Synthesising* is when you step back, ask what you now understand better, and how it fits into your larger worldview. This final step—so often skipped—is what transforms information into wisdom. *Without synthesis, curiosity becomes intellectual hoarding.*

Ultimately, staying curious in crypto without getting hooked is about *returning to first principles*. What are you here to learn? What decisions will this learning inform? What kind of thinker do you want to become? These questions are more than philosophical—they're practical shields against the entropy of the attention economy. Crypto culture will always try to rush you, distract you, seduce you. But you can choose how, when, and why to engage. You can be a tourist, a student, or a sovereign learner. The difference lies not in what you know, but in *how you choose to know it.*

Sustainable curiosity requires intentional rhythm, deliberate filters, and boundaries that honour your cognitive energy. You don't need to be the first to know. You need to be the one who understands *why it matters*. And that understanding only comes when you slow down enough to think clearly, act deliberately, and *choose signal over noise—again and again.*

About the Author

Ethan Rowe writes to make complex systems simple and relevant for everyday thinkers. With a deep interest in how technology reshapes trust, value, and decision-making, he focuses on topics where hype and misunderstanding often cloud clarity. Ethan's work reflects a calm, skeptical curiosity—always grounded in the belief that smart questions matter more than fast answers. He doesn't speak from a pedestal; he writes for the reader who wants to feel informed, not overwhelmed. His previous books explored digital life, modern focus, and behavioral economics in everyday choices. With Understand Crypto Before You Invest, Ethan brings that same clarity and care to one of the most misunderstood shifts in modern finance.

www.ingramcontent.com/pod-product-compliance
Lightning Source LLC
Chambersburg PA
CBHW031343230926
51848CB00002B/362